ROUTLEDGE LIBRARY EDITION: SYNTAX

Volume 21

COMPARATIVE CONSTRUCTIONS IN SPANISH AND FRENCH SYNTAX

COMPARATIVE CONSTRUCTIONS IN SPANISH AND FRENCH SYNTAX

SUSAN PRICE

LONDON AND NEW YORK

First published in 1990 by Routledge

This edition first published in 2017
by Routledge
4 Park Square, Milton Park, Abingdon, Oxon OX14 4RN
605 Third Avenue, New York, NY 10017

Routledge is an imprint of the Taylor & Francis Group, an informa business

© 1990 Susan Price

All rights reserved. No part of this book may be reprinted or reproduced or utilised in any form or by any electronic, mechanical, or other means, now known or hereafter invented, including photocopying and recording, or in any information storage or retrieval system, without permission in writing from the publishers.

Trademark notice: Product or corporate names may be trademarks or registered trademarks, and are used only for identification and explanation without intent to infringe.

British Library Cataloguing in Publication Data
A catalogue record for this book is available from the British Library

ISBN: 978-1-138-21859-8 (Set)
ISBN: 978-1-315-43729-3 (Set) (ebk)
ISBN: 978-1-138-69846-8 (Volume 21) (hbk)
ISBN: 978-1-138-69847-5 (Volume 21) (pbk)
ISBN: 978-1-315-51893-0 (Volume 21) (ebk)

Publisher's Note
The publisher has gone to great lengths to ensure the quality of this reprint but points out that some imperfections in the original copies may be apparent.

Disclaimer
The publisher has made every effort to trace copyright holders and would welcome correspondence from those they have been unable to trace.

Comparative Constructions in Spanish and French Syntax
Susan Price

London and New York

First published 1990
by Routledge
11 New Fetter Lane, London EC4P 4EE

Simultaneously published in the USA and Canada
by Routledge
a division of Routledge, Chapman and Hall, Inc.
29 West 35th Street, New York, NY 10001

© 1990 Susan Price

Data conversion by
Columns Design and Production Services Ltd, Reading
Printed in Great Britain by
T.J. Press, Cornwall

All rights reserved. No part of this book may be reprinted or
reproduced or utilized in any form or by any electronic,
mechanical, or other means, now known or hereafter invented,
including photocopying and recording, or in any information
storage or retrieval system, without permission in writing from
the publishers.

British Library Cataloguing in Publication Data
Price, Susan
  Comparative constructions in Spanish and French syntax.
  (Romance linguistics series)
  1. Romance languages. Syntax
  I. Title
  440

ISBN 0-415-01024-1

Library of Congress Cataloging in Publication Data
Price, Susan
    Comparative constructions in Spanish and French / Susan Price.
      p. cm. — (Romance linguistics series)
    Includes bibliographical references and index.
    ISBN 0-415-01024-1 (hb)
    1. Romance languages—Comparison. 2. Grammar, Comparative—
  Spanish and French. 3. Grammar, Comparative—French and Spanish.
  4. Spanish language—Comparison. 5. French language—Comparison.
  I. Title. II. Series.
  PC133.P75   1990
  465—dc20   90-8683

Contents

Acknowledgements	vii
1 The nature of comparative constructions	1
1.1 Recent studies	2
1.2 The mental representation of comparison	6
1.3 Types of comparative constructions: of inequality and equality	8
1.4 Kinds of comparison: full and partial	9
1.5 Realization of comparison in Spanish	11
1.6 Realization of comparison in French	16
1.7 Focus of comparison	20
1.8 Marker of comparison	22
1.9 Summary	24
Notes	25
2 Comparative constructions in Spanish	26
2.1 Expression of full comparison	27
2.2 Expression of partial comparison	39
2.3 The pleonastic or expletive negative	58
2.4 The clause introducers	60
2.5 Summary	62
Notes	64
3 Comparative constructions in French	68
3.1 Expression of full comparison	70
3.2 Expression of partial comparison	89
3.3 Expletive ne	103
3.4 The clause introducer	130
3.5 Summary	133
Notes	136

4 Variation between Spanish and French comparative constructions and a consideration of other Romance languages	143
4.1 Comparative constructions in Italian	146
4.2 Comparative constructions in Portuguese	191
4.3 Comparative constructions in Rumanian	200
4.4 Comparative constructions in Catalan	209
4.5 Comparative constructions in Galician, Friulan, Occitan, and Walloon	222
4.6 Summary	226
Notes	233
References	239
Further reading	244
Index	248

Acknowledgements

I should like to thank all those who helped by giving me their native-speaker judgements on the numerous examples used in this study, particularly Rafael Sala (for Spanish and Catalan), Luis Domínguez (for Spanish), and Mohammed Khane and Luc Gouzland (for French). I am also grateful to Giulio Lepschy, Graham Mallinson and Max Wheeler for their valuable comments on the sections on Italian, Rumanian and Catalan comparatives, respectively. Finally, particular thanks are due to the editors of the series, Martin Harris and Nigel Vincent, and also to John Green, for their helpful and informed comments on the work as a whole.

1 The nature of comparative constructions

'If the realm of language is seen as a cosmos, vast, largely unexplored and sometimes bewildering, then the comparative construction must be a microcosmos, reflecting all the complexity of the whole.'

(Hoeksema 1984: 93)

The comparative construction has been the subject of numerous studies, in which both its syntax and semantics have been exhaustively analysed.[1] Recent contributions to this field include two major general works, Andersen (1983) and Stassen (1985), in which comparative constructions are treated within the framework of word-order typology, as well as Hellan (1981), a more restrictive study, in which an integrated analysis of the syntax and semantics of the comparative construction is attempted, though this bears almost exclusively on English. The aims of the present study are rather different and more modest in scope; they are, in brief, to present a comprehensive description of the comparative constructions of Spanish and French, and show that the apparently numerous differences in their syntactic realizations can be accounted for by general constraints on the expression of comparison. Reference will also be made to parallel constructions in other Romance languages, in an attempt to show that these languages display a range of constructions not divergent from the suggested pattern of possibilities resulting from the general constraints proposed.

As the intention is to present a descriptive analysis of the constructions concerned, the approach will be neutral in terms of syntactic model, observations being couched rather in terms of traditional grammatical theory. However, it is impossible to avoid the use of certain terms which may appear inextricably linked with particular theoretical approaches. This is particularly the case with regard to the term 'deletion'. Nevertheless, I intend to use this term as a convenient label for the consistent relationships which exist between sentence types, following Stassen (1985: 21): 'when I use the term "deletion" it should not be inferred that I claim that a specific procedure of string-derivation by means of deletion rules should be part of a grammar.' My use of the term 'deletion' will correspond broadly to the more traditional term 'ellipsis'.

1.1 RECENT STUDIES

Andersen (1983: 118), basing his analysis on a representative sample of the world's languages, establishes five different types of comparative construction:

1 juxtaposition: A is big, B is small/not(big)
2 adpositional: A is bigger FROM B
3 case: A is big(ger) B-FROM
4 particle: A is bigger THAN B
5 verbal: A SURPASSES B

Examples of juxtaposition comparatives are given from Dakota (p. 108), Mosquito (p. 109), Hittite (p. 112) and Classical Sanskrit (p. 113). The Mosquito example follows:

(1) Jan almuk, Sammuel almuk apia
    John old   Samuel   old   not
    John is older than Samuel

Examples of adpositional comparatives (where the adposition may be either pre- or post-posed), are given from Nuba and Hindi (pp. 109, 113), Modern Greek (pp. 110, 113) and Japanese (p. 125). A Hindi example follows:

(2) Mohan se   barā
    Mohan from big
    bigger than Mohan

Latin (pp. 111, 113) is given as an example of a case comparative, where the relation between the second compared category and the adjective is expressed through the case ending:

(3) te   maior
    you-from bigger
    bigger than you

Latin, German, Finnish, Old Indic and French (pp. 111, 117–18) are given as examples of particle comparatives, where a separate lexeme connects the compared category and the adjective; the following is one of the Latin examples:

(4) maior quam tu
    bigger than you

Examples of verbal comparatives, where a verb meaning 'to surpass' explicitly contains the comparative idea, are given from Homeric Greek (pp. 111, 131), Old Indic, English and German (p. 131). The German example follows:

(5) Er übertrifft ihn an Körperkraft
    He surpasses him in strength

For Andersen, then, Spanish and French will fall into group 4, the particle constructions, 'particle' here being a term for the item which links the two clauses of a comparative construction containing the terms of comparison.

However, Andersen distinguishes between an adpositon and a particle on very specific grounds. Both adpositions, which may be either preposition or postposition, and particles serve to connect the compared category to the adjective; these he terms 'links'. However, he also introduces the concept of 'marker', defined as 'that specific element which distinguishes a comparison of inequality from a comparison of equality. It is, therefore, that element which expresses the specific result of inequality as opposed to the only other result possible, namely, that of equality (p. 116). Adpositions, he claims, serve as both links and markers (as do case endings). Particles, on the other hand, serve only as links, and not as markers, given that, according to his evidence, 'the particle does not distinguish comparisons of inequality ... from comparisons of equality'. For example, *que* in French acts as the 'comparative particle' in both comparatives of inequality and equality. The evidence from Spanish, however, would contradict this assertion, given that the 'particles' *que* and *como* do serve to distinguish between the two types of comparison. This may suggest that particle comparatives are not an entirely discrete category, a point which will be taken up again in section 1.8.

4   *Comparative Constructions in Spanish and French Syntax*

Stassen (1985: 39–44) also posits the existence of five major types of comparative construction, though there is no one-to-one correspondence with Andersen's list:

1 the separative comparative
2 the allative comparative
3 the locative comparative
4 the exceed comparative
5 the conjoined comparative

Separative comparatives are defined as instances of 'fixed-case adverbial comparative constructions', with one of the compared NPs 'encoded as a constituent part of an adverbial phrase with a . . . separative interpretation' (p. 39). Examples are given from Japanese, Carib and Mundari, the latter of which (his (11)) follows:

(6) Sadom-ete hati   mananga-i
    horse-from elephant big   -PRES.3SG.
    The elephant is bigger than the horse

Thirty-two languages are listed as exhibiting separative comparatives as their primary structural option and nine, including Old French, as having a secondary separative comparative.

Allative comparatives are also fixed-case adverbial comparatives, defined as 'the mirror-image of the Separative Comparative', but with the compared NP 'encoded as a constituent part of a . . . goal-phrase' (p. 40). Examples are given from Breton and Maasai; the latter (his (14)) follows:

(7) Sapuk ol-kondi to l -kibulekeny
    is-big the-deer to the-waterbuck
    The deer is bigger than the waterbuck

Seven languages are listed as exhibiting allative comparatives as their primary structural option and three as having a secondary allative comparative.

Locative comparatives are also fixed-case adverbial comparatives, but the compared NP is 'a constituent of an adverbial phrase which is marked by an element that indicates spatial or non-spatial contact' (p. 41). Formally it is similar to the previous two types of comparative. Examples are given from Chuckchee and Salinan, the second of which (his (17)) follows:

The nature of comparative constructions 5

(8) Ragas-mo in   luwa ti-hek
    surely-you more man on-me
    You are more of a man than me

Seventeen languages are listed as primary in this class and eight as secondary.

Stassen's separative, allative and locative comparatives appear to correspond to Andersen's single group of adpositional comparatives.

Exceed comparatives are also fixed-case constructions, with the compared NP 'constructed as the direct object of a special transitive verb, the meaning of which can be glossed as "to exceed" or "to surpass"' (p. 42). Examples are given from Yoruba, Hausa, Swahili and Vietnamese; the Vietnamese example (his (19)) follows:

(9) Vang qui   hon   bac
    gold valuable exceed silver
    Gold is worth more than silver

Twenty languages are listed as having some variant of the exceed comparative as their primary option and six as being secondary in this class. The exceed comparatives are equivalent to Andersen's verbal comparatives.

Conjoined comparatives are derived-case constructions in which 'NP-comparison is typically effected by means of the adversative coordination of two clauses . . . this type of comparative involves two grammatically independent clauses, which are connected in such a way that a gradation between the two objects can be inferred' (p. 44). Examples are given from Hixkaryana and Sika, the latter of which (his (22)) follows:

(10) Dzarang tica gahar, dzarang rei kesik
     horse   that big   horse   this small
     That horse is bigger than this horse

Twenty primary languages are given for this class and six secondary languages. Stassen's conjoined comparatives appear to correspond to Andersen's juxtaposition comparatives.

These five major types exclude the phenomenon of particle comparatives, a type of comparative construction which, unlike Andersen, for whom they constitute a major type, he considers problematic: they cannot fall under the heading of conjoined comparative (type 5), as they do not necessarily consist of two grammatically independent clauses. Stassen (1985: 46) also notes that

a typical characteristic of all Particle Comparatives is the presence of a specific *comparative particle* . . . there are also indications that the Particle Comparative is not a homogeneous category. The internal diversification of this set of comparatives is brought out by the fact that the comparative particles which are involved in the various constructions cannot be shown to have the same origin or categorial status for all of the languages in this class. One gets the impression that the class of Particle Comparatives . . . has assembled its members from a large variety
of sources and that . . . the formation of the comparative construction has, so to speak, '**gone wrong along the way**'. (my emphasis)

He states that this type of construction is an areal phenomenon, largely confined to the languages of the European 'Sprachbund', and eventually concludes that particle comparatives are 'a kind of "intermediate" category between the "optimal" categories of adverbial comparatives [i.e. separative, allative, locative] . . . and conjoined comparatives' (1985: 313). Eighteen languages, including French, are listed as primary in this class, and two as secondary.

While both Spanish and French clearly fall under this heading of particle comparatives, scant mention is made of the Spanish construction in either Stassen or Andersen (Andersen 1983, in fact, refers only once to Spanish (p. 101), and in a different context); nor does the construction in Italian merit very much greater consideration (again, only one mention in Andersen (p. 110)). Both authors prefer to concentrate their attention on the French construction, as being representative of the group. However, as I hope to show, a comparison of the detail of the Spanish and French constructions reveals major differences, which remain hidden within the framework of their broader analyses.

1.2 THE MENTAL REPRESENTATION OF COMPARISON

Stassen attempts a representation of the cognitive structure of comparisons. Following various others,[2] he sees this cognitive structure as a spatial configuration, in which 'the parameter of the comparison . . . is pictured as an axis, which is marked for positive–negative polarity' (1985: 262). The objects of comparison are then placed on the axis, the object which possesses the higher degree of the relevant quality being nearer to the positive side of the axis than the object with which it is being compared:

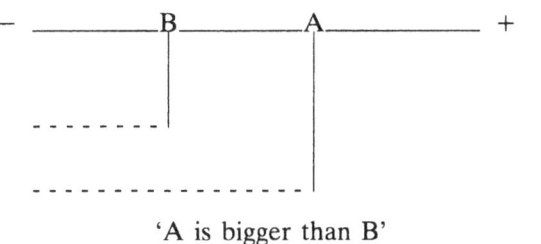

'A is bigger than B'

(Stassen 1985: 263)[3]

This cognitive representation, he claims, is

> language-independent. That is, we take it that the cognitive structure representing the mental operation of comparison is *essentially the same for all speakers of all natural languages . . . the cognitive representation of comparison presented above is indeed valid for all languages*

(1985: 264).

Hellan (1981: 42–3) conceives of this relation as linear, referring to such an axis as representing 'quality dimensions . . . along which an individual can manifest a given quality to a greater or lesser extent. . . . Let us call such dimensions *linear*.' Cresswell (1976: 266)
also states 'when we make comparisons, we have **in mind** points on a scale' (my emphasis). This idea of a linear, or spatial, representation of comparison has underpinned, more or less explicitly, many analyses of comparison in French, being adduced as explanation for the presence of an otherwise apparently extraneous marker of negation in the second clause of the comparison; the expletive negative is often held to indicate the position of the second compared item towards the '−' or negative end of the scale, as in, for example, (11):

(11) Marie est plus intelligente que Jean ne peut l'être
    Marie is more intelligent than Jean is capable of being

In (11) the presence of *ne* is taken to indicate that, with reference to the quality of intelligence, Jean is closer to the '−' end of the scale than Marie. Whatever the truth about the mental representation of comparison, and it seems unlikely that the mysterious nature of cognitive representations will be elucidated in the near future, to take as the basis for a syntactic analysis an unproven and probably, by its very nature, unprovable hypothesis seems an unsound method of investigation.

1.3 TYPES OF COMPARATIVE CONSTRUCTIONS: OF INEQUALITY AND EQUALITY

There are two types of comparative constructions: comparatives of inequality and of equality. Andersen's analysis of comparative constructions considers only one kind of comparison, that 'involving only two entities and one quality or property: *John is taller than Mary*' (1983: 99). In other words, he explicitly proposes to discuss only the adjectival comparative of inequality. Stassen, too, is 'concerned exclusively with cases of the comparison of inequality' and, again, restricts discussion to adjectival comparison: 'I have found it useful to confine my typology to those cases of comparative constructions in which *two objects or individuals (typically expressed in the form of NPs)* are being graded against each other' (1985: 25). Finally, Hellan (1981) also concentrates on adjectival comparison, particularly with reference to the comparative of inequality, though he does give some consideration to the comparative of equality (p. 150), considering, for example, the analysis of a sentence like (12) (his (16b)):

(12) John is three times as tall as Bill

This narrow consideration of only the comparative of inequality is a feature of many studies of comparison, perhaps reflecting the opinion evinced by Huttenlocher and Higgins in a paper on the psychological aspects of comparison: 'The most common way to compare two items, classes, or events is the "more" form, as in "more beautiful", "more friendly", etc.' (1971: 493).

Indeed, under the rubric of 'comparative of inequality' only the 'more than' comparative of superiority is usually considered, the 'less than' comparative of inferiority being excluded from the discussion on the (spurious) grounds that what holds for the former will of necessity hold for the latter. While this may be largely true in terms of the syntax of the construction, it cannot be said to be equally relevant where the semantics is concerned. Many of the semantic explanations offered for the presence of an expletive negative element in French comparative constructions rely exclusively on consideration of the comparative of superiority, e.g. (13):

(13) Pierre est plus intelligent que Marie ne l'est
Pierre is more intelligent than Marie is

Here the presence of the expletive negative is held to indicate that the speaker's assumption, that Marie is intelligent, is false. Once the comparative of inferiority is also considered, however, the arguments may not go through quite so smoothly; consider the following sentence:

(14) Pierre est moins intelligent que Marie ne l'est
Pierre is less intelligent than Marie is

In (14) the expletive negative may still occur, despite the fact that the speaker's assumption, again that Marie is intelligent, has not been demonstrated to be false.

The comparative of equality, on the other hand, rarely merits a mention, though it is self-evident that a complete study of comparison cannot exclude this type. Moreover, analysis of the comparative of equality may throw otherwise unshed light on the structure of the comparatives of inequality. This group of three construction types, of equality and of superior or inferior inequality, forms a homogeneous whole, of which any detailed study of comparison must, therefore, be prepared to take account. In this study equal attention will be paid to both the comparatives of inequality and the comparative of equality.

1.4 KINDS OF COMPARISON: FULL AND PARTIAL

To quote Andersen (1983: 99):

> Comparison can involve a number of parameters, the two most important being the number of entities compared and the number of qualities or properties used . . . there are only two basic results which can be expressed, i.e., (a) identity or similarity and (b) difference. If the result shows that the two entities in question do not differ with respect to the quality or property, we are dealing with a *comparison of equality* . . . if, on the other hand, the two entities do indeed differ, then the result will be termed a *comparison of inequality*.

In speaking of the conceptual content of a comparative construction, Stassen quotes Small (1929: 12–13):

> The speaker who uses comparison as a means of indicating the intensity of a given quality in an object casts about in his mind for a second object . . . which has that same quality . . . . If he is fortunate enough to hit upon a second object that . . . has the quality in exactly the *same* degree as the object he is discussing,

he may indicate the intensity of the quality by equating the first object with the second, thus: John is as tall as the gate-post . . . . Instead of a second *object* of comparison the speaker may also refer to a second *condition* of the first object itself, thus: John is just as accurate as he was in the rifle match a year ago. This way of pointing out the intensity of a given attribute may be termed the *comparison of equality*. Should the hypothetical speaker be unable to hit upon a second object or condition that exactly matches the first in the quality observed . . . he will call up to the attention of the hearer another object having the same quality, but either in a higher or a lower degree of intensity. Thus: John is taller than Mary . . . . The patient *is* now weaker than he *was* . . . . This sort of thing may best be referred to as the *comparison of inequality*.

(Stassen 1985: 24–5)

He also offers his own definition of the notion 'comparative construction': 'a construction in a natural language counts as a comparative construction . . . if that construction has the semantic function of assigning a graded (i.e. non-identical) position on a predicative scale to two (possibly complex) objects' (1985: 24).

Comparison may, however, be of two different kinds: full or partial. Full comparison involves comparing two categories which are identical with regard to lexical features, though they may be referentially distinct, in the case of nouns. Partial comparison, on the other hand, involves comparing categories which are necessarily lexically distinct.[4] As Doherty and Schwartz (1967: 904) put it with reference to adjectival comparison in English,

The comparison of attributes usually assumes some common scale of measurement . . . . But it seems that the attributes need not be on the same scale, and, furthermore, that the scales need not be specifiable, as in

[10] This table is more decorative than it is useful.

In addition, the categories which may be the objects of comparison range over nouns, adjectives, adverbs, prepositional phrases, verbs and even whole clauses. In this study, comparative constructions expressing both full and partial comparison involving each of these categories will be discussed. However, I shall omit consideration of potentially related constructions, such as superlatives and other degree constructions.[5]

1.5 REALIZATION OF COMPARISON IN SPANISH

By way of introduction to the analysis proper, possible realizations of the comparative construction in Spanish will now be exemplified. The most salient fact about comparatives in Spanish is that in a comparative of inequality the first half of the comparison may be linked to the second half by either *que* or (some variant of) *de lo que*, depending on syntactic considerations which will be discussed in detail in Chapter 2. Those comparatives of inequality in which *que* is the linking element will be referred to as 'sentential comparatives', while those in which this role is fulfilled by *de lo que* will be termed 'phrasal comparatives'.

A sentential comparative is a construction in which the complementizer, in the case of Spanish comparatives of inequality, *que*, introduces a clause; this clause may be full, in which case it will contain a tensed verb, or it may be reduced, with the tensed verb (and, optionally, other elements) omitted. The former type will be referred to as 'full sentential constructions' and the latter as 'reduced sentential constructions'.

A phrasal comparative, by contrast, is a construction in which the 'comparative particle' does not introduce a clause, either full or reduced. Rather, the category following the 'comparative particle' is generated directly as its complement and is not, as in the case of a reduced sentential construction, the 'survivor' of a full clause, the other elements of which have been deleted. It is not possible, in such cases, to 'reconstitute' a hypothetical comparative clause. This is the distinction, for example, between (15) and (16) in English (ignoring other possible considerations, such as register/style):

(15) He is older than I
(16) He is older than me

Example (15) may be analysed as a reduced sentential construction, in which the verb *am* could optionally be supplied: while (16) may be considered to be a phrasal construction, with *me* the complement of *than*.

This is reminiscent of the distinction made in Hoeksema (1984: 94) between oblique and sentential comparatives: 'a syntactic distinction should be made between comparatives with a noun phrase complement (let us call these oblique comparatives) and comparatives with a sentential complement (let us call those sentential comparatives)'. He sets up this distinction on the basis of the difference in English between sentences (17) and (18):

(17) Bill is taller than Mary
(18) He is bigger than we are

He also extends this analysis to include the Italian comparative construction (on the basis of the distinction between *di* and *che* as complementizers). It might, therefore, be expected that the same approach could work for Spanish. However, there are major differences between both Spanish and English and Spanish and Italian in this respect. Moreover, the situation with regard to Italian is not so clear-cut as it appears to be in Hoeksema's article.[6] Consequently, I prefer not to use the term 'oblique' for the Spanish *de lo que* comparative, retaining instead the term 'phrasal'.

Clearly, in Spanish comparatives of inequality involving *de lo que*, a clause does occur following *que*. Nonetheless, it is *lo* itself which is the complement of the 'comparative particle', *de*; hence such constructions may accurately be considered phrasal. The clause is in fact a relative clause, rather than a comparative clause, with *lo* as the head. Thus, strictly speaking, these structures are relativized phrasal constructions, a relative clause being constructed on the complement of the comparative particle. These constructions are analysed in detail in Chapter 2. For the sake of simplicity, they will occasionally be labelled 'phrasal', rather than the lengthier, but more accurate, 'relativized phrasal', constructions.

On the other hand, phrasal comparative constructions which are not relativized, for example, (16) in English, will be termed 'oblique phrasal comparatives', borrowing Hoeksema's terminology. This labelling will serve to differentiate unambiguously between the two types of phrasal comparative constructions.

1.5.1 Expression of full comparison

I shall begin with examples of comparative constructions expressing full comparison, i.e. comparison involving two categories which are identical with regard to lexical features. In each case the category which is the object of comparison will be an adjective.

The comparatives of inequality

With regard to the comparative of inequality,[7] there are two possible constructions:

The nature of comparative constructions

1 a reduced sentential construction, i.e. one in which a tensed verb does not appear in the second half of the comparison, e.g. (19):

(19) Un perro es más feroz que   un gato
     a dog is more fierce than   a cat

2 a (relativized) phrasal construction, involving *de lo que*, e.g. (20):

(20) Un perro es más feroz de   lo que puede ser un gato
     a dog is more fierce than it that may be a cat
     A dog is more fierce than a cat may be

The comparative of equality

The comparative of equality, by contrast, allows three types of construction:

1 a reduced sentential construction, e.g. (21):

(21) La chica es tan inteligente como su   amiga
     the girl is as intelligent as   her friend

2 a full sentential construction, i.e. one in which a tensed verb does appear in the second half of the comparison, after *como*, e.g. (22):

(22) La chica es tan inteligente como su   amiga parece ser
     the girl is as intelligent as   her friend seems to be

3 a (relativized) phrasal construction, e.g. (23):

(23) La chica es tan inteligente como lo que creen   sus padres
     the girl is as intelligent as   it that believe her parents
     The girl is as intelligent as her parents believe

1.5.2 Expression of partial comparison

The range of possibilities for constructions expressing partial comparison, i.e. comparison involving categories which are necessarily lexically distinct, is somewhat wider. Again, the following examples will demonstrate partial comparison involving only the category of adjective.

14   *Comparative Constructions in Spanish and French Syntax*

The comparatives of inequality

For the comparative of inequality, there are three possible constructions:

1 a reduced sentential construction, e.g. (24):

(24) La mesa es más larga que ancha
 the table is more long than wide

2 a full sentential construction, where the second compared category appears clause-initially in the second clause (this I will term a 'topicalized sentential construction'; the grounds for a topicalization analysis will be explored in Chapter 2), e.g. (25):

(25) La mesa es más larga que ancha es la puerta
 the table is more long than wide is the door
 The table is longer than the door is wide

3 a (relativized) phrasal construction, e.g. (26):

(26) La mesa es más larga de   lo que la   puerta es ancha
 the table is more long than it that the door   is wide
 The table is longer than the door is wide

The comparative of equality

The comparative of equality allows four types of construction:

1 a reduced sentential construction, e.g. (27):

(27) El chico es tan guapo   como listo
 the boy is as handsome as   clever

2 a topicalized sentential construction, e.g. (28):

(28) El chico es tan guapo   como listo es su hermano
 the boy is as handsome as   clever is his brother
 The boy is as handsome as his brother is clever

3 a full sentential construction with declarative word order in the second clause, e.g. (29):

The nature of comparative constructions 15

(29) El chico es tan guapo   como su hermano es listo
    the boy is as handsome as   his brother is clever

4 a (relativized) phrasal construction, e.g. (30):

(30) El chico es tan guapo   como lo que su hermano es listo
    the boy is as handsome as   it that his brother is clever
    The boy is as handsome as his brother is clever

While there are certain differences between the preceding construction types with regard to level of appropriateness and extent of use, they are all fully grammatical.

1.5.3 The clause introducers

Clearly, the range of constructions allowed by the two types of comparison, those of inequality and equality, differs both for full and partial comparison. In each case, the comparative of equality displays one more option than the corresponding comparative of inequality. One of the more obvious differences between the comparatives of inequality and the comparative of equality is the existence of different clause introducers, *que* and *como*.

According to the analysis in Stassen (1985: 188–97), the category of particle comparatives, which he does not consider a major type, contains at least seven different types of particle comparative:

1 where there is 'a straightforward parallel between the comparative and the expression of *and-coordination*' (p. 189): for example Javanese, where the element *karo* functions with both the meanings 'than' and 'and';
2 where the comparative particle 'is also used as an adverbial element in a balanced consecutive chain' (p. 189): for example Toba Batak, where the element *asa* functions with both the meanings 'than' and 'then' or 'after that';
3 where the comparative particle 'is represented by an item which has also the function of marking adversative relation between coordinated sentences or clauses' (p. 190): for example Basque, where *baino/bainan* functions as equivalent to both 'than' and the adversative conjunction 'but';
4 where the comparative particle also functions 'as the marker for negative coordination "nor"' (p. 190): for example Scottish Gaelic, where the particle *na* has both these functions;
5 where the comparative particle 'is identical to the item which

connects balanced disjunctive clauses or phrases' (p. 191): for example Classical Greek, where *ē* has this dual function;
6 where the comparative particle is also used 'as an element with the meaning "like" or "as"' (p. 191): for example Modern Hungarian, where the element *mint/amint* has both the meanings 'than' and 'like';
7 where the comparative particle 'has its etymological origin in *an oblique case form of the relative/interrogative pronoun*' (p. 195), but does not occur as an item meaning 'like'.

This implies that the Spanish comparative of equality belongs to his sixth group of particle comparatives. The comparatives of inequality, however, will belong to the seventh group of particle comparatives, in which he also places French. It seems possible that the varying availability of construction types for the two types of comparison may be the consequence of *que* having been selected as the clause introducer, or 'particle', for comparatives of inequality, while *como* fulfils this function in comparatives of equality. This possibility will be discussed more fully in Chapter 2.

1.6 REALIZATION OF COMPARISON IN FRENCH

Turning now to French, examples will be given in a similar fashion. The most salient fact about the comparative constructions in French is the possible appearance of a pleonastic negative element, *ne*, in the second clause of the comparison, particularly in comparatives of inequality, but also in the comparative of equality. In addition, paralleling the case in Spanish, there is a possible alternation between *que* and *que ce que* as the element linking the two clauses. Those comparatives in which *que ce que* introduces the second clause will be termed 'phrasal', as was the case for the Spanish *de lo que* comparatives, though their status is somewhat different.

1.6.1 Expression of full comparison

I shall begin with constructions expressing full comparison; once again, all examples involve an adjective as the compared category.

The comparatives of inequality

The following are examples of the comparative of inequality constructions.[8] There are three possible construction types:

1 a reduced sentential construction, e.g. (31):

(31) Le père   est plus   riche qu'   auparavant
     the father is   more rich   than before
     The father is richer than before

2 a full sentential construction, e.g. (32):

(32) Le père   est plus   riche que le   fils ne   l' était
     the father is   more rich   than the son neg. it was
     The father is richer than the son was

3 two types of phrasal construction:

(a) a construction corresponding to Hoeksema's oblique comparative, which I shall term the 'oblique phrasal construction', e.g. (33):

(33) Son père   est plus   riche que   lui
     his father is   more rich   than him
     His father is richer than him

(b) a (relativized) phrasal construction involving *que ce que*,[9] e.g. (34):

(34) Le père   est plus   riche que   ce   que   le   fils croyait
     the father is   more rich   than that which the son believed
     The father is richer than the son believed

The comparative of equality

For the comparative of equality there are also three construction types:

1 a reduced sentential construction, e.g. (35):

(35) La jeune   fille est aussi contente qu' auparavant
     the young girl is   as   happy   as   before

2 a full sentential construction, e.g. (36):

(36) La jeune   fille est aussi contente que l' était le   petit garçon
     the young girl is   as   happy   as   it was the little boy
     The young girl is as happy as the little boy was

18 *Comparative Constructions in Spanish and French Syntax*

3 two types of phrasal construction:

(a) an oblique phrasal construction, e.g. (37):

(37) La jeune fille est aussi contente que lui
 the young girl is as happy as him

(b) a *que ce que* (relativized) phrasal construction,[10] e.g. (38):

(38) La jeune fille est aussi contente que ce que le petit
 the young girl is as happy as that which the little
 garçon voulait
 boy wished
 The young girl is as happy as the little boy wished

1.6.2 Expression of partial comparison

Where the expression of partial comparison is concerned, the range of possibilities may be wider.

The comparatives of inequality

The comparative of inequality allows four construction types:

1 a reduced sentential construction, e.g. (39):

(39) Le travail est plus détaillé que difficile
 the work is more detailed than difficult

2 a full sentential construction with declarative word order in the second clause, e.g. (40):

(40) Le travail est plus difficile que le contrat n' est
 the work is more difficult than the contract neg. is
 détaillé
 detailed
 The work is more difficult than the contract is detailed

3 a topicalized sentential construction,[11] e.g. (41):

(41) Le travail est plus difficile que détaillé est le contrat
 the work is more difficult than detailed is the contract
 The work is more difficult than the contract is detailed

4 a (relativized) phrasal construction,[12] e.g. (42):

(42) Le travail est plus difficile que ce que le contrat est
the work is more difficult than that which the contract is
détaillé
detailed
The work is more difficult than the contract is detailed

The comparative of equality

The same situation holds for the comparative of equality, which has an identical range of possibilities:

1 a reduced sentential construction, e.g. (43):

(43) La vie est aussi dure que transitoire
life is as hard as transitory
Life is as hard as it is transitory

2 a full sentential construction with declarative word order in the second clause, e.g. (44):

(44) La vie est aussi transitoire que la mort est permanente
life is as transitory as death is permanent

3 a topicalized sentential construction,[13] e.g. (45):

(45) La vie est aussi transitoire que permanente est la mort
life is as transitory as permanent is death
Life is as transitory as death is permanent

4 a (relativized) phrasal construction,[14] e.g. (46):

(46) La vie est aussi transitoire que ce que la mort est
life is as transitory as that which death is
permanente
permanent
Life is as transitory as death is permanent

1.6.3 The clause introducer

The preceding examples show clearly that, for French, the range of constructions available for the expression of comparison does not vary in accordance with the type of comparative construction, be it a comparative of inequality or equality. This would appear to be related to the fact that for both types the clause introducer, or comparative particle, is *que*. In other words, both types fall under the heading of Stassen's seventh group of particle comparatives: 'the Particle Comparatives in Russian, Finnish and French . . . may be viewed as a *seventh* group . . . . Modern French has a primary Particle Comparative in which the standard NP or clause is preceded by the item *que*' (1985: 195–6). In this respect the French and Spanish constructions differ greatly.

1.6.4 The expletive negative

Further, the appearance of an expletive negative element in the second clause of some comparatives in French distinguishes these constructions from their Spanish equivalents.[15] In connection with this, Seuren (1984: 109) refers to the 'intimate relationship of the comparative in English and most other European languages with negation'. And Stassen (1984: 178) speaks of 'strong evidence for the claim that, in a number of particle comparatives, an *underlying negative element* is present. This negative element . . . may crop up in comparatives as an independent item . . . (as in French . . .)', while Stassen 1985 goes further: 'in French the negative particle *ne* shows up obligatorily in a comparative clause if that clause contains a finite verb' (p. 217). It is one of the aims of this work to show that such a bald statement cannot be said to reflect the true nature of the phenomenon.

1.7 FOCUS OF COMPARISON

The diversity of construction types available in Spanish and French, which have been briefly sketched, and the variation found both within and between the two languages, would seem to point to complex and intricate differences in the ways in which comparison is realized. My aim, however, is to show that the various syntactic effects in the Spanish and French constructions are partially conditioned by a general constraint on comparison: that some element in the subordinate clause of the comparison must act as a focus.

The notion of 'focus of comparison' is referred to in Flores D'Arcais (1970), where it is described as an 'intuitive and vague' notion (p. 319). For Flores D'Arcais, the way in which a comparison is 'focussed' is a 'cognitive factor' (p. 308) and may involve either the matrix or subordinate clause category of comparison. Pinkham (1982: 102–3) also refers to 'foci for comparison', but offers no specific definition. However, the examples given there (reproduced below) seem to indicate that such foci are simply contrasting items and may or may not involve one of the objects of comparison:

(47) Il passe plus d'heures avec ses étudiants que toi de minutes
He spends more hours with his students than you (spend) minutes (with yours)
(48) Paul donne plus d'argent à la Croix Rouge que Marie à UNICEF
Paul gives more money to the Red Cross than Marie (gives) to UNICEF

Pinkham considers both *toi* and *de minutes* in (47) and *Marie* and UNICEF in (48) to be foci. However, these sentences are dissimilar, (47) being an expression of partial comparison, and (48) an expression of full comparison. In (47), therefore, *de minutes* is the second compared category, that is, the category for which a preceding quantifier must be inferred, while the status of *toi* is simply that it contrasts with *il* in the matrix. In (48), neither *Marie* nor UNICEF is the compared category; this does not appear, but must be inferred, and is a quantified expression involving the noun *argent*, parallel to the phrase *plus d'argent* of the matrix. *Marie* and UNICEF simply contrast with *Paul* and *la Croix Rouge* in the matrix. Pinkham's definition of a focus item, therefore, must be considered to range over both valid compared categories and categories which simply contrast.

This is not the case in Kuno (1981: 142–4), where a syntactic rule of focus of contrast raising is proposed as being involved in the derivation of comparatives. While the precise details of the rule are not relevant here, it is interesting in that it involves an element defined as constituting a focus of contrast. Although exactly what this 'contrastive element' is is not clearly defined, an explanation of what it is not is offered: it is not the category in the subordinate clause specified by a quantifier. In other words, it is not the second object of comparison, whether lexicalized (as in partial comparison) or deleted (as in full comparison). So Kuno's notion of focus of contrast may involve only those categories which are not involved in the comparison proper, unlike Pinkham's focus of comparison, which may involve almost any category, whatever its precise status.

Andersen (1983: 156–62) also refers to a 'process of Focus' as being essential in some types of comparative, which may be 'marked by means of the use of a focussing particle', while Zaslawsky (1977: 70) refers to one of the compared objects in a comparison as acting as the focus, without making it clear which of these (the matrix or subordinate term) he is referring to, or whether such status is variable.

The notion of focus in expressions of comparison, then, is often invoked in the literature, but in rather vague terms. I intend to use the label 'focus of comparison' to refer only to the second compared category in a comparison: that is, to the category in the second half of the comparison modified by an (inferable) quantifier, corresponding to an overtly quantified category in the matrix. This category will be lexicalized in expressions of partial comparison, but necessarily deleted in expressions of full comparison (though it may, of course, be represented by a proform). Any other category directly involved in the comparison by virtue of paralleling a category in the matrix (for instance, *toi* in (47), *Marie* and UNICEF in (48)) will be referred to as a 'focus of contrast', following Kuno. These notions of foci of comparison and contrast and their interaction with the comparative constructions of Spanish and French will be elaborated and shown to play a role in accounting for the diversity of construction types in the two languages.

1.8 MARKER OF COMPARISON

Andersen (1983) also considers the concept of the marker of comparison. He cites Greenberg 1966 (on p. 101) and Friedrich 1975 (on p. 105) as defining the marker of comparison as corresponding to English *than*. Lehmann (1974), on the other hand, is cited as referring to comparative suffixes, e.g. *-er* in English, as markers, preferring to term *than* a 'pivot' (Andersen 1983: 104). Andersen himself defines the marker of comparison as

> that specific element which distinguishes a comparison of inequality from a comparison of equality. It is, therefore, that element which expresses the specific result of inequality as opposed to the only other result possible, namely, that of equality. In the juxtapositional construction the marker [may be] the negative element NOT.

(1983: 116)

He then considers what the marker of comparison is in the particle construction: 'We know already that the particle is the link, but is it

The nature of comparative constructions

also that element which distinguishes this construction from a comparison of equality?' (p. 117). On the basis of brief examples of comparatives of equality and inequality in Latin, German, Finnish, Old Indic and French, he decides that, as the particle in both types of comparative is the same (*quam*, *wie*, *kuin*, *yac* and *que*, respectively),

> the particle does not distinguish comparisons of inequality . . . from comparisons of equality . . . ; hence the particle, although being the link, is not a marker. Generalizing from examples found in a number of languages, I would now say that the sole marker in the particle construction is the comparative morpheme of the adjective.
>
> (1983: 118)

However, it is not the case that in all languages classed as particle comparatives the particle does not distinguish between comparisons of equality and of inequality. In Spanish, quite clearly, *que* might be viewed as having this function, since the equative 'particle' is *como*. Even in one of the languages Andersen cites this is so: in Standard German the particle *als* is used in comparatives of inequality, while *wie* is the particle in equative constructions (Andersen admits in a note (p. 140) that his comparison of inequality with *wie* is actually a dialectal form). So *als* in German and *que* in Spanish, at least, might have a claim to be considered as markers of comparison as well as 'particles'.

In French this is clearly not the case, as *que* plays the role of particle in both types of comparison and therefore is not distinctive in comparatives of inequality. It is interesting, however, to note that Andersen's previous definition of a marker of comparison, as a negative element in juxtapositional comparatives, might easily be extended to French, where expletive *ne* occurs in sentential comparatives of inequality. Despite being a language with particle comparatives, rather than juxtapositional constructions, then, French might well be viewed as using an, at least formally, negative element as a marker of comparison. This leads to the hypothesis that languages with particle comparatives may use either the particle (where this is distinctive in comparatives of inequality) or a negative element (where the comparative particles are non-distinct) as a marker of comparison. If this is accepted, then particle comparatives must be a less homogeneous group than Andersen suggests, a point made by Stassen (1985) (see section 1.1). Interestingly, Stassen does suggest that particle comparatives are intermediate between the categories of adverbial and conjoined comparatives and, as I have already shown, Stassen's category of conjoined comparatives appears to correspond to Andersen's category of juxtaposition comparatives. The suggestion that the expletive negative may act as a marker of comparison, then, could act as a bridge between the two theories.

Hence, in Spanish, where there are two 'comparative particles', *como* and *que*, *que* may be regarded as a marker of comparison; in French, on the other hand, where there is only one 'particle', *que*, this particle may not be regarded as a marker (according to Andersen's definition), but the additional expletive negative particle may be. This provides a possible explanation for the role of *ne* in French and also makes an interesting prediction: languages in which the same particle occurs in comparatives of inequality and equality will require an expletive negative element to act as a marker of comparison, while languages with two distinctive particles will not. This prediction will be tested against data from Spanish and French, as well as a number of other Romance languages. The fact that the marker of comparison may be homonymic with the tensed clause complementizer (e.g. Spanish *que*) means that the situation is somewhat less clear-cut; nevertheless it will be shown that there is a great deal of evidence to support this contention regarding the reason that an expletive negative may be required. This suggests that a further constraint on comparison exists: that there must be a suitable marker of comparison in comparative expressions. Moreover, together with considerations of focus, the concept of a marker of comparison can account for otherwise inexplicable structural contrasts between Spanish and French.

1.9 SUMMARY

The nature of comparative constructions has been considered and a brief review of recent studies given. It has been shown that for both Andersen (1983) and Stassen (1985) French and Spanish belong to the group of languages exhibiting particle comparatives (though this is not a major type for Stassen). The differences between types of comparative constructions (of inequality and of equality) and kinds of comparison (full and partial) have been illustrated and the range of construction types available in Spanish and French exemplified, though without detailed comment. These will be considered more fully in Chapters 2 and 3 respectively, where the relevance of the notions of focus of comparison and marker of comparison will also be demonstrated. It will be shown that these two simple concepts can account for the wide range of structures found in both languages.

To borrow a quote from von Stechow (1984a: 199) in a slightly different context: 'These principles are very simple. The amazing complexity of comparative constructions arises if we consider their interaction with other relevant principles of syntax and semantics.' Stassen (1985: 6) appears to feel that the comparative construction in particle comparative languages has 'gone wrong along the way' and, indeed, asks himself 'why Particle Comparatives should exist at all' (p. 197), yet the comparative constructions of Spanish and French constitute a fruitful and interesting field of study. Moreover, this is a field where, as I hope to demonstrate, a comparative approach will show the wealth of detail to be predictable on the basis of simple generalizations.

NOTES

1 See Hoeksema (1984) for a concise statement of the major controversies.
2 See Stassen (1985: 262).
3 See Joly (1967) for an almost identical suggestion.
4 Full comparison and partial comparison within a model of grammar including (the concept of) syntactic deletion rules have traditionally been referred to as examples of comparative deletion versus comparative subdeletion, respectively. See Bresnan (1973, 1975).
5 For a discussion of degree constructions in Spanish, see S.A. Price (1982).
6 Discussion of the Italian construction can be found in Chapter 4.
7 For now, only examples involving the comparative of superiority will be given. In each case, substitution of *menos* for *más* will have no effect on the syntax.
8 As for Spanish, only examples of the comparative of superiority will be given here.
9 This construction is felt to be somewhat marginal.
10 See note 9.
11 This construction is very limited, due to word-order restrictions.
12 See note 9.
13 See note 11.
14 See note 9.
15 Discussion of the (limited) possibility of a pleonastic negative in Spanish comparatives may be found in Chapter 2.

2 Comparative constructions in Spanish

Any discussion of the comparative constructions of Spanish must be prepared to take into account the notable differences in structure between the comparatives of inequality and the comparative of equality, differences which have already been sketched in the preceding chapter. Nevertheless, it is by no means true that existing studies always accept or even refer to this fact. As is so often the case, examination of the comparative construction in Spanish is limited to consideration of the comparatives of inequality, e.g. Saenz (1940), Bolinger (1950, 1953), De Mello (1977), Rivero (1979), Solé (1982), Studerus (1982) and Knowles (1984). Butt and Benjamin (1989: 57) even go so far as to claim confidently that 'comparison in Spanish is not particularly complex'. In fact, the expression of comparison is complex and what is striking about these constructions in Spanish is precisely this possibility for both types of comparative to enter into different syntactic configurations and the ways in which these possibilities are restricted.

The following discussion will begin by examining the constructions expressing full comparison, in the sense which has already been defined, both for comparatives of inequality and the comparative of equality. Constructions expressing partial comparison, with regard to both types of comparative, will be considered next. I will then discuss the extent to which a pleonastic or expletive negative element may be found in the Spanish constructions and what its status might be, before finally proceeding to draw conclusions as to the nature of the construction exemplified and, specifically, to attempt to link the (normal) inability of a tensed verb to surface after *más/menos* with the general constraints on comparison mentioned in Chapter 1: that an element acting as the focus of comparison occurs in the second half of a comparative construction and that a marker of comparison must be present in comparatives of inequality.

2.1 EXPRESSION OF FULL COMPARISON

2.1.1 The comparatives of inequality[1]

It was stated in the preceding chapter that there are two possible constructions:

1 a reduced sentential construction, exemplified there by the following:

(1) Un perro es más feroz que un gato
    A dog is more fierce than a cat

2 a relativized phrasal construction, involving *de lo que*:[2]

(2) Un perro es más feroz de lo que puede ser un gato
    A dog is more fierce than a cat may be

In fact, the position may seem slightly more complex than this. There is a well-known alternation in Spanish between the preposition *de* and *que* after *más/menos* when the second half of the comparison contains a number or refers to a quantity, e.g.:

(3) Tengo más de/que mil pesetas
    I have more than a thousand pesetas

There may be a slight semantic difference in the choice of alternant in that the variant with *de* implies that what is possessed in excess of 1,000 pesetas is also numerical, as in (4):

(4) Tengo más de mil pesetas; tengo dos mil
    I have more than a thousand pesetas; I have two thousand

The variant with *que*, on the other hand, does not necessarily have this implication, e.g.:

(5) Tengo más que mil pesetas; tengo mis tarjetas de crédito
    I have more than a thousand pesetas; I have my credit cards

Additionally, *de* and *que* are said to alternate freely in sentences like (3) if they are negated, e.g.:

(6) No tengo más de/que mil pesetas
    I do not have more than a thousand pesetas

Nevertheless, native speakers frequently use the two interchangeably, though the construction with *de* is more frequent 'when the comparative cooccurs with an overt or covert numerical estimate' (Solé 1982: 615). Interestingly, when the comparative is preceded by a negative, (as in (6)), *que* is usually preferred to *de*. This gives rise to a somewhat confusing picture, usually summed up as in Solé (1982: 618): '*más/menos* . . . *que* versus *más/menos* . . . *de* can be said to be in complementary distribution, that is, where one occurs the other does not, and vice versa.' That this is not strictly true has already been exemplified. The position is rather that *de* is preferred to *que* when the second half of the comparison contains a numerical reference, except when the main clause is negated, when the opposite preference holds. It seems clear that, in any case, such constructions are not true comparatives, in the sense in which the term is being used here. A construction expressing comparison is one in which two categories which are identical with regard to lexical features are being compared (full comparison) or involving the comparison of two categories which are necessarily lexically distinct (partial comparison). In sentences such as (3) no category is actually being compared; it exhibits no gap semantically.

The reduced sentential construction

That the construction type exemplified in (1) is indeed a reduced sentential construction rather than some kind of oblique phrasal comparative is easily demonstrated. While in English there is a clear opposition between sentences like (7) and (8), there is no such opposition in Spanish:

(7) He is bigger than I
(8) He is bigger than me[3]

The Spanish version of (7) is (9), while directly translating (8) gives the ungrammatical (10):

(9) Es más grande[4] que yo
(10) *Es más grande que mí

In other words, *que* may only be followed by the subject form of the personal pronoun, unlike English *than*, which may be followed either by the subject form or by the object form of the pronoun, thus indicating the possibility of two separate structures, despite the fact that in actual usage this difference may be felt by speakers to be purely stylistic. Only one of these appears to be a reduced sentential structure, that is, the structure exhibited in (7). In the Spanish construction, only the reduced sentential structure is grammatical. Sentences (1) and (9), then, are reduced sentential constructions. It should be noted that they are obligatorily reduced; while the element following *que* need not be a personal pronoun, as shown by (11), it is never possible for a tensed verb to appear in the second half of the comparison, as shown by (12–14):

(11) Es más grande que antes
    He is bigger than before
(12) *Un perro es más feroz que es un gato
    A dog is more fierce than a cat is
(13) *Es más grande que yo soy
    He is bigger than I am
(14) *Es más grande que antes era
    He is bigger than he was before

Notice that the person and tense of the verb are irrelevant, as is its lexical content. The sentence is equally ungrammatical whether the subject of the verb of the subordinate clause is identical to the matrix subject or not, and irrespective of tense or meaning:

(15) *Es más grande que creíamos
    He is bigger than we thought

It may appear an easy matter to construct comparative sentences of this type which do indeed allow a tensed verb to appear after *que*, e.g. (16):

(16) Vende menos que compra
    He sells less than he buys

Example (16) is perfectly grammatical. Notice, however, that the superficially parallel (17) is ungrammatical:

(17) *Vende menos que tiene
    He sells less than he has

The grammatical version of (17) is (18):

(18) Vende menos de lo que tiene

Interestingly, equally grammatical is (19):

(19) Vende menos de lo que compra

What is the difference between (16) and (19), and (17) and (18)? Both (18) and (19) are relativized phrasal comparative constructions involving *de lo que* and are grammatical, as expected. However, (16) and (17) appear to be full sentential constructions involving a tensed verb after *que* and therefore might be expected to be ungrammatical, given that, as has been demonstrated, a tensed verb seems unable to appear in this position. This is, in fact, the case for (17). Why, then, do there appear to be two acceptable variants for (16), but only one for (17), i.e. (18)? Firstly, it must be realized that what is being compared in each of these four sentences is not exactly the same. *Vender* and *comprar* are optionally transitive verbs and in (16) the category undergoing comparison is the verb itself. Thus the verbs are interpreted intransitively and it is the extent of selling which is being compared to the extent of buying. In (19) the compared category is the lexically unspecified object of *vender*. The verbs are interpreted transitively: the amount sold is being compared to the amount bought. *Tener*, however, is an obligatorily transitive verb. As a result, it may only enter into a construction like (18), where *vender* is interpreted as a transitive verb, just as in (19), and the amount sold is being compared to the amount possessed. Sentence (17) is necessarily ungrammatical as like is not being compared with like; *vender* is intransitive and constitutes the category of comparison, while *tener* may not do so: there is no 'extent' of possession. The difference in acceptability between these four sentences is, therefore, explicable on the basis of exactly what the comparative *menos* is modifying: the verb or its unspecified object. It may still seem surprising, however, that a sentence like (16) should be acceptable, appearing, as it does, to break the proposed rule that a tensed verb may not follow *que* in these constructions. This is because (16) is actually an example of partial comparison, i.e. the compared categories (the verbs *vender* and *comprar*) are lexically distinct. In this section only examples of full comparison are being considered in detail. As will be shown in the section dealing with examples of partial comparison, such constructions are crucially different from those expressing full comparison; this apparent irregularity in fact forms part of a wide and very regular pattern.

Sentence (1) was an example of a reduced sentential comparative where the category undergoing comparison was the adjective, *feroz*. The following examples show simple reduced sentential comparatives exhibiting comparison of the noun, verb, adverb and prepositional phrase, respectively:

(20) Juan tiene más hermanos que María
Juan has more brothers than Maria
(21) A causa de sus problemas, mi padre duerme menos que antes
Because of his problems, my father sleeps less than before
(22) La chica bailaba más elegantemente con su novio que con su padre
The girl danced more elegantly with her boyfriend than with her father
(23) Un avión vuela más por encima de los tejados que un pájaro
A plane flies further (lit. 'more') above the rooftops than a bird

The relativized phrasal construction

The second type of construction, the relativized phrasal construction exemplified in (2), exhibits the sequence: preposition[5] – pronoun – *que* + tensed verb. The characteristics of this type of comparative are very different. First, this construction, unlike the reduced sentential type, displays no gap in the second half of the comparison. In other words, it is not reduced. In fact, the sequence pronoun – *que* + tensed verb is identical to the sequence found in relative constructions, e.g.:

(24) Este hombre es el que llegó ayer
This man is the one who arrived yesterday

It seems, then, that the phrasal construction involving *de lo que* might best be analysed as involving a pronoun (*lo*), which is the complement of *de* and heads a restrictive relative clause, parallel to the restrictive relative clause in a sentence like (24).[6]

This noun phrase complement of *de* is always pronominal, one of the following forms of the pronoun:

	singular	plural
+*masculine*	el	los
+*feminine*	la	las
−*masculine*/−*feminine*	lo	

The features on the pronoun complement of *de* in the second half of phrasal comparatives allow reconstruction of the features of the matrix noun to which it corresponds (lexically, that is; obviously they are not referentially identical as this would preclude comparison). Clearly, this applies only when the categories being compared are nouns. Equally clearly, only *el/los* and *la/las* could occur in such a comparison, as nouns in Spanish are always marked for gender. Given that *lo* is unmarked for gender, it evidently cannot correspond to any lexical noun in the matrix; in all cases where the category involved in the comparison is other than a noun the complement of *de* will be *lo*. That this is so may easily be demonstrated.

The following is an example of a relativized phrasal comparative involving an adjective:

(25) Este vestido es más corto de lo que era
 This dress is shorter than it was

Lo may act as a pronominal copy for an adjective in other contexts too, e.g.:

(26) ¿Es corto el vestido?
 Is the dress short?
 Lo es
 It is

Example (27) is an example of a relativized phrasal comparative involving an adverb as the compared category:

(27) Pedro come más ruidosamente de lo que come Juan
 Pedro eats more noisily than Juan eats

Here *lo* refers to the matrix adverb.

An example of a relativized phrasal comparative involving the category of prepositional phrase is given in (28):

(28) El avión está volando más por encima de los tejados de lo que antes volaba
 The plane is flying further (lit. 'more') above the rooftops than it flew before

Lo here is equivalent to the prepositional phrase *por encima de los tejados* in the matrix. *Lo* may also act as a pronominal anaphor for a prepositional phrase in other contexts, e.g.:

(29) ¿Está el pájaro por encima de su jaula?
 Is the bird on top of its cage?
 Lo está
 It is

Here *lo* replaces the prepositional phrase *por encima de su jaula*.

In the following example the verb is the compared element:

(30) Duerme más de lo que dormía
 He sleeps more than he used to sleep

However, it seems that *lo* in (30) cannot correspond to the verb in the matrix as this is repeated in the restrictive relative clause, hence there could be no coherent interpretation of the sentence under such an analysis. In fact, in a sentence like (30), although the verb is the category undergoing comparison, what is actually being compared is not the verb itself, but rather an underlying quantifier or measure phrase contained within the adverb *más*. It seems uncontroversial to assume that *más* and *menos* may be thought of as being synthetic realizations of *más mucho* and *menos mucho*; in other words, the latter correspond, respectively, to their semantic content. It can then be claimed that, in cases of relativized phrasal comparatives involving the verb as the category of comparison, what is actually being compared is this underlying quantifier, the semantic content of *mucho*, and it is to this that *lo* refers: it is impossible for a tensed verb to be the element compared in a phrasal comparative.[7]

The verb *dormir* is intransitive. Notice that if the verb involved is optionally transitive, e.g. *vender*, the phrasal comparative should be ambiguous between an interpretation of *lo* as corresponding to *mucho* or as referring to a lexically unfilled object of the verb. That this is the case is shown by a sentence like (31):

(31) Vende más de lo que vendía
He sells more than he used to sell

Example (31) is ambiguous between the first reading – the *extent to/frequency with which he is involved in the act of selling is greater than it was* – and the second – *the quantity of goods he sells is greater than it was*. The second reading will normally be preferred as being generally a more relevant statement, but the first is quite possible, given an appropriate context.[8]

Example (31) also shows that when the pronoun following *de* corresponds to a lexically empty object of the verb in the matrix, it takes the form *lo*, the form which is unmarked for gender and number.[9]

The noun as the compared category

The pronominal forms corresponding to a lexical matrix noun in phrasal comparatives have been given as *el/los*, *la/las*. The following examples contain instances of each of these forms:

(32) Gana menos dinero del[10] que quería
He earns less money than he wanted
(33) Hay más problemas de los que se cree
There are more problems than one thinks
(34) Existe menos bondad de la que se necesita
There exists less goodness than one needs
(35) Vio más mesas en el almacén de las que pensaba que existían
He saw more tables in the store than he thought existed

In each case the pronoun following *de* clearly allows for reconstruction of the gender and number of the matrix noun to which it corresponds. However, other versions of (32-4) are possible,[11] as exemplified by (36) (an alternative version of (32)):

(36) Gana menos dinero de lo que quería

It seems that in such cases, where *lo* appears instead of the gender-marked version of the pronoun, it refers to the *mucho* part of the nominal modifier *más/menos*, rather than to the lexical noun itself, just as in the case of the verbal comparison already discussed; in other words, *lo* may also correspond to the quantifier contained within the comparative modifier, *más/menos*, of the nominal antecedent. Where a noun is the category involved in a phrasal comparative, the pronoun following *de* may correspond **either** to the lexical noun **or** to the quantifier modifying the noun.[12] In the first case it will be marked for the same gender and number as the matrix noun, in the second it will be *lo*.

It is also possible for the matrix object noun to be compared with a prepositional object in the subordinate clause, e.g.:

(37) Gana   menos dinero de   con el que contaba
he earns less   money than with it that he counted
He earns less money than he was counting on
(38) Tiene más títulos en su lista de   sobre los   que ha
he has more titles   on his list   than on   those that has
hablado su profesor
spoken his teacher
He has more titles on his list than his teacher has spoken about
(39) Han   destrozado más árboles de   en los   que se   había
they have destroyed more trees   than on those that one had
puesto la   cruz blanca
put   the cross white
They have destroyed more trees than had had the white cross placed on them

These constructions are felt to be somewhat inelegant by native speakers, due to the (normally unacceptable) sequence of *de* + another preposition. That such a sequence is actually possible in such structures is directly related to the fact that *de* is not functioning here as a preposition, but as a 'comparative particle'. Such constructions would normally be avoided by the use of some periphrasis, but they are perfectly grammatical. Note that it is not possible for the positions of the preposition and pronoun to be reversed, giving, for example, *menos dinero del con que*, in (37). These constructions follow the pattern for normal restrictive relative clauses in Spanish, where material is not allowed to intervene between the pronoun heading the relative clause and the relative pronoun, e.g.:

(40) Mire   usted en lo que yo me   entretengo (Azorín)
     look at you in it that I myself amuse
     Look at how I am amusing myself

The rule being obeyed in examples (37–9) is therefore a general rule applying to restrictive relative clauses of all types.

2.1.2 The comparative of equality

It was claimed in the preceding chapter that, unlike the comparatives of inequality, there exist three possible types of construction for the comparative of equality. These were exemplified as follows:

1 a reduced sentential construction, e.g. (41):

(41) La chica es tan inteligente como su amiga
     The girl is as intelligent as her friend

2 a full sentential construction, e.g. (42):

(42) La chica es tan inteligente como su amiga parece ser
     The girl is as intelligent as her friend seems to be

3 a relativized phrasal construction, e.g. (43):

(43) La chica es tan inteligente como lo que creen sus padres
     The girl is as intelligent as her parents believe

The reduced sentential construction

The reduced sentential construction is straightforwardly the same for the comparative of equality as for the comparatives of inequality. The following are examples of reduced sentential constructions involving, as the object of comparison, the categories of noun, verb, adjective, adverb and prepositional phrase:

(44) Juan tiene tantos[13] libros como su hermano
Juan has as many books as his brother
(45) Pedro grita tanto como siempre
Pedro shouts as much as ever
(46) La abuela está tan triste como el abuelo
The grandmother is as sad as the grandfather
(47) Mi primo corre tan rápidamente como un leopardo
My cousin runs as fast as a leopard
(48) La crueldad está tan en nuestras entrañas como la generosidad
Cruelty is as much in our hearts as generosity

In each of these examples there is no tensed verb form following the comparative 'particle' *como*.

The full sentential construction

However, as has already been pointed out, the principal difference between the comparative of equality and the comparatives of inequality is that there exists no tensed verb constraint as regards the former. Hence, examples (44–8) may be expanded to form the following, equally grammatical, sentences:

(49) Juan tiene tantos libros como tiene su hermano
Juan has as many books as his brother has
(50) Pedro grita tanto como siempre gritaba
Pedro shouts as much as he always shouted
(51) La abuela está tan triste como parece el abuelo
The grandmother is as sad as the grandfather seems
(52) Mi primo corre tan rápidamente como puede correr un leopardo
My cousin runs as fast as a leopard can run
(53) La crueldad está tan en nuestras entrañas como está la generosidad
Cruelty is as much in our hearts as generosity is

None of the equivalent sentences constructed as comparatives of inequality would be grammatical; the only possible construction would be the relativized phrasal construction with *de lo que*. This construction is also possible for the comparative of equality, as will be demonstrated. However, the tensed verb constraint does not apply to the comparative of equality construction and this accounts for the fact that the subordinate clause of an equative construction is not obligatorily reduced, giving rise to the possibility of this second type of construction, the full sentential construction.

Given this difference between the comparative of equality and the comparatives of inequality, it might be expected that the grammatical status of comparative of equality sentences corresponding to examples (16–19) (repeated here for convenience) would not be the same.

(16) Vende menos que compra
(17) *Vende menos que tiene
(18) Vende menos de lo que tiene
(19) Vende menos de lo que compra

The equivalent sentences are:

(54) Vende tanto como compra
(55) Vende tanto como tiene
(56) Vende tanto como lo que tiene
(57) Vende tanto como lo que compra

Examples (54–7) are all grammatical. In particular, (55) is perfectly acceptable, whereas its equivalent, (17), is not. This is a direct result of the lack of applicablity of the tensed verb constraint to the equative construction. Recall that (17) was ungrammatical just because of the tensed verb constraint as a tensed verb follows *que* ((16) is an example of partial comparison, and as a result the tensed verb may escape the constraint in a manner to be discussed in the section on partial comparison). The only grammatical version of (17) is (18), the phrasal construction.

Notice that (54) is ambiguous and has two possible readings: under one the verbs *vender* and *comprar* are interpreted as being intransitive, *tanto* being a verbal modifier; and under the second *vender* and *comprar* are interpreted as transitive verbs, with *tanto* a nominal modifier, that of the lexically empty object of the verbs. In other words, in (54) either the extent/frequency of the acts of selling and buying is being compared (this is partial comparison), or the amounts being sold and bought are being compared (full comparison). The first of these readings, the partial comparison reading, is the only one available for 16, hence the tensed verb may appear, as the constraint may be avoided in expressions of partial comparison. The second reading, that involving full comparison, is found in (19), the relativized phrasal construction. That (54) is ambiguous, unlike (16), is a direct result of the non-applicability of the tensed verb constraint. The fact that a tensed verb may always follow *como* can also have the effect, therefore, of sometimes making it difficult to detect the difference between full and partial comparison in equative constructions.

Given that a tensed verb form may appear after *como*, it is obvious that the second half of a comparison of equality may involve more than one clause, within the limits of comprehensibility. The following set of examples[14] illustrates this:

(58) Desde luego, pueden emplear a tantas mujeres como antes empleaban
Of course, they can employ as many women as they employed before

(59) Desde luego, pueden emplear a tantas mujeres como antes les permitía el gobierno emplear
Of course, they can employ as many women as the government permitted them to employ before

(60) Desde luego, pueden emplear a tantas mujeres como antes pensaba el gobierno en permitirles emplear
Of course, they can employ as many women as the government was considering permitting them to employ before

(61) Desde luego, pueden emplear a tantas mujeres como antes consintió el gobierno en pensar en permitirles emplear
Of course, they can employ as many women as the government agreed to consider permitting them to employ before

(62) Desde luego, pueden emplear a tantas mujeres como antes parecía que el gobierno consentiría en pensar en permitirles emplear
Of course, they can employ as many women as it seemed that the government would agree to consider permitting them to employ before

(63) Desde luego, pueden emplear a tantas mujeres como antes quería el gobierno que pareciese que consintiese en pensar en permitirles emplear
Of course, they can employ as many women as the government wished it to seem that it would agree to consider permitting them to employ before

None of these sentences is possible as a sentential comparative of inequality, due to the constraint against the occurrence of a tensed verb after *más/menos . . . que*.

The relativized phrasal construction

As already stated, a relativized phrasal construction involving *como lo que* is also possible for the comparative of equality. It is not, however, required as a kind of 'escape hatch' from a tensed verb constraint, as it is for the comparatives of inequality. The following examples are the phrasal equivalents of (49–53):[15]

(64) Juan tiene tantos libros como los que tiene su hermano
(65) Pedro grita tanto como lo que siempre gritaba
(66) La abuela está tan triste como lo que parece el abuelo
(67) Mi primo corre tan rápidamente como lo que puede correr un leopardo
(68) La crueldad está tan en nuestras entrañas como lo que está la generosidad

The grammatical status of this type of construction is the same as for the comparatives of inequality. As they constitute an alternative means of expression, however, due to the availability of a sentential construction, they are less highly valued than when they are a unique means of expression, as is the case for the comparatives of inequality, and, therefore, are considerably less frequent.

2.2 EXPRESSION OF PARTIAL COMPARISON

Partial comparison, unlike full comparison, involves comparing referentially and lexically distinct categories (though they must still be non-distinct with regard to categorial features).

2.2.1 The comparatives of inequality

It was claimed in Chapter 1 that there are three possible constructions:

1 a reduced sentential construction, exemplified there by the following (repeated here for convenience):

(69) La mesa es más larga que ancha
 The table is more long than wide

2 a full sentential construction where the second compared category appears clause-initially in the second clause, which I have termed a 'topicalized sentential construction':

(70) La mesa es más larga que ancha es la puerta
 The table is longer than the door is wide

3 a relativized phrasal construction:

(71) La mesa es más larga de lo que la puerta es ancha
 The table is longer than the door is wide

Clearly, option 2 is additional to the options available for the expression of full comparison.

If the defining characteristic of partial comparison is that what is being compared is not lexically identical categories, then the comparison must involve some modifier of the lexemes. Logically, therefore, the comparison must involve the actual comparison of inequality modifiers, *más/menos*, themselves, rather than the category they modify. If the semantic content of *más* is taken to be equivalent to *más mucho*, and that of *menos* as equivalent to *menos mucho*, then it is this quantifier element, *mucho*, which is actually the object of comparison and an equivalent quantifier must be inferred as modifying the compared category in the second half of the comparison.[16] These quantification-type modifiers themselves are the real objects of comparison, rather than the categories they modify. As simple proof of the existence of this second modifier, notice that when *mucho* appears in a partitive phrase it is followed by the preposition *de*:

(72) mucho de este trabajo
 much of this work

When the compared constituents in an expression of partial comparison are partitive phrases, *de* appears in both clauses:

(73) Hay más de aquellas mujeres en la tele que de estos hombres
 There are more of those women on TV than of these men

Equally, another quantifying expression may not appear before the second compared category, whereas it can appear elsewhere in a comparative clause. Contrast (74) and (75):

(74) *El año que viene admitiremos a tantas mujeres como muchos hombres[17]
Next year we will admit as many women as many men
(75) El año que viene admitiremos a tantas mujeres como muchas universidades admitirán a hombres
Next year we will admit as many women as many universities will admit men

In (74) *muchos* is barred from modifying *hombres*, one of the compared categories, but may modify *universidades* in (75) (with feminine gender marking) since this noun phrase is not the object of comparison.

The reduced sentential construction

To make this discussion more concrete, there follow four examples of (simple) sentences expressing partial comparison:

(76) Nada menos que corre
He swims less than he runs
(77) Come más manzanas que naranjas
He eats more apples than oranges
(78) Parece más feliz que triste[18]
He seems more happy than sad
(79) Viste menos elegante que funcionalmente
He dresses less elegantly than functionally

Each of these examples (except, necessarily, (76), which demonstrates comparison involving the verb) is of type 1, the reduced sentential construction, i.e. there is no tensed verb following *más/menos*, in accordance with the tensed verb constraint. Unlike expressions of full comparison, however, features other than categorial of the second compared category may vary; for example, a singular noun may be compared with a plural noun, a feminine adjective with a masculine adjective and two verbs, the persons of whose subjects differ, may be compared, as illustrated by (80–2) (which, for expository reasons, are full sentential constructions):

(80) Juan tiene menos dinero que deudas tiene María
Juan has less money than Maria has debts
(81) Esta iglesia es más vieja que modernos son esos pisos
This church is older than those flats are modern
(82) El atleta corre más que nadan sus amigos
The athlete runs more than his friends swim

The only feature of the second compared category which is relevant to its appropriateness in an expression of partial comparison is its syntactic category; features such as number and gender are irrelevant. This is because the term of comparison is, as already stated, the quantifying modifier and not the category so modified.

Phrasal versus sentential constructions

In the discussion of constructions expressing full comparison it was seen that the relativized phrasal construction with *de lo que* was required principally in order to express a comparison in which a tensed verb appears in the subordinate clause of a comparative of inequality. As might be expected, phrasal alternatives exist for examples (76–9):

(83) Nada menos de lo que corre
(84) Come más manzanas de lo que come de naranjas
(85) Parece más feliz de lo que parece triste
(86) Viste menos elegantemente de lo que viste funcionalmente

All of these examples illustrate the relativization of a pronoun anaphoric to the quantifying modifiers *más/menos*. They will be considered in more detail on pages 50–4, as they clearly differ in certain respects from their full comparison equivalents, but suffice for now to show that the expected sentential/phrasal structure alternation is found for expressions of partial comparison.

The full sentential construction

Examples (77–9) illustrate reduced sentential constructions expressing partial comparison involving the categories of noun, adjective and adverb. Sentence (76), involving comparison of the verb, is structurally parallel to the following sentence (repeated):

(87) Vende menos que compra

This is the only example of partial comparison to be discussed in any kind of detail so far. However, while an explanation for the ambiguity of this sentence was proposed, the question of why it, and example (76), escape the tensed verb constraint has not been answered. In other words, why does the appearance of an overt tensed verb in the subordinate clause not mark the sentence as ungrammatical?

Examples (76–9) are very simple sentences. Constructing slightly more complex examples, the following judgements regarding grammatical status are found:

(88) a. Mi tío duerme más que dormía mi tía
 b. *Mi tío duerme más que mi tía dormía
 My uncle sleeps more than my aunt used to sleep
(89) a. Mi padre vende más libros que discos compra mi madre
 b. *Mi padre vende más libros que mi madre compra discos
 My father sells more books than my mother buys records
(90) a. La mesa es más larga que ancha es la puerta
 b. *La mesa es más larga que la puerta es ancha
 The table is longer than the door is wide
(91) a. El crío gatea más cuidadosamente que descuidadamente anda su hermana
 b. *El crío gatea más cuidadosamente que su hermana anda descuidadamente
 The baby crawls more carefully than his sister walks carelessly
(92) a. La crueldad está más en nuestras cabezas que en nuestras entrañas está la generosidad
 b. *La crueldad está más en nuestras cabezas que la generosidad está en nuestras entrañas
 Cruelty is more in our heads than generosity is in our hearts

In every case the (b) version is judged ungrammatical compared to the perfectly acceptable version in (a).

In each of the (a) examples the structure of the subordinate clause appears to be a kind of 'mirror-image' of the matrix clause, as opposed to the (b) examples, where the word order of the subordinate clause is exactly as in the matrix. However, it is not the case that only 'mirror-image' subordinate clauses are acceptable; the following, while felt to be somewhat inelegant, are nonetheless acceptable:

(93) ?Mi padre vende más libros que discos mi madre compra
(94) ?La mesa es más larga que ancha la puerta es
(95) ?El crío gatea más cuidadosamente que descuidadamente su hermana anda
(96) ?La crueldad está más en nuestras cabezas que en nuestras entrañas la generosidad está

The difference between these sentences and the (b) examples of (88–92) is clearly felt: the former are rather clumsy, while the latter are totally ungrammatical. Examples (93–6), however, do not exhibit a 'mirror-image' of the matrix in the subordinate clause. Such word-order considerations are clearly not crucial.

In attempting to isolate exactly what differentiates them and why an overt tensed verb is acceptable in the (a) sentences, but not in the (b) sentences, several hypotheses suggest themselves.

Coordinate structure

One possibility might be to claim that comparative constructions expressing partial comparison have a radically different structure from that of full comparatives, being coordinate structures rather than examples of a matrix clause plus subordinate clause structure. This does not seem too implausible given the importance of poorly understood notions of parallelism in such constructions. That such notions do play an important part in partial comparison structures is shown by examples like the following:

(97) Los chicos de la escuela de la esquina comen más
     the boys   of the school of the corner eat   more
     manzanas que zumos de naranja beben las chicas de la
     apples   than juices of orange drink the girls of the
     iglesia de la   plaza
     church of the square
     The boys from the school on the corner eat more apples than the girls from the church in the square drink orange juice

In (97) no fewer than five separate and parallel contrasts are set up between the first clause and the second. Notice that any change which results in a lowered parallelism of contrasts will significantly alter the sentence's acceptability:

(98) ?Los chicos de la escuela de la esquina comen más manzanas que himnos cantan las chicas de la iglesia de la plaza
     The boys from the school on the corner eat more apples than the girls from the church in the square sing hymns

As Kuno (1981: 152) notes, difficulties arise in such constructions when the constituents following the quantified element 'cannot be interpreted contrastively or emphatically'. Given such complex semantic constraints relating to parallelism between the two clauses, the proposal seems plausible that these are not subordinate structures but coordinate structures, where similar constraints of parallelism/symmetry may apply. Quoting from Stockwell,

Schachter and Partee (1973: 315), the definition of coordination given there, 'speakers choose to conjoin constituents . . . only when they wish to express some relation between these constituents. (The relation may be one of similarity, contrast . . . etc.)', looks as though it might apply straightforwardly to this construction since the relation between the two clauses in expressions of partial comparison is one of contrast. However, in a coordinate structure the conjunction is not linked to either of the coordinates, whereas in comparative constructions *que* is clearly connected with *más/menos* in the first clause.

Position of compared categories

It can be observed that (88a–92a) and (93–6) have in common that in each case the compared categories directly precede and follow *que*. Nevertheless, this is clearly not a requirement, as (99–103) are equally grammatical:

(99) Más duerme mi tío que dormía mi tía
(100) Más libros vende mi padre que discos compra mi madre
(101) Más larga es la mesa que ancha es la puerta
(102) Más cuidadosamente gatea el crío que descuidadamente anda su hermana
(103) Más en nuestras cabezas está la crueldad que en nuestras entrañas está la generosidad

Ordering of the second compared category

Only the first part of the above suggestion as to the structure of these constructions is invalidated by examples (99–103). In other words, although there is clearly no requirement for the compared category in the matrix to directly precede *que*, the second compared category does immediately follow *que*. That this is the case is demonstrated by example (104), where both conditions of the previous suggestion are unfulfilled:

(104) *Más duerme mi tío que mi tía dormía

Equivalent rearrangement of the constituents of (100–3) will also result in ungrammaticality. Therefore, it seems to be a requirement that the second compared category must immediately follow the comparative particle *que* in full sentential expressions of partial comparison. The remaining question, then, is why these constructions appear to escape the effects of the tensed verb constraint normally operative in comparatives of inequality.

An additional constraint

Before a detailed examination of these constructions is attempted, an additional problem should be noted. The following sentence is ungrammatical:

(105) *Mi padre duerme más que dormía
     My father sleeps more than he used to sleep

The only grammatical version is (106), a phrasal construction:

(106) Mi padre duerme más de lo que dormía

It appears, therefore, that the tensed verb constraint has applied here, even though this is clearly an example of partial comparison. It is structurally parallel to examples (107) and (108) (repeated), which are perfectly grammatical:

(107) Duerme más que sueña
     He sleeps more than he dreams
(108) Vende menos que compra
     He sells less than he buys

Various reasons suggest themselves as an explanation of this fact. It could be that the reason for the ungrammaticality of (105) is lexical, namely, that the fact that the same lexical verb appears in both the matrix and subordinate clauses is the reason for its unacceptability. We should not, in this case, expect to find expressions of partial comparison with the same verb in both clauses. However, this is not the case, as shown by the following example:

(109) Mi padre duerme más que duermen mis hermanos
     My father sleeps more than my brothers sleep

It is not the case that the subjects of the two verbs must differ for the construction to be grammatical, as shown by (107) and (108). It is also unrelated to the differing tenses of the verbs in (105), present and imperfect, respectively, as the tense of the subordinate clause verb in (109) may be changed without loss of grammaticality:

(110) Mi padre duerme más que dormían mis hermanos

The unacceptability of (105) can also not be linked to the number of categories following the comparative particle, as a solitary verb follows in (107) and (108) also.

Nonetheless, there are grounds for considering that whatever accounts for (105) must be linked to the tensed verb constraint, particularly as constructing the parallel example using the comparative of equality results in a grammatical sentence:

(111) Mi padre duerme tanto como dormía
My father sleeps as much as he used to sleep

In addition, notice that a sentence exhibiting what is often referred to as 'verb-gapping' is grammatical:

(112) Criticó más libros que yo ensayos
He criticized more books than I (did) essays

Yet in this case the second compared category, *ensayos*, does not immediately follow *que*, as has been shown to be required in such expressions of partial comparison. This is a direct consequence of the fact that the verb of the subordinate clause has been 'gapped'. Notice that if the tensed verb is not omitted in such cases the sentence becomes ungrammatical:

(113) *Criticó más libros que yo critiqué ensayos
He criticized more books than I criticized essays

In (113) the presence of the tensed verb *critiqué* in the subordinate clause renders the sentence ungrammatical. Grammaticality may, of course, be restored by placing the second compared category immediately after *que*:

(114) Criticó más libros que ensayos critiqué yo

In (114) the presence of the tensed verb *critiqué* no longer leads to ungrammaticality.

Whatever accounts for these apparently anomalous facts relating to the expression of partial comparison in comparatives of inequality must somehow be connected with the tensed verb constraint.

Topicalization

It has been established that the single most important factor in determining the grammaticality of a comparative of inequality construction expressing partial comparison is the position of the second compared category: it must immediately follow the comparative particle. There exists another type of construction in which just such a configuration is found, namely, constructions which have undergone the process often referred to as topicalization.[19] Topicalization can be said to have taken place when a category appears in a marked position at the beginning of a clause or sentence as, for example, in (115):

(115) Dicen que enemigos, parece que tiene
    They say that enemies, it seems that he has

The noun *enemigos* has been placed in a clause-initial position, in the marked or 'topic' position, which has the effect of focussing on the fronted category. In Spanish, nouns, adjectives, adverbs, prepositional phrases and verbs may be topicalized and this is exactly the position of the second compared category in full sentential constructions expressing partial comparison; in (88a–92a) the compared categories of the subordinate clause immediately follow *que*, rather than appearing in a more natural and unmarked position. Analysing this as being the result of a process of topicalization makes it an unsurprising and expected result, falling out as a natural consequence. Andersen (1983: 66) quotes Enkvist (1976: 9–11) to the effect that word order may be affected by the 'expression of focus . . . ; this is linked with emphasis'. The analysis, then, seems intuitively satisfying, given that the phenomena under discussion are evidently dependent on the notion of 'focus of comparison' (see examples (97–8)) and a constituent which has been topicalized is always in an emphatic position. Seeing the full sentential constructions in terms of a process of topicalization thus provides an explanation for the obligatory position, directly following *que*, of the second compared category. What still remains to be explained is the apparent inapplicability of the tensed verb constraint to such structures. The answer to this question appears to be linked to the notion of focus just introduced.

Focus of comparison

If it is assumed to be the case that there exists a semantic requirement for a focus of comparison, that is, a second compared category, in comparative constructions, and that therefore each and every comparative construction must contain an element capable of bearing the focus of comparison, then we may have a solution to the apparent problem. If a tensed verb may not normally appear in the second half of comparatives of inequality, it can be claimed that it may not appear in this position unless it is felt to be acting as a focus of comparison. In expressions of partial comparison, therefore, a tensed verb may appear when it, or rather its modifying quantifier, is the category of comparison, as in (88a) (repeated):

(88) a. Mi tío duerme más que dormía mi tía

This is because in this case it appears in a topic position at the front of the clause and bears the focus of comparison since it is, in fact, the second compared category. A tensed verb may also appear when it is not itself the topicalized category, but rather follows this category, since it is then no longer within the scope of the comparison proper, being outside the topic position. This is the case in partial comparison involving any other category (see (89a–92a)). In other words, a tensed verb may appear in the subordinate clause of a comparative of inequality in only two specific contexts: firstly, if the verb itself is the focus-bearing element, in which case it will appear in clause-initial topic position; secondly, if it clearly falls outside the scope of the comparison proper, which I am defining here as meaning that (a) there is some other category in topic position and (b) the tensed verb follows this category. This suggests that the topic position here is one of very strong focus, since its properties of focus derive from two sources: firstly, from the fact that the topic position is always associated with strong emphasis and secondly, from the fact that the category occupying the topic position is itself the focus of the comparison, being the second compared element. The strength of this focus position, then, appears to override the normal prohibition against an ensuing tensed verb. In expressions of full comparison, however, a tensed verb may never appear, as it will be unable to act as a focus of comparison itself. This is because there is no topicalized variant available for this construction (as there is nothing to topicalize – the second compared constituent has no lexical content and does not appear). Moreover, there is, in such constructions, no focus position, such as the topic position, strong enough apparently to override the tensed verb prohibition. The constraint in operation appears to be, not simply that a tensed verb may never appear after comparative *que*, but rather that it may not normally do so. This constraint may be overridden when the second compared element is topicalized (i.e. in expressions of partial comparison), since the tensed verb may then itself be the compared category, in topic position, or otherwise be felt to fall outside the scope of the comparison proper, due to the strong focus associated with topic position.[20] Clearly, rather more needs to be said about this and I will return to this point in section 2.5.

A semantic constraint Returning to example (105) (repeated), an explanation has still to be given for its ungrammaticality:

(105) *Mi padre duerme más que dormía

It seems that the reason must be semantic rather than syntactic and linked to the properties of foci. Bearing in mind that partial comparison constructions, particularly the more complex types, involve a (potentially) infinite number of foci of contrast, as well as the constituent in topic position acting as the focus of the comparison, it appears that what is problematic in (105) is the status of tense alone as a suitable focus element. Kuno (1981: 154) remarks that 'the constituent that appears after the deletion site is highly contrastive.' *Dormía*, following the site of the deleted quantifier, is not, in fact, highly contrastive; the only element of contrast here is tense. Hence (109) is grammatical because of the presence of an additional focus of contrast, the subject *mis hermanos*, as is (107) because of the additional lexical content of the verb *sueña*. Therefore, it appears that the tensed verb of the subordinate clause, when topicalized and therefore constituting the focus of comparison, must be accompanied by further foci of contrast; this may either be the lexical content of the verb itself, distinct from the matrix verb, or may derive from there being a distinct subject from that of the matrix verb, or, of course, both. Tense alone is not an appropriate or sufficient focus of contrast and the operative constraint in (105) is not syntactic, but semantic.

The phrasal construction

That a relativized phrasal alternative exists alongside the full sentential construction has already been indicated.[21] The following are the relativized phrasal equivalents of (88–92):

(116) Mi tío duerme más de lo que mi tía dormía[22]
(117) Mi padre vende más libros de lo que mi madre compra de discos
(118) La mesa es más larga de lo que la puerta es ancha
(119) El crío gatea más cuidadosamente de lo que su hermana anda descuidadamente
(120) La crueldad está más en nuestras cabezas de lo que la generosidad está en nuestras entrañas

Although the phrasal construction is no longer required as a means of escaping the tensed verb constraint in this construction, as it has been shown that this may be achieved via topicalization, there are nonetheless instances where it will be the preferred construction. As there is no tensed verb constraint in topicalized structures, *que* may be followed by more than one clause, i.e. the topicalized category may be linked to a position indefinitely far down in ensuing clauses. This is so only in principle. In practice, when the length of the sentence is perceived, due to performance factors, as being excessive, a phrasal alternative is used. The following example is grammatical, but unacceptable on other grounds:

(121) ?María está más deprimida que triste me dijo Juan que le había informado Pedro que parecía antes
Maria is more depressed than Juan told me that Pedro had informed him that she seemed sad before

The phrasal alternative will be preferred:

(122) María está más deprimida de lo que me dijo Juan que le había informado Pedro que parecía triste antes

The analysis of *lo* in these relativized phrasal constructions expressing partial comparison is as before in that it is anaphoric to an element in the matrix clause and heads the following relative clause. As what is actually being compared in such constructions is the quantifying modifier of the matrix and subordinate categories, it is to this, the semantic content of *más/mucho*, that *lo* refers.[23] This has already been discussed on pages 31–5. However, the position with regard to partial comparison involving nouns is a little different from the case of full comparison.

Phrasal comparatives involving nominals

When the phrasal construction expressing partial comparison involves comparison of two nouns, the structure typically includes a preposition, *de*, preceding the noun in the subordinate relative clause, as in (117). This example will be ungrammatical without *de*:
(123) *Mi padre vende más libros de lo que mi madre compra discos

Moreover, unlike the case in full phrasal comparison involving the noun, the pronoun *lo* is invariable. The following example demonstrates this:

(124) Pedro tiene menos valentía de lo que se dice que Juan tiene de fuerza
Pedro has less courage than they say Juan has strength

Here the nouns *valentía* and *fuerza* are both feminine singular. Replacing *lo* with the feminine singular pronoun *la* would make the sentence ungrammatical. *Lo* cannot, therefore, be considered to be anaphoric to any noun head, being rather an anaphor related to the semantic content of the (non-lexical) quantifier modifying the second noun of the comparison, *discos* in (117) and *fuerza* in (124).

Pseudo-partitive constructions A similar structure, N–*de*–N, is found in Spanish in pseudo-partitive constructions like the following:

(125) un grupo de niños
a group of children

It seems reasonable, then, to assume that the equivalent bit of structure in these phrasal comparatives, *lo . . . de discos* in (117), *lo . . . de fuerza* in (124), is also a pseudo-partitive structure, whence the appearance of *de*. It clearly is semantically parallel to a standard pseudo-partitive construction. As this makes *lo*'s syntactic status that of a noun, its non-marking for gender and number is unexceptional, given that the position is unmarked for these features, being lexically unspecified.

Some apparent exceptions Native speakers will usually judge sentences like the following to be acceptable:

(126) Juan encontró a más chicas de lo que María encontró a chicos
Juan met more girls than Maria met boys

(127) El chiquito juega con más juguetes de lo que la chiquita se divierte con muñecas
The little boy plays with more toys than the little girl amuses herself with dolls

(128) El profesor criticó menos libros de lo que yo hablé de ensayos
The teacher criticized fewer (lit. 'less') books than I talked about essays

(129) Interpola a menos hombres de lo que habla con mujeres
He interrupts fewer (lit. 'less') men than he speaks to women

In none of these examples, except (128), is the noun in the relative clause preceded by *de*, as expected. In (128) its appearance is not connected with *lo*, but with the verb *hablé*. However, in each case the noun in question is preceded by some preposition, though for differing reasons. In (126) *chicos* is preceded by the so-called 'personal *a*'; in (127) *muñecas* is preceded by *con* as a result of the comparison involving a prepositional object in the matrix and in the relative clause; in (128) *ensayos* is preceded by *de* because it is a prepositional object, being compared with a direct object, *libros*, in the matrix; in (129) *mujeres* is preceded by *con* for similar reasons. Evidently, then, although the noun undergoing comparison in the subordinate clause of a phrasal construction expressing partial comparison must normally be preceded by *de* as a result of its pseudo-partitive structure, when the noun in question is already preceded by a preposition, as in (126–9), this is impossible. Recall that in the case of the relativized phrasal constructions expressing full comparison (pp. 33–5) it was shown that the sequence *de* + preposition is possible (examples (37–9)). It might, therefore, seem surprising that the same sequence is not allowed here. In fact, the sequences are not identical. *De* may be followed by a preposition in the relativized phrasal constructions expressing full comparison because it is not actually functioning as a preposition, but rather as a 'comparative particle', an alternant of *que*, as in (37) (repeated):

(37) Gana menos dinero de con el que contaba
He earns less money than he was counting on

Thus the sequence *de con* in (37) is not a sequence of two prepositions. Nonetheless, the fact that, superficially, it appears to contain such a sequence does make it a highly unusual construction. In the constructions expressing partial comparison under discussion here, on the other hand, the role of *de* is very different. It occurs in a pseudo-partitive structure and is, therefore, a preposition. (It is the first instance of *de*, preceding *lo*, which is the 'comparative particle'.) The normal restriction against a sequence of two prepositions therefore applies.[24]

It seems that in these sentences, which are somewhat marginal, the semantic interpretation is different. Taking (126) as typical, what is actually being compared here is not the two object noun phrases; rather, the noun phrase *más chicos* in the matrix is being compared with the verb *encontró* in the subordinate clause. In other words, the number of girls Juan met is beng compared to the extent to which Maria met boys. Obviously, the two constituents being compared are now categorially distinct. Semantically, this is odd, but it does allow speakers to form phrasal constructions expressing partial comparison involving, for example, both direct and prepositional objects. This possibility, together with the increasing tendency on the part of native speakers to view *de lo que* as a simple conjunction in phrasal comparatives, accounts for the apparently grammatical status of (126–9).

2.2.2 The comparative of equality

I have claimed that for the comparative of equality there are four possible means of expressing partial comparison, one more than for the comparatives of inequality. These are the following:

1 a reduced sentential construction, exemplified by the following:

(130) El chico es tan guapo como listo
The boy is as handsome as clever

2 a topicalized sentential construction:

(131) El chico es tan guapo como listo es su hermano
The boy is as handsome as his brother is clever

3 a full sentential construction with declarative word order in the second clause:

(132) El chico es tan guapo como su hermano es listo
The boy is as handsome as his brother is clever

4 a relativized phrasal construction:

(133) El chico es tan guapo como lo que su hermano es listo
The boy is as handsome as his brother is clever

Option 2 is additional to those available for the expression of full comparison, while option 3 is the option not available to the comparatives of inequality, due to the operation of a tensed verb constraint.

The reduced sentential construction

The reduced sentential construction is, as before, the variant in which a tensed verb does not follow *como*. Unlike the case for the comparatives of inequality, however, where this reduction is obligatory, reduction of sentential comparatives expressing a comparison of equality is always optional. The following are simple examples of this type of construction involving, as the categories of comparison, the noun, adverb and prepositional phrase ((130) is an adjectival example):

(134) Come tantas manzanas como naranjas
 He eats as many apples as oranges
(135) Corre tan enérgica como rápidamente
 He runs as energetically as quickly
(136) El odio está tan en nuestras entrañas como en nuestras cabezas
 Hatred is as much in our hearts as in our heads

The topicalized sentential construction

As for the comparatives of inequality, there exists the option of a full sentential construction including a tensed verb following the particle *como*, where the second compared category is placed in the topic focus position immediately after *como*. The following are examples of such constructions, involving the categories of noun, adverb, prepositional phrase and verb:

(137) Este hombre tiene tantos   enemigos como amigos posee
 this man   has   as many enemies as   friends possesses
 aquella mujer
 that   woman
 This man has as many enemies as that woman has friends
(138) María canta tan alegremente como tristemente llora Juan
 Maria sings as cheerfully   as   sadly   cries Juan
 Maria sings as cheerfully as Juan cries sadly
(139) El odio está tan   en nuestras cabezas como en nuestras
 hatred is   as much in our   heads   as   in our
 entrañas está el amor
 hearts   is   love
 Hatred is as much in our heads as love is in our hearts
(140) El jefe descansa tanto   como trabajan los empleados
 the boss rests   as much as   work   the employees
 The boss rests as much as the employees work

As these are full sentential constructions, the verb itself may participate as the category of comparison, as in (140).

The sentential construction with declarative word order

It has been shown that the construction with topicalization constitutes a means whereby the comparatives of inequality may escape the tensed verb constraint which is normally operative, as a result of the interaction of the notion of focus of comparison, together with the focus associated with topic position, with the tensed verb. However, as there is no tensed verb constraint operating on comparative of equality constructions, it might be expected that the word order of the subordinate clause would not be crucial in equative constructions. This is indeed the case, as exemplified by the following sentences, equivalent to (137–40):

(141) Este hombre tiene tantos enemigos como aquella mujer posee amigos
(142) María canta tan alegremente como Juan llora tristemente
(143) El odio está tan en nuestras cabezas como el amor está en nuestras entrañas
(144) El jefe descansa tanto como los empleados trabajan

Due to the lack of a tensed verb constraint, the second compared category need not immediately follow *como*; the equivalent sentences constructed using the comparatives of inequality will be ungrammatical.

This explains the following constellation of data:

(145) La mesa es tan larga como ancha es la puerta
(146) La mesa es tan larga como la puerta es ancha
(147) La mesa es más larga que ancha es la puerta
(148) *La mesa es más larga que la puerta es ancha

Only the equative construction allows both topicalized and non-topicalized sentential structures.

As the option of a subordinate clause with declarative word order exists for equatives, the second compared category in an equative expressing partial comparison may occur indefinitely far down in the clauses following *como*, subject to the obvious restrictions, as the following example shows:[25]

(149) Desde luego, pueden emplear a tantas mujeres como antes quería el gobierno que pareciese que consintiese en pensar en permitirles emplear a hombres
Of course, they can employ as many women as the government wished it to seem that it would agree to consider allowing them to employ men before

Tense as an inadequate focus element

On pages 46–7 it was pointed out that a sentence like (105) (repeated) is ungrammatical:

(105) *Mi padre duerme más que dormía

This was explained on the basis that *dormía* is in topic position and the only available focus element is tense. This seems never to be an adequate focus element unless accompanied by further foci of contrast. Example (105) can easily be made grammatical by the addition of further suitable foci of contrast (different verb, subject, etc.). However, the equivalent comparative of equality sentence is fully grammatical:

(150) Mi padre duerme tanto como dormía

While this may seem surprising, in reality it follows from the preceding analysis: as a full sentential construction with declarative word order in the subordinate clause, i.e. **without** topicalization, is available for the equative, it may be assumed that cases like (150) actually exemplify this type of construction. In other words, nothing has been topicalized in (150), therefore the suitability of tense alone as a focus element is not relevant. This contrasts with (105), where the verb must have been topicalized in order to appear at all.

The relativized phrasal construction

As has been noted, there also exists the option of a relativized phrasal construction. A phrasal alternative could be substituted for (149):

(151) Desde luego, pueden emplear a tantas mujeres como lo que antes quería el gobierno que pareciese que consintiese en pensar en permitirles emplear de hombres

Note that as *lo* enters into a pseudo-partitive structure in such phrasal constructions involving nouns as the categories of comparison, as already explained, *de* appears before *hombres*. For the comparatives of inequality, a construction parallel to (151) would be the only option (apart from an exceedingly clumsy topicalized structure, as in (152)):

(152) *??Desde luego, pueden emplear a más mujeres que a hombres antes quería el gobierno que pareciese que consintiese en pensar en permitirles emplear

Of course, they can employ more women than the government wished it to seem that it would agree to consider allowing them to employ men before

As the analysis of the phrasal construction for the expression of partial comparison in the comparatives of inequality holds true for the comparative of equality, I shall restrict myself to giving five examples of the phrasal construction. It should be noted, however, that their stylistic status does differ, as does their frequency of occurrence, as they constitute a fourth option for the equative. The following examples are the phrasal equivalents of (131) and (137–40):

(153) El chico es tan guapo como lo que su hermano es listo
(154) Este hombre tiene tantos enemigos como lo que aquella mujer posee de amigos
(155) María canta tan alegremente como lo que Juan llora tristemente
(156) El odio está tan en nuestras cabezas como lo que el amor está en nuestras entrañas
(157) El jefe descansa tanto como lo que los empleados trabajan

Further discussion of the relative status of these constructions can be found in section 2.5.

2.3 THE PLEONASTIC OR EXPLETIVE NEGATIVE

It seems that the possibility exists in Spanish for an expletive negative element, superficially similar to the expletive negative of French mentioned in Chapter 1, to appear in some kinds of comparative expression. However, unlike the position in French, these constructions are marginal and acceptable to only a minority of native speakers. This expletive *no* is mentioned briefly in Rivero (1970: 655) as an optional constituent, and Butt and Benjamin (1989: 277) also state that 'In informal language redundant *no* is often unnecessarily used in comparisons.' Bolinger (1950: 57), in his detailed survey of constructions expressing comparison in Spanish, states that in his corpus 'there are no expressions of a redundant *no* . . . such as are described in the Academy Grammar', and goes on to cast doubt on the very existence, let alone acceptability, of this 'redundant' *no*. Bolinger's position, then, is that this expletive negative element does not exist in Spanish. The weaker position, that it does indeed exist, but is extremely marginal at best, will be the one taken here.

Accepting, therefore, that there is the possibility of an expletive negative, however slight, the relevant question must be, where does it occur? It has already been established that it is unlike the French expletive negative in terms of frequency of occurrence. In fact, it can also be shown that in terms of distribution it has nothing in common with the equivalent French negative, as we would expect given the fundamental differences between the constructions in the two languages.

Of all the constructions so far examined for Spanish, both for the expression of full and partial comparison, and ranging over the equative and the comparatives of inequality, there is only one type of structure in which such an expletive element may occur and that is the reduced sentential construction expressing full comparison in a comparative of inequality construction,[26] i.e. the very first construction dealt with in this chapter and perhaps the simplest of all. In other words, alongside example (1) (repeated), there exists, for some speakers, the marginal alternative (158):

(1) Un perro es más feroz que un gato
(158) Un perro es más feroz que no un gato

Expletive *no* may never appear followed by a tensed verb; that is to say, it may not appear in a non-reduced sentential comparative or a phrasal comparative of inequality; Butt and Benjamin (1989: 278), though they do not point it out, admit this implicitly by giving four examples of comparative constructions including 'redundant' *no*, in none of which a tensed verb appears in the subordinate clause. Also, it never appears in any type of equative construction. This is so even for speakers for whom (158) would be acceptable. It is clear from this that, despite a superficial resemblance to the French expletive negative in such constructions, there are no parallels to be drawn between the two elements. The Spanish negative is only marginally acceptable, whereas the opposite case holds in French, and it appears precisely where it could never occur in French, i.e. in a clause lacking a tensed verb. A more detailed treatment of the French construction will be given in the next chapter, but these comments should suffice for now to illustrate that the two negative elements are in no sense comparable.

Notice that the fact that this expletive negative never appears with a tensed verb is compatible with considerations of potential ambiguity. In such a context it could then be interpreted as a full negative, being isomorphic with the standard sentential negative in

Spanish. While ambiguity is common in natural languages, it might nevertheless be expected that where an alternative, unambiguous structure is available to a language it will be selected in preference to one which is ambiguous. Again, the situation in French is not the same: the disjoint sentential negative *ne* . . . *pas* could not be confused with the pleonastic element *ne*, thus freeing the latter to appear unambiguously before a tensed verb. Moreover, recall that it was suggested in Chapter 1 (section 1.8) that an expletive negative element may be used by some languages to act as a marker of comparison where no other marker is available, i.e. where the comparative particle for both the comparatives of inequality and the comparative of equality is the same. Since in Spanish *que* may act as a marker of comparison (by virtue of being distinct from *como*), Spanish has no need of a further marker. Again, this is not true of French.

While it must be stressed that this expletive negative in Spanish is only marginally acceptable for some speakers, nonetheless the restrictions governing its appearance have been shown to follow from and be predictable on the basis of the analysis for comparative constructions suggested.

2.4 THE CLAUSE INTRODUCERS

As has already been pointed out in Chapter 1, the Spanish comparative constructions are unlike their French equivalents in not sharing a clause-introducer, or 'comparative particle'. This fact, if the analysis of particle comparatives in Stassen (1985) is taken as a model, requires that they be members of two different groups: the comparative of equality belonging to his sixth group of Particle Comparatives, where the particle in question, in the case of Spanish, *como*, also has the meaning 'like' or 'as'; and the comparatives of inequality falling under his seventh group, along with French comparatives, where the particle derives from an oblique case form of the relative/interrogative pronouns. This would be rather surprising and must cast some doubt on the validity of Stassen's subgroupings. Why the two types of comparatives should have selected different clause introducers is not the point at issue, but does mean that *que* is able to act as a marker of comparison; moreover, the increased availability of structural possibilities for the comparative of equality in Spanish (in each case one more construction type than for the comparatives of inequality) does seem to be linked to this difference, as indeed does the existence of what

I have chosen to term the tensed verb constraint. Thus this historical divergence of Spanish and French with regard to eventual choice of 'comparative particles' may well be linked to synchronic structural differences, an interesting hypothesis, which unfortunately falls beyond the scope of the present work.

The most obvious syntactic reason for the existence of a tensed verb constraint in the comparatives of inequality appears to be that the presence of a tensed verb in the second half of the comparison might lead to a preferential interpretation of the clause as an ordinary tensed clause introduced by the standard subordinator *que*. That the *que* which occurs in comparatives of inequality is a different lexical item, which just happens to be homonymic with the subordinator, is easily demonstrated. It may be followed by a pronoun, as in the *que lo que* alternant for *de lo que*; it may be followed by an infinitive; in fact, the one item by which it may not be followed is a tensed verb, unlike the subordinator *que*, which must be followed by a tensed verb form. As it is this tensed verb constraint which accounts for the additional constructions into which the comparative of equality may enter, we may have a simple explanation for the difference noted: where a clause is introduced by *como* there is no risk of misinterpretation as there is no separate subordinating item *como*. Hence it is the, coincidental, fact that the marker of comparison and the standard tensed clause complementizer in Spanish are homonymic which means that a tensed verb may not normally appear in the subordinate clause of a comparative of inequality. This constraint may appear to have been overridden in comparatives of inequality expressing partial comparison.

It might be expected that the choice of a unique comparative particle *que* in French, unable to act as a marker of comparison, would have produced a similar range of constraints throughout the comparative constructions. That this is not so is due in very large measure to a single factor: the existence of expletive *ne*, which may act as a marker of comparison. This element also prevents the kind of surface ambiguity to which the Spanish comparatives of inequality would be prone without the tensed verb constraint. The French constructions will be examined in detail in Chapter 3, where it will be shown that the situation regarding expletive *ne* is actually rather more complex than suggested here, but these remarks should suffice for now to indicate that a unified treatment of these construction types must rely on an interplay of syntactic and semantic considerations, concentrating on their synchronic function, rather than on their diachronic bases, however suggestive.

2.5 SUMMARY

Constructions expressing both full and partial comparison, involving the comparatives of inequality and the comparative of equality, have now been exemplified and discussed. The apparently complex variations in structure between the various types of comparatives have been shown to be predictable on the basis of relatively simple constraints. In particular, the major distinction to be made with regard to Spanish comparatives has been given as the available choice between what I have termed sentential and relativized phrasal comparatives.

For the expression of full comparison, these two structures can be seen to be in complementary distribution where the comparatives of inequality are concerned (due to the tensed verb constraint), whereas for the equative they act as alternatives of equal grammatical status.

When the expression of partial comparison is considered, however, the picture appears somewhat less clear. Once more, both relativized phrasal and sentential constructions are available. Additionally, an extra sentential option, essentially involving a process of topicalization of the compared category in the second half of the comparison, has been shown to be available, due in part to the differing semantics of this type of comparison. Again, for the comparative of equality, the relativized phrasal structure is simply an alternative to the sentential options (whether topicalized or not). For the comparatives of inequality, on the other hand, this phrasal construction is in (almost) complementary distribution with the sentential structures. That the distribution is not fully complementary is due to the existence of the topicalized sentential option, which constitutes an additional (to the relativized phrasal construction) means of escape from the tensed verb constraint. Since these various possibilites are available, it would be natural for some order of preference to exist among native speakers. This seems to be as follows:

1 for a relatively 'short' comparison:
   (a) a sentential structure with topicalization of the compared category in the subordinate clause (for both comparatives of inequality and equality)
   (b) a sentential structure with declarative word order in the subordinate clause (only available for the comparative of equality);

2 for a more complex comparison:
(a) a relativized phrasal structure (for both types of comparative)
(b) a non-topicalized sentential structure with a potentially infinite number of embedded clauses (for the comparative of equality only and subject to processing/performance limitations).

These preferences may depend on perceptual factors. In other words, in 'short' comparisons a clause-initial topicalized position for the compared category in the subordinate clause will be preferred because of the stronger semantic focus of this position and the fact that it will be easy to associate the category with its normal, 'unmarked' position in the clause. For longer comparisons the distance between the topic position and the unmarked position of the category will be considerably greater and it will consequently be more difficult to retrieve the correct association. Therefore, the simpler option of inserting (invariable) *de lo que* between the first half of the comparison and the second half, with subsequent declarative word order, will be taken.

It is unsurprising that the situation regarding the expression of partial comparison should be more complex. In particular, these types of construction appear to become more unacceptable as the length and complexity of the sentence increases, to an extent which is not evidenced by constructions expressing full comparison. This general fact about comparative constructions has been noted many times in the literature and is usually assumed to be the result of the relative semantic complexity of the two construction types. It is clear that expressions of partial comparison crucially involve a comparison of contrasts and that both the notions of focus of comparison and focus of contrast which I have proposed are, if anything, even more relevant to a description of expressions of partial comparison in Spanish than to a description of expressions of full comparison.

I have suggested that what I have termed the 'tensed verb constraint' is closely connected with constraints on suitable foci of comparison in such structures; a tensed verb may not appear in the subordinate clause of a comparative of inequality unless it is acting as a focus of comparison, i.e. unless it is itself the second compared category. In expressions of partial comparison a tensed verb may therefore appear when it, or rather its (lexically empty) quantifying modifier, is the category of comparison, in which case it will be in topic position, a position of strong focus. However, it may also appear when another syntactic category is the object of comparison; in this case it will follow the topicalized category and lie outside the scope of the comparison proper. I have suggested that this is due to the strength of the focus associated with topic position, which derives from two sources: the focus normally associated with topic position; and the focus of comparison borne by the compared category in topic position. This strong focus, then, overrides the tensed verb constraint, causing constituents following the topicalized category to be defocussed and therefore outside the comparison proper. In fact, this semantic explanation may be rephrased syntactically, if we consider the topic position to lie outside the following clause. In this case, the tensed verb, when it is not functioning as the topicalized constituent (i.e. the compared category), will not, in any case, occur in the clause introduced by *que*, the comparative clause, but will lie outside this. The only true constituent of the comparative clause will be the topicalized category itself. Hence the tensed verb constraint is irrelevant, since no tensed verb appears in the clause introduced by *que*, the sole constituent of this clause being the topicalized category.

In expressions of full comparison the verb will always fall within the scope of the comparison, given the logical impossibility of a topic position in such constructions. Naturally, the verb may always appear with impunity in a relativized phrasal construction as the focus of comparison in these structures is the pronoun (some form of *lo*) following *de*, which represents the second compared category. The content of the following relative clause is automatically defocussed just because the clause is a relative, rather than comparative, clause. Hence the tensed verb, here again, does not appear in the clause introduced by *que*. While I have claimed that this tensed verb constraint is syntactically linked to the potential ambiguity of the marker of comparison *que*, it seems beyond doubt that no full explanation of the various structural possibilities for the comparatives of Spanish is possible without reference to a semantic notion of focus of the type proposed.

NOTES

1 For ease of exposition, examples will sometimes involve *más*, sometimes *menos*, with no particular relevance attached to this choice.
2 The variant *que lo que* also exists, as noted by De Mello (1977: 511), but is uncommon.
3 Taken from Hankamer (1973).

4 There exist a small number of morphogical comparative adjectives and adverbs:

mejor	más bueno/más bien
peor	más malo/más mal
menor	más pequeño
mayor	más grande

The forms on the left have the semantic content of the analytical forms on the right.

5 Solé (1982: 618) claims that *de lo que/que lo que* freely alternate in this type of comparative, subject to a simple rule:

> *De* and *que* alternate ... the selection of one or the other is motivated by the embedded clause constituents. If the embedded clause contains the relator *que*, the clause is introduced by *de* .... Conversely, if the embedded clause contains a noun phrase introduced by *de*, the clause is introduced by *que*.

As proof of this assertion he gives the following examples:

[57] *Es más inteligente que lo que yo esperaba
[58] Es más inteligente de lo que yo esperaba
[63] *Su casa es más grande de la de Pedro
[64] Su casa es más grande que la de Pedro

He has clearly missed the point here; examples [57] and [58] are not equivalent to [63] and [64]. The first pair are phrasal comparatives, the second pair are reduced sentential comparatives; this is the source of any discrepancy in acceptability (which is not, in fact, so clear-cut, [57] being considerably better than [63]).

6 Bolinger (1950: 49), referring to the example *Quizás te conviene más de lo que tú crees*, speaks of the 'accompanying clause' (i.e. *que tú crees*) as being a 'modifier of *lo*'.

7 That this must be so is self-evident: a pronominal anaphor may not exist for a tensed verb as long as its presence is required for sentence grammaticality.

8 Examples (16–19), earlier, are of a somewhat different type and will be discussed further on pages 36–9 and 42–50.

9 Although the object is unspecified lexically, it must be partially specified as singular, since the following are also possible: *Vende más de los/las que vendía*.

10 *Del* is the contracted form of *de el*.

11. *Lo* may not replace *las* in (35). This is because *las* also functions as the subject of the verb *existían*, whose plurality excludes *lo*.

12 Studerus (1982: 47), discussing similar cases, states that this *lo* occurs 'where it relates **less directly** to a nominal antecedent' (my emphasis). My claim that *lo* may correspond to the quantifier modifying the nominal antecedent improves upon this somewhat indeterminate formulation and has the virtue of being empirically testable.

13 When acting as a verbal or nominal modifier *tan* is realized as *tanto*, with appropriate number and gender marking in the latter case.

14 These examples are adapted from examples given for English in Bresnan (1977).
15 The forms in (64–8) sound rather clumsy, but are fully grammatical.
16 That this must be so has been demonstrated convincingly for English in Bresnan (1975), where she points out that while (a) below is not contradictory, (b) is perceived as such:
   (a) The table is longer than the door is wide – in fact, the door is quite narrow.
   (b) *The door is wide – in fact, it is quite narrow.
17 It is necessary to use a comparative of equality construction to illustrate this point as the interaction of the tensed verb constraint with comparatives of inequality might obscure the point at issue.
18 This type of partial comparative immediately disproves the claim in De Mello (1977: 510–11) that '*que* is used in comparisons involving two different entities, while *de* is required when reference is to a single entity.' His example is a full comparison:
   (1.1) Juan es más alto que Pedro
   Rephrasing this as a partial comparison might give, for example,
   Juan es más alto que grueso
   Here, reference is still to a single entity, Juan, but *de* is not allowed.
19 A syntactic rule of topicalization in Spanish is discussed in Rivero (1980b).
20 Saenz (1940: 329) offers an explanation of these facts as follows: ' "Than" is translated by *que* when both members of the comparison are of the same nature . . . . If the members of the comparison are verbs, use *que* only when the value of one term is not part of the other: *Canta más que duerme. Juega más que trabaja.*' The first part of this assertion is obviously insufficient to account for all the structural possibilities; the second part, which is equivalent to my tensed verb constraint, is couched in terms so vague as to be non-explanatory. If, as I assume, in referring to the value of the terms he means that the verbs must be lexically distinct, this is immediately falsified by examples like (109).
21 Butt and Benjamin (1989: 61) explain the difference between the relativized phrasal construction and the sentential construction as follows: 'This apparently unwieldy construction, i.e. *gasta más de lo que gana* "he spends more than he earns", is necessary in Spanish since *gasta más que gana* usually means "he spends more (i.e. 'rather') than earns".' They do not explain why this should be so, and that the difference is in fact related to what is being compared (the modifiers of the intransitive verbs, i.e. a comparison of frequency or extent, in the second case, but the lexically unspecified objects of the transitive verbs, i.e. a comparison of quantity, in the first). Nor do they point out that the *más . . . que* + tensed verb construction is only possible when a partial comparison is being expressed, but impossible when full comparison is being expressed; as they do not distinguish between the two types of comparison they are, in fact, unable to do so. This fact is presented as largely accidental and apparently inexplicable.

Comparative constructions in Spanish 67

22 Notice that while the other syntactic categories may be involved in relativized phrasal comparatives expressing both full and partial comparison, the verb may only be involved in expressions of partial comparison, as a direct result of the lack of a pronominal anaphor for a tensed verb.

23 Bolinger encounters a problem when considering this point. In a note he states:

> Though theoretically there can be no absolute semantic identity where differences of form exist, I have been unable to pin down whatever difference in meaning there may be between *Juan duerme más que trabaja* and *Juan duerme más de lo que trabaja* (I suspect, however, that *lo* quantifies it, suggesting more strongly an AMOUNT of time).
>
> (1950: 58)

His suspicion is correct and is borne out by my analysis; the difference between the two examples he gives is precisely that, in the phrasal version with *de lo que, lo* corresponds and refers overtly to the quantifier modifying the first verb, *duerme*. Within his analysis, on the other hand, there is no way of explaining this fact, which must be considered a surprising oddity.

24 A sequence of two prepositions, though not involving *de*, is occasionally possible in Spanish, for example (taken from Butt and Benjamin (1989: 350)):

> Es muy cariñoso (para) con su mujer
> He's very affectionate towards his wife

Here *para* may optionally be included.

25 See note 14.

26 There is another context in which an expletive *no* may appear, as illustrated by the following example:

> Dice más a menudo que nos engañamos que no que tenemos razón
> He says more often that we are mistaken than that we are right

Here *no* has been inserted for the sake of euphony, as a means of avoiding a sequence *que que*, and appears to be a phonetic reflex. A structurally parallel example constructed as an equative displays no such reflex:

> Dice tan a menudo que nos engañamos como que tenemos razón
> He says as often that we are mistaken as that we are right

Nonetheless, the question of why it is this expletive *no* which appears in such contexts is interesting and suggests some link between expletive *no* and the expression of comparison in Spanish despite the infrequency of its occurrence, due to its not being required as a marker of comparison.

3 Comparative constructions in French

The comparative constructions of French, unlike Spanish, do not display marked differences in structure: the comparatives of inequality and the comparative of equality share the same clause introducer or 'comparative particle' *que* and enter into similar syntactic configurations. This may provide an explanation for the fact that studies of comparison in French, e.g. Moignet (1970), Milner (1978), Pinkham (1982) and Muller (1983), rarely refer to the equative construction. However, as has already been stated, studies of comparison in general tend to treat only the comparatives of inequality and often restrict themselves to a consideration of the comparative of superiority. This is particularly true of studies of the French construction, a fact noted by De Boer (1954: 172), who quotes Brunot:

> Sitôt qu'on a ôté les oeillères que la tradition nous impose, que de découvertes! . . . *plus grand, plus petit* sont des comparatifs de supériorité. N'y a-t-il donc pas de comparatifs d'infériorité: *moins grand*? Et les comparatifs d'égalité? Pourquoi sont-ils à peu près escamotés? Sans doute parce qu'ils ne jouent qu'un rôle effacé. En effet! Ils contiennent seulement toutes les équations des sciences. Quantité négligeable! Seulement ils n'avaient pas de formes spéciales en Latin!

Jonas (1971: 272) also remarks, 'En effet, les phrases comparatives en *moins* sont assez rares et on en cherche souvent vainement des exemples dans les grammaires.' If the origins of this bias lie in the influence of Latin grammar, it is nonetheless the case that a number of synchronic analyses supporting a particular view of the role of expletive *ne* in such constructions are based solely on a specific interpretation of the comparative of superiority, which can be extended to the comparative of inferiority only with difficulty, and cannot possibly apply to the comparative of equality. These arguments and their relevance to the other comparative constructions will be considered in detail below (see pages 103–29).

Expletive or pleonastic *ne* appears in a rather wide range of other construction types, as well as the comparative, in French and it is usually considered to be a homogeneous phenomenon, susceptible to a single analysis. I consider the expletive *ne* of the French comparative construction to be unrelated to other occurrences of expletive *ne* and will attempt to justify this view.

It is, in fact, the existence of this expletive *ne* which chiefly differentiates the comparative constructions of French from those of Spanish and which seems to serve to differentiate between the comparatives of inequality and the comparative of equality in French itself. The situation is not, however, as clear-cut as this, as will be shown.

Another distinctive feature of the French constructions is the availability of the anaphoric elements *en* and *le*, which may appear in the second half of the comparative construction when the object of comparison is a noun or adjective (or, marginally, a prepositional phrase), respectively. Spanish lacks a proform equivalent to French *en* and does not make parallel use of *lo*, the equivalent of *le*, in these constructions.

The discussion of the means available for the expression of comparison in French will follow the same pattern as the discussion of the Spanish constructions: an examination of constructions expressing full comparison, followed by consideration of constructions expressing partial comparison, involving both the comparatives of inequality and the comparative of equality. The role of the expletive element *ne* in these constructions, interacting in a subset of comparison types with the anaphoric proforms *en* and *le*, will then be discussed and contrasted with its role in other, unrelated, constructions. This discussion will draw heavily at times on three studies of negation and comparison by Muller (1978, 1983, 1984), one of a small set of authors to have considered these constructions in detail. Finally, it will be shown that there is little evidence to support the traditional view of this expletive element as a marker of negation and that, far from being an element of negation, *ne* in comparative constructions serves as a marker of comparison. It is the availability of this extra marker element which, it will be claimed, accounts for the homogeneity of the French construction types, in contrast to the Spanish constructions, and for the fact that no tensed verb constraint appears to operate in French comparatives of inequality.

3.1 EXPRESSION OF FULL COMPARISON

3.1.1 The comparatives of inequality

In Chapter 1 it was stated that there are three possible construction types:

1 a reduced sentential construction,[1] exemplified there by the following:

(1) Le père est plus[2] riche[3] qu'auparavant
    The father is richer than before

2 a full sentential construction:[4]

(2) Le père est plus riche que le fils ne l'était
    The father is richer than the son was

3 two types of phrasal construction:

(a) an oblique phrasal construction:[5]

(3) Son père est plus riche que lui
    His father is richer than him

(b) a relativized phrasal construction involving *que ce que*:[6]

(4) Le père est plus riche que ce que le fils croyait
    The father is richer than the son believed

As in Spanish, there is also an alternation between the preposition *de*[7] and *que* after *plus/moins* when the second half of the comparison contains a number or refers to a quantity, e.g.:

(5) J'ai plus de/que cent francs
    I have more than one hundred francs

Again, as in Spanish, the variant with *de* implies that what is possessed in excess of 100 francs is also numerical, as in (6):

(6) J'ai plus de cent francs; j'en ai deux cents
I have more than one hundred francs; I have two hundred

The variant with *que*, on the other hand, does not necessarily have this implication:

(7) J'ai plus que cent francs; j'ai mes cartes de crédit aussi
I have more than one hundred francs; I have my credit cards as well

Where *que* occurs in a sentence like (6) the usage is described by Muller (1983: 279) as 'populaire'.

The reduced sentential construction

It has already been demonstrated in Chapter 2 that the construction type exemplified in (1) is a reduced sentential construction rather than some kind of oblique phrasal comparative. Commenting on the possible structure of a reduced subordinate clause, Muller (1983: 276) states that 'le complément n'est jamais effacé seul, il est effacé *avec* le verbe qui le commande. C'est ce qui fait que le seul complément qu'on trouve généralement dans ces constructions soit le sujet de la subordonnée.' This is clearly not the case in an example such as (1), though the category following *que* may of course be the subject, as (8) shows:

(8) Le père est plus riche que le fils
The father is richer than the son

In fact, almost any category may 'survive' after *que*; the only restriction in such cases is that a tensed verb may not appear without a subject. However, in cases of this type we are no longer dealing with a reduced clause at all. This is in marked contrast to the Spanish construction, where a tensed verb form can never appear in the second half of such a comparison, as already noted.

Sentence (1) was an example of a reduced sentential comparative where the category undergoing comparison was the adjective, *riche*. The following examples show simple reduced sentential comparatives exhibiting comparison of the noun, verb, adverb and prepositional phrase:

(9) Pierre possède moins de voitures que son frère
Pierre owns fewer cars than his brother

(10) Les travailleurs protestent plus maintenant que dans le passé
    The workers protest more now than in the past
(11) On obtient la promotion moins facilement qu'avant
    One achieves promotion less easily than before
(12) La générosité est plus dans nos coeurs que la cruauté
    Generosity is more in our hearts than cruelty

The full sentential construction

The full sentential construction, exemplified in (2), has no equivalent in Spanish, where only a relativized phrasal structure is available. Muller (1983: 275) defines such sentential complements as follows: 'le complément ne comporte pas de terme lexical corrélé à X', where X is the category of comparison in the matrix. This is obviously not entirely true of expressions of full comparison involving a noun, adjective or prepositional phrase as the object of comparison, since the anaphoric proforms *en* or *le*, directly linked to the category of comparison in the matrix, will appear in the subordinate clause (though as proforms they may not qualify under Muller's definition of 'terme lexical'); nor is this true of expressions of partial comparison involving any category at all, since there will by definition be a lexical item acting as the second term of the comparison in the subordinate clause, e.g. sentence (40) of Chapter 1 (repeated):
(1:24) Le travail est plus difficile que le contrat n'est détaillé
    The work is more difficult than the contract is detailed
This is a full sentential structure expressing partial comparison, with the nouns *le travail* and *le contrat* the objects of comparison. Clearly, the subordinate clause, or 'complément', does contain a 'terme lexical corrélé à X': *le contrat* is correlated with *le travail*.

Sentence (2) was an example of a full sentential construction in which the category undergoing comparison was the adjective. The following examples, the full sentential versions of (9–12), show full sentential comparatives exhibiting comparison of the noun, verb, adverb and prepositional phrase:

(13) Pierre posssède moins de voitures que son frère n'en possède
    Pierre owns fewer cars than his brother owns

The variant displaying subject–verb inversion in the subordinate clause is also possible:

(14) Pierre possède moins de voitures que n'en possède son frère

The tendency towards subject–verb inversion in the second half of the comparison is noted by Le Bidois and Le Bidois (1938: 40): 'Le rapport de différence . . . se marque par les adverbes *plus*, *moins* . . . en corrélation avec *que*. La présence de cette dernière conjonction amène fréquemment l'inversion dans le second membre du système.' However, this applies only when the subject of the subordinate clause is a noun, as pointed out in Ferrar (1984: 179): 'Where the subject of the *que* clause is a noun, inversion is frequent.' Indeed, this construction appears to be preferred if the verb *posséder* is replaced by the verb *avoir*, (15) being considered better than (16):

(15) Pierre a moins de voitures que n'en a son frère
(16) Pierre a moins de voitures que son frère n'en a

This preference may be connected to the proportional 'weights' of the verb and subject noun phrase.

G. Price (1971: 263) speaks of subject–verb inversion as being a stylistic variant: 'the choice is determined by rhythmic considerations and there is little or no difference of meaning or emphasis.' It is these 'rhythmic considerations' which must account for the preference of (15) over (16): *a* is felt to be too short a form to bear the stress associated with its position, unlike *possède*.

Example (17) is the full sentential version of (10), with the verb as the compared category:

(17) Les travailleurs protestent plus maintenant qu'ils ne protestaient dans le passé
The workers protest more now than they protested in the past

Example (18) shows comparison involving the adverb:

(18) On obtient la promotion moins facilement qu'on ne l'obtenait avant
One achieves promotion less easily than one achieved it before

Finally, in (19) the prepositional phrase is the object of comparison:

(19) La générosité est plus dans nos coeurs que ne l'était la cruauté
Generosity is more in our hearts than cruelty was

Here, subject–verb inversion has again occurred in the subordinate clause. Example (19) is preferred to (20), for reasons already outlined, though (20) is grammatical:

(20) La générosité est plus dans nos coeurs que la cruauté ne l'était

The anaphoric proforms

An item anaphoric to the compared category appears in the subordinate clause of a number of the full sentential constructions just exemplified, *le* appearing in sentences (2), (19) and (20) and *en* appearing in sentences (13–16). In (2) *le* is anaphoric to the adjective *riche* in the matrix clause, in (19) and (20) it bears the same relation to the prepositional phrase[8] *dans nos coeurs* of the matrix. In (13–16) *en* is an anaphor of *de voitures* in the matrix.

As has been pointed out, Spanish has no equivalent to French *en* and makes no use in these contexts of the proform *lo*, broadly equivalent to French *le*. These forms appear in French comparatives where in the Spanish constructions there is simply a gap; 'instead of a gap in the comparative clause, we find a proform replacing the compared element ... the compared element is an anaphor of the compared element in the main clause' (Pinkham 1982: 4). Both *en* and *le*, then, act as foci of comparison, representing the second compared category, which must be fully deleted in Spanish. *En* must occur whenever the object of comparison is a noun in the matrix and, as Pinkham observes, is simply an instance of the standard clitic proform. However, this clitic normally replaces a prepositional phrase; how, then, can it be said to be an anaphor of a noun phrase? The answer lies in the structure of the matrix noun phrase *moins de voitures*. This can be seen to be a partitive structure, *de voitures* being the complement of the quantifier *moins*.[9] In the subordinate clause *en* is the proform replacing the prepositional phrase *de voitures*[10] and a quantifier parallel to *moins* will be inferred. Thus it is not entirely accurate to speak, as Pinkham does, of there being no gap in such comparatives; rather, the gap represents the quantifier, much as in constructions expressing partial comparison.

The use of *en* in comparatives where the object of comparison is a noun is obligatory. Pinkham (1982: 16) points out that this is true in two ways: 'it must be used instead of the element it is intended to "replace" and ... it cannot be omitted.' The following three examples (Pinkham's (43–5)) illustrate this:

(21) Ces jours-ci, il a plus d'argent qu'il n'en avait
      These days, he has more money than he used to have
(22) *Ces jours-ci, il a plus d'argent qu'il n'avait d'argent

(23) *Ces jours-ci, il a plus d'argent qu'il n'avait

The proform *le*, unlike *en*, seems able to act as a 'replacement' for both adjectives and prepositional phrases.[11] As for *en*, a quantifier modifying the proform must be inferred, parallel to the quantifier in the matrix. Pinkham (1092: 18) claims that the anaphor *le* is also obligatory in comparisons involving an adjective and gives the following examples (Pinkham's (49)):

(24) Jean est plus grand que je ne le suis
 Jean is taller than I am
(25) *Jean est plus grand que je ne suis grand
(26) *Jean est plus grand que je ne suis

However, native speakers appear to find constructions like (26) less unacceptable than constructions like (23). In particular, the unacceptability of (26) is closely linked to the fact that no new information is given by the verb of the subordinate clause, as a result of which an oblique phrasal construction would be preferred:

(27) Jean est plus grand que moi
 Jean is taller than me

If new information is included in the second half of the comparison, for instance by changing the verb tense, a sentence structurally similar to (26) becomes more acceptable:

(28) ?Jean est plus grand que je n'étais à son âge
 Jean is taller than I was at his age

Notice it is not being claimed that sentences like (28) are fully acceptable, but rather that they are felt by native speakers to be less unacceptable than sentences like (23), where the clitic *en* is omitted.

As Pinkham's study ignores comparatives involving prepositional phrases, the question of whether an anaphoric element exists for these categories is not addressed. Nor are comparatives involving the verb[12] as the object of comparison, as in (17), considered. Such constructions also lack a pronominal anaphor in the second half of the comparison. It is, however, pointed out that adverbs, as in (18), lack a 'replacement' proform in the subordinate clause, though this is considered an 'exceptional case' in that here 'we observe a gap' (Pinkham 1982: 17). In fact, comparative constructions where the adverb is the object of comparison are not exceptional in displaying a gap, or, in other words, in requiring some category to be inferred in the subordinate clause. All sentential comparatives in French require this for their interpretation; it is just that those categories with available proforms (nouns, adjectives, prepositional phrases) require rather less to be inferred, having a morphological marker, referring back to its matrix antecedent, in the subordinate clause. The quantifier itself must still be inferred.

The expletive *ne*

Expletive *ne* appears in all the examples of full sentential constructions. Without this element in the subordinate clause, the sentences become considerably less acceptable and, in fact, ungrammatical for most native speakers. I have suggested that it is this expletive *ne* which in some sense licenses the appearance of the tensed verb in the French constructions. The lack of an equivalent expletive element in Spanish accounts for the inability of a tensed verb to appear in the subordinate clause of such constructions, sentential comparatives of inequality expressing full comparison being obligatorily reduced in this language. *Ne* in French appears, as predicted, to act as a marker of comparison, essential for most of the native speakers I have consulted.

Example (29) exemplifies the scale of acceptability which may apply for most native speakers:

(29) a. *??Il est plus riche qu'il était
    b. ??Il est plus riche qu'il l'était
    c. ?Il est plus riche qu'il n'était
    d. Il est plus riche qu'il ne l'était
       He is richer than he used to be

For most of the speakers I consulted (29a) is ungrammatical. Equally, for most speakers (29c), with expletive *ne*, but without the anaphoric proform, is preferable to (29b), with the proform, but without *ne*; (29d) is the only version which is fully acceptable to all speakers. These judgements point clearly to a certain amount of interaction between *ne* and the anaphoric proforms (where available), which, as indicated, are foci of comparison. The role of expletive *ne* in comparatives and its subtle interdependence with the anaphoric proforms will be discussed in detail in section 3.3.7.

Comparison over an unbounded context

As a tensed verb may surface freely after *que* in French comparatives of inequality, it is possible for the second half of such a comparison to involve more than one clause, within the limits of comprehensibility. This is unlike the case in Spanish, where such multi-clause constructions (without *de lo que*) are restricted to the comparative of equality.

Interestingly, where more than one tensed verb follows comparative *que*, the position of expletive *ne* is not fixed. Muller (1983: 296) gives the following two examples:

(30) Max est plus riche que tu n'as cru qu'il l'était
 Max is richer than you thought he was
(31) ?Max est plus riche que tu as cru qu'il ne l'était

Here (31) is the less acceptable variant. Yet if *ne* were a truly negative element it might be expected to modify the second verb more naturally than the first. If, however, *ne* is a marker of comparison rather than negation, its position before the first verb would seem more natural as it marks the construction as expressing comparison immediately after the appearance of (potentially ambiguous) *que*. Negative raising is clearly not a possible analysis of this phenomenon.

Sentences (32) and (33) also appear to be equally acceptable:

(32) Marie est plus déprimée que Jean ne m'a dit que Pierre lui avait expliqué qu'elle le paraissait auparavant
 Marie is more depressed than Jean told me that Pierre had explained to him that she seemed before
(33) Marie est plus déprimée que Jean m'a dit que Pierre lui avait expliqué qu'elle ne le paraissait auparavant

In (32) *ne* appears with the first verb after *que*, to mark the comparison. In (33) it appears with the verb which expresses the natural contrast of the comparison. In fact, (34) is also possible, at least for some native speakers:

(34) Marie est plus déprimée que Jean ne m'a dit que Pierre lui avait expliqué qu'elle ne le paraissait auparavant

In (34) *ne* appears twice. It seems that here the first *ne* has the role of comparative marker, while the second *ne* reinforces the contrast expressed by the second half of the comparison. For speakers who accept (34) *ne* seems to be totally divorced from any idea of negativity, hence it appears automatically as a conditioned marker of comparison as soon as possible in the second half of the comparison and must then be repeated with the verb expressing the natural contrast of the comparison, in the final clause. It is quite clear that the positioning of *ne* in these examples has nothing to do with the idea of negativity. If *ne* were a negative particle, its position might be expected to be relatively stable. As a marker of comparison, its relative instability, with a definite preference for a position early in the second half of the comparison, is exactly what we would expect.[13]

The following set of examples[14] illustrate more fully the ability of the second half of a comparison of inequality to involve more than one clause, within the limits of comprehensibility:

(35) Evidemment, ils peuvent employer plus de femmes qu'ils n'en employaient auparavant
Obviously, they can employ more women than they employed before

(36) Evidemment, ils peuvent employer plus de femmes que le gouvernement ne leur permettait d'en employer auparavant
Obviously, they can employ more women than the government allowed them to employ before

(37) Evidemment, ils peuvent employer plus de femmes que le gouvernement ne pensait à leur permettre d'en employer auparavant
Obviously, they can employ more women than the government thought of allowing them to employ before

(38) Evidemment, ils peuvent employer plus de femmes que le gouvernement ne consentait à penser à leur permettre d'en employer auparavant
Obviously, they can employ more women than the government agreed to think of allowing them to employ before

(39) Evidemment, ils peuvent employer plus de femmes qu'il ne paraissait que le gouvernement consentît à penser à leur permettre d'en employer auparavant
Obviously, they can employ more women than it seemed that the government agreed to think of allowing them to employ before

(40) Evidemment, ils peuvent employer plus de femmes que le gouvernement ne voulait qu'il parût qu'il consentît à penser à leur permettre d'en employer auparavant
Obviously, they can employ more women than the government wanted it to seem that it agreed to think of allowing them to employ before

In each of these examples *ne* appears attached to the first verb of the second half of the comparison. As the comments above indicate, this is not the only possible position for it; it is, however, the preferred position.

The phrasal constructions

The oblique phrasal construction

The oblique phrasal construction has been exemplified in (3) (repeated for convenience):

(3) Son père est plus riche que lui
    His father is richer than him

I have chosen to analyse this as a phrasal construction, with *lui* the complement of *que*, rather than a reduced sentential construction, because of the appearance of the disjunctive form of the masculine pronoun. If it were a reduced sentential construction, the subject form of the pronoun might be expected:

(41) *Son père est plus riche qu'il

This is impossible, given the inability of weak subject pronouns to appear without an associated verb, though it might also be possible to analyse (3) as a reduced sentential construction, with the strong form of the pronoun appearing as a result of the deletion of the verb. Recall that the oblique phrasal construction does not exist in Spanish, where superficially similar examples must be reduced sentential constructions parallel in structure to (41), not (3); this may be because the subject pronouns of Spanish, unlike French, are able to appear without an associated verb. It seems, then, that while English allows both a phrasal and a reduced sentential structure to express such comparisons, Spanish allows only a reduced sentential structure, while French allows only a phrasal structure.

Notice that when the noun following *que* is a full lexical item both sources will presumably be available:

(42) Son père est plus riche que Jean
     His father is richer than Jean

Example (42) may be either a reduced sentential construction, parallel to (1), or an oblique phrasal construction, parallel to (3).

The phrasal construction involving *que ce que*

The relativized phrasal construction involving *que ce que* is exemplified in (4) (repeated):

(4) Le père est plus riche que ce que le fils croyait

This construction appears, superficially, to be the equivalent of the Spanish construction with *de lo que*. It displays no gap in the second half of the comparison. As with *lo que*, the sequence *ce que* + tensed verb following the comparative subordinator *que* looks like the sequence pronoun – *que* + tensed verb found in relative uctions, e.g.:

(43) Je ne suis pas d'accord avec ce que tu crois
    I do not agree with what you believe

It seems, then, that the *que ce que* phrasal construction might be analysed along parallel lines as involving a pronoun (*ce*), which is the complement of *que* and heads a restrictive relative clause. However, unlike the Spanish *de lo que* construction, the French phrasal construction is not required as a means of escaping from a tensed verb constraint. The meaning of (4) might just as easily be expressed as (44):

(44) Le père est plus riche que le fils ne croyait

There is no difference in meaning between (4) and (44). Sentence (44) may, however, be felt to be more emphatic. This is a consequence of the presence of the marker of comparison *ne*, marking the construction more overtly as a comparative.[15] As a result, the acceptability of such phrasal comparatives in French varies considerably, according to a number of factors, among them the nature of the category being compared. The following are simple[16] phrasal comparatives involving the categories of noun, verb, adverb and prepositional phrase:

(45) Il a plus d'amis que ce[17] qu'il avait
    He has more friends than he had
(46) Il travaille plus que ce qu'il travaillait
    He works more than he used to work
(47) ?L'enfant mange moins goulûment que ce qu'il mangeait
    The child eats less greedily than he used to eat
(48) ?La générosité est plus dans nos coeurs que ce qu'on pourrait penser
    Generosity is more in our hearts than one might think

Examples (47) and (48), comparisons involving the adverb and prepositional phrase, are felt to be less acceptable. For some

speakers, phrasal comparatives seem improved by the addition of an anaphoric proform and/or expletive *ne*:
(49) a. ?Le père est plus riche que ce que le fils ne croyait
     b. ??Le père est plus riche que ce que le fils ne le croyait
(50) a. ?Il a plus d'amis que ce qu'il n'avait
     b. *Il a plus d'amis que ce qu'il n'en avait
(51) ?Il travaille plus que ce qu'il ne travaillait
(52) ?L'enfant mange moins goulûment que ce qu'il ne mangeait
(53) ?La générosité est plus dans nos coeurs que ce qu'on ne pourrait penser

Judgements as to the acceptability of sentences like (49–53) vary greatly: for some speakers, the version including *ne* is more acceptable than the version without *ne*; for others, the addition of *ne* makes the sentence totally unacceptable; yet others find versions including an anaphoric element much improved. In fact, strictly speaking, neither *ne* nor a proform is allowed in this construction. The proform is unacceptable because in phrasal comparatives there is no gap, the pronominal *ce* acting as the head of an ensuing relative, rather than comparative, clause. *Ne* is unacceptable for the same reason: it is the marker of a comparative subordinate clause, never occurring in a relative clause. However, it is not unexpected that some speakers should prefer the addition of one or both of these elements, given the essentially marginal nature of phrasal comparatives in French. The existence of a parallel full sentential construction makes them redundant. Hence the features most closely identified with constructions expressing comparison, expletive *ne* and possibly an anaphoric proform, may be 'imported' by some speakers into the phrasal construction in an attempt to make it seem more acceptable. This reinforces my argument that *ne* is essentially a marker of comparison, dissociated from any idea of negativity; its occurrence in relativized phrasal constructions is the result of a process of attraction.

Discussing similar constructions, Muller (1983: 284–6) points out 'l'impossibilité d'y faire figurer un pronom'; he also demonstrates that expletive *ne* may not occur and that the relative clause may not be reduced, giving as an example:

(54) *Pierre a bu moins d'eau que ce que Paul[18]
     Pierre has drunk less water than Paul

He does not, however, consider examples involving categories other than noun and adjective as the object of comparison, nor does he mention that the restrictions on the appearance of *ne* and the proforms in such constructions may not hold for all speakers. He also fails to grasp the significance of the fact that expletive *ne* does not generally occur in the phrasal construction. This, for his analysis, is problematic for two reasons. First, he is attempting to defend the hypothesis that the sentential construction is derived from the phrasal *que ce que* construction via deletion of the head of the relative clause.[19] This hypothesis is not only unworkable but actually indefensible, since it ignores the fact that there is a gap in the sentential construction or, to put it another way, the fact that something extra must be inferred in the subordinate clause of such constructions, while in the phrasal construction there is no gap as the very element he wishes to delete, *ce*, the head of the following relative clause, is what allows retrieval of the information relevant to the comparison. In other words, it 'replaces' the gap. If sentential constructions are derived from phrasal constructions, as he is claiming, where does *ne* come from?

Second, as he believes expletive *ne* is a truly negative item, there is no reason to expect that it should not occur in phrasal comparatives, which can hardly be more or less negative than the equivalent sentential construction. Notice that it is his belief, widely shared, that *ne* is actually a negative marker, that causes the problem. My claim that *ne* is a marker of comparison makes it natural that it should not occur in phrasal comparatives, since these are actually relative clauses, and yet unsurprising that for some speakers it seems acceptable there, since for them the marginal acceptability of such phrasal constructions is improved by the addition of a marker of comparison.

Returning to example (46), a phrasal comparative involving the verb as the compared category, although, as has been pointed out in chapter 2, what is actually being compared is not the verb itself, but rather an underlying quantifier or measure phrase contained within *plus*,[20] notice that the verb *travailler* is intransitive. If the verb involved is optionally transitive, e.g. *vendre*, the phrasal comparative should be ambiguous between an interpretation of *ce* as corresponding to the idea of the underlying quantifier in *plus* or as referring to a lexically unfilled object of the verb:

(55) Il vend plus que ce qu'il vendait
    He sells more than he used to sell

Example (55) is ambiguous between the first reading – *the extent to/frequency with which he is involved in the act of selling is greater than it was* – and the second – *the quantity of goods he sells is greater than it was*. The second reading will normally be preferred as being a more natural interpretation, but, given an appropriate context, the first is possible. This is parallel to the case for example (31) in Chapter 2 (repeated for convenience):

(2:31) Vende más de lo que vendía

Nonetheless, there is an important difference. The perceived ambiguity of sentence (55) can be resolved using a full sentential construction for each of the two interpretations

(56) Il vend plus qu'il ne vendait
(57) Il en vend plus qu'il n'en vendait

Sentence (56) has the 'extent' interpretation and (57) the 'quantity' interpretation. These constructions would, therefore, normally be preferred. The non-existence of a full sentential construction in Spanish (linked to the lack of both an expletive element like *ne* and an anaphoric proform) means that the ambiguity of the Spanish example cannot be resolved.

3.1.2 The comparative of equality

For the comparative of equality there are also three construction types, as for the comparatives of inequality. These were exemplified in Chapter 1 as follows:

1 a reduced sentential construction:

(58) La jeune fille est aussi contente qu'auparavant
    The young girl is as happy as before

2 a full sentential construction:

(59) La jeune fille est aussi contente que l'était le petit garçon
    The young girl is as happy as the little boy was

3 two types of phrasal construction:

(a) an oblique phrasal construction

(60) La jeune fille est aussi contente que lui
    The young girl is as happy as him

(b) a *que ce que* relativized phrasal construction

(61) La jeune fille est aussi contente que ce que le petit garçon voulait
The young girl is as happy as the little boy wished

The reduced sentential construction

The reduced sentential construction is straightforwardly the same for the comparative of equality as for the comparatives of inequality. The following are examples of simple reduced sentential constructions involving, as the object of comparison, the categories of noun, verb, adjective, adverb and prepositional phrase:

(62) On trouve autant[21] de problèmes économiques en Angleterre qu'en France
One finds as many economic problems in England as in France
(63) Les femmes travaillent autant que les hommes
Women work as much as men
(64) Un président est aussi puissant qu'un roi[22]
A president is as powerful as a king
(65) Il court aussi lentement qu'auparavant
He runs as slowly as previously
(66) La cruauté est autant dans nos coeurs que la générosité[23]
Cruelty is as much in our hearts as generosity

Aussi may be replaced by *si* and *autant* by *tant* after a negative or interrogative matrix clause, e.g.:

(67) Un président n'est pas si puissant qu'un roi
A president is not as powerful as a king
(68) Les femmes ne travaillent pas tant que les hommes
Women do not work as much as men

However, this usage 'n'a rien d'obligatoire' according to Le Bidois and Le Bidois (1938: 259); for Gougenheim (1939: 253) it is 'une variation stylistique'; and for Moignet (1981: 202) 'il n'y a pas d'emphase dans l'emploi de *si* en phrase négative appelant une comparative.' In fact, both alternatives are possible after interrogative and negative matrix clauses, as exemplified in Ferrar (1984: 179). They cannot, therefore, be said to be in fully complementary distribution, *si* and *tant* constituting optional alternatives in the contexts mentioned.

The full sentential construction

Sentence (59) was an example of a full sentential construction in which the category undergoing comparison was the adjective. The following examples are full sentential versions of (62–6) and involve comparison of the noun, verb, adjective, adverb and prepositional phrase:

(69) On trouve autant de problèmes économiques en Angleterre qu'on en trouve en France
One finds as many economic problems in England as one finds in France

(70) Les femmes travaillent autant que travaillent les hommes[24]
Women wok as much as men work

(71) Un président est aussi puissant que l'est un roi
A president is as powerful as a king is

(72) Il court aussi lentement qu'il courait auparavant
He runs as slowly as he ran previously

(73) La cruauté est autant dans nos coeurs que l'était la générosité
Cruelty is as much in our hearts as generosity was

These examples are constructed in a parallel fashion to the full sentential examples involving the comparatives of inequality. The distinction between the comparatives of inequality and the comparative of equality which is found in Spanish, i.e. the existence of a tensed verb constraint for the former but not the latter, does not, therefore, exist in French.

The expletive *ne*

A distinction is, however, usually made between the equative construction and the comparatives of inequality on the basis of the appearance or non-appearance of expletive *ne* in the subordinate clause. It has already been shown that for most speakers a full sentential comparative involving *plus/moins* is ungrammatical without *ne* in the subordinate clause. Yet *ne* does not appear in the equative full sentential examples (69–73).

Most of those who have analysed comparison state that a negative element may not appear in the second half of an equative. According to Bergmans (1982: 112), 'Generally, the markers of the

COMPARATIVE NEGATION seem to be limited to THAN-constructions' (Bergman's emphasis). This is a widely held view. In analyses of French this restriction is based on the negative import of *ne*, which makes it unsuited to comparisons where a relation of equality is posited. Muller (1983) states that 'une négation (non explétive) n'est pas impossible dans les comparatives phrastiques d'égalité (qui par contre ne prennent pas . . . de *ne* explétif)' (p. 287) and that 'si l'on fait de *ne* une négation constitutive de la relation d'inégalité, il est normal qu'il n'apparaisse que dans ce cas' (p. 295). This view of expletive *ne* as being solely a negative item cannot allow its appearance in an equative. Yet expletive *ne* does appear in equatives, as Muller implicitly admits: 'Il va de soi que *ne* n'apparaît guère dans les comparatives d'égalité' (p. 295). Ferrar (1984: 179) gives no example of an equative with *ne* in the subordinate clause, but states in a footnote, 'No *ne* is present in the que clause in sentences of this kind [equatives] when the main clause is negative.' This is equivalent to allowing that *ne* can appear in positive equatives, but, again, this is implied, rather than explicit. Jonas (1971: 271) is explicitly opposed to such an idea: 'C'est un fait bien connu, et il est inutile de s'y appesantir, que ce *ne* n'apparaît que dans les systèmes qui comportent dans le premier terme une marque de disparité (*plus* . . .) et jamais dans ceux qui renferment dans le premier terme une marque d'égalité.'

Against this, Napoli and Nespor (1977: 89) give as acceptable the sentence *Il est aussi bon qu'ils ne puissent l'être*, and Gaatone (1971:97), speaking of the equative construction and the comparatives of inequality, states: 'La similarité des constructions entraîne . . . l'emploi de *ne*, dans le second terme d'une comparaison d'égalité, soit positive, soit négative.' In fact, expletive *ne* may appear in the subordinate clause of the comparative of equality as well as in the comparatives of inequality. The general reluctance to accept this is owed to the fact that such an admission will not allow a description of *ne* as a negative item in these constructions to go through unproblematically. Examples (74–8) are (69–73) repeated, but including *ne*:

(74) On trouve autant de problèmes économiques en Angleterre qu'on n'en trouve en France.
(75) Les femmes travaillent autant que ne travaillent les hommes
(76) Un président est aussi puissant que ne l'est un roi
(77) Il court aussi lentement qu'il ne courait auparavant

(78) La cruauté est autant dans nos coeurs que ne l'était la générosité

For most of the speakers I have consulted, (74–8) are fully acceptable. This is inexplicable if *ne* is a negative item. If, however, it is a marker of comparison, it is unsurprising. I shall return to this point on pages 99–100.

Comparison over an unbounded context

As with the comparatives of inequality, the second half of a comparative of equality may involve more than one clause. The following examples,[25] parallel to examples (35–40), illustrate this:

(79) Evidemment, ils peuvent employer autant de femmes qu'ils en employaient auparavant
(80) Evidemment, ils peuvent employer autant de femmes que le gouvernement leur permettait d'en employer auparavant
(81) Evidemment, ils peuvent employer autant de femmes que le gouvernement pensait à leur permettre d'en employer auparavant
(82) Evidemment, ils peuvent employer autant de femmes que le gouvernement consentait à penser à leur permettre d'en employer auparavant
(83) Evidemment, ils peuvent employer autant de femmes qu'il paraissait que le gouvernement consentît à penser à leur permettre d'en employer auparavant
(84) Evidemment, ils peuvent employer autant de femmes que le gouvernement voulait qu'il parût qu'il consentît à penser à leur permettre d'en employer auparavant

Ne may also appear in such multi-clause comparatives, e.g.:

(85) a. La table est aussi grande que Marie ne croit que Pierre avait dit qu'elle l'était
b. La table est aussi grande que Marie croit que Pierre n'avait dit qu'elle l'était
c. La table est aussi grande que Marie croit que Pierre avait dit qu'elle ne l'était
The table is as big as Marie believes that Pierre had said that it was

For native speakers who accept expletive *ne* in equatives, the three versions in (85) seem equally acceptable. Thus the position of *ne* in equatives is as unstable as in comparatives of inequality of this type.

The phrasal constructions

The oblique phrasal construction

The oblique phrasal construction has been exemplified in (60) (repeated for convenience):

(60) La jeune fille est aussi contente que lui

This is exactly parallel to the oblique phrasal construction involving the comparatives of inequality. That constructions like (60) are indeed phrasal, rather than reduced sentential constructions, has already been demonstrated.

The phrasal construction involving *que ce que*

The relativized phrasal construction involving *que ce que* is exemplified in (61) (repeated):

(61) La jeune fille est aussi contente que ce que le petit garçon voulait

The phrasal construction has already been discussed in some detail in the section on comparatives of inequality (pp. 79–83). The following are simple phrasal comparatives involving the categories of noun, verb, adverb and prepositional phrase:

(86) ??Il possède autant de chevaux que ce qu'il possédait
    He owns as many horses as he used to own
(87) ??Elle sortait autant que ce qu'elle était sortie auparavant
    She went out as much as she had gone out before
(88) ??Les élèves se comporteront aussi bien que ce qu'ils se comportent maintenant
    The pupils will behave as well as they behave now
(89) ??La générosité est autant dans nos coeurs que ce qu'on pourrait penser
    Generosity is as much in our hearts as one might think

In fact, examples (86–9) are considerably less acceptable than the equivalent constructions involving the comparatives of inequality. For some speakers I have consulted, they are marginally acceptable;

for others they are totally ungrammatical. In each case a full sentential construction would be the acceptable replacement. This is not unexpected, as the existence of another possible construction makes the phrasal option superfluous. It is interesting, however, to draw parallels between French and Spanish here. In Spanish, recall, the phrasal construction is required for comparatives of inequality (to escape the tensed verb constraint) and possible for the comparative of equality, but not required and therefore not usually found, the sentential construction being preferred. In French, the phrasal construction is not required for either the comparatives of inequality or the comparative of equality as both allow a sentential construction, due to the inapplicability of the tensed verb constraint (linked to the presence of *ne*). Yet the phrasal construction still appears to be more acceptable with the comparatives of inequality than for the expression of a comparative of equality. This may be linked to the fact that *ne* is much less frequent in sentential equative constructions, making the relativized phrasal structure, which is an alternative to the sentential structure containing expletive *ne*, redundant. In this respect the situation in French is remarkably similar to the situation in Spanish despite other, more obvious, differences.

3.2 EXPRESSION OF PARTIAL COMPARISON

As pointed out in Chapter 2, partial comparison involves comparing referentially and lexically distinct categories which are non-distinct with regard to categorial features.

3.2.1 The comparatives of inequality

In Chapter 1 it was claimed that there are four possible construction types for the expression of partial comparison involving the comparatives of inequality:

1 a reduced sentential construction:

(90) Le travail est plus détaillé que difficile
    The work is more detailed than difficult

2 a full sentential construction with declarative word order in the subordinate clause:

(91) Le travail est plus difficile que le contrat n'est détaillé
The work is more difficult than the contract is detailed

3 a topicalized sentential construction:

(92) Le travail est plus difficile que détaillé est le contrat
The work is more difficult than the contract is detailed

4 a relativized phrasal construction:

(93) Le travail est plus difficile que ce que le contrat est détaillé
The work is more difficult than the contract is detailed

Option 3 appears to be additional to the options available for the expression of full comparison.

Recall that in expressions of partial comparison what is actually being compared is not the lexically distinct categories, but rather their modifier: the semantic content of the comparative modifier, in this case *plus/moins*, is compared with an equivalent quantification modifier of the second compared category, this modifier being inferred.[26] This has been discussed in more detail in Chapter 2.

The reduced sentential construction

The following are examples of (simple) sentences expressing partial comparison, involving the categories of noun, adjective, adverb and prepositional phrase:

(94) Il possède moins de chevaux que de chiens
He owns fewer horses than dogs
(95) Elle paraît plus triste que contente
She seems more sad than happy
(96) Jean danse plus énergiquement qu'élégamment
Jean dances more energetically than elegantly
(97) La cruauté est plus dans nos têtes que dans nos coeurs
Cruelty is more in our heads than in our hearts

The full sentential construction

Examples (94–7) are simple sentences, lacking a tensed verb in the subordinate clause. As there is no restriction on the appearance of a tensed verb in French comparatives, more complex examples can easily be constructed:

(98) Jean vend plus de bicyclettes que Pierre n'achète de voitures

Jean sells more bicycles than Pierre buys cars
(99) La table est plus longue que la porte n'est large
The table is longer than the door is wide
(100) Mon oncle dort moins que ne dormait ma tante[27]
My uncle sleeps less than my aunt slept
(101) Le bébé rampe plus soigneusement que son frère ne marche négligemment
The baby crawls more carefully than his brother walks carelessly
(102) La cruauté est moins dans nos têtes que la générosité n'est dans nos coeurs
Cruelty is less in our heads than generosity is in our hearts

Naturally, the anaphoric proforms *en/le* will not appear, since the second object of comparison is a full lexical item.[28] Expletive *ne* appears along with the tensed verb in each case.

A constraint was noted with regard to such constructions in Spanish. In Chapter 2 it was pointed out that while a sentence like (105) (repeated) is not acceptable, (110) (repeated) is:

(2:105) *Mi padre duerme más que dormía
(2:110) Mi padre duerme más que dormían mis hermanos

The ungrammaticality of (105) was explained on the grounds that the only available focus of comparison in the subordinate clause is the verb tense and that verb tense alone is not a sufficient focus and requires additional foci of contrast. Notice that the equivalent constructions in French are both grammatical:

(103) Mon père dort plus qu'il ne dormait
(104) Mon père dort plus que ne dormaient mes frères[29]

Why should (103), in which comparison, as in the Spanish example, involves the verb tense only, be acceptable? The difference between (103) and (2:105) is the presence of expletive *ne*. This element provides the extra contrast required; the lack of such an element in Spanish condemns (2:105) to ungrammaticality. An analysis of *ne* as a marker of negativity cannot explain this contrast. The French sentence is not more 'negative' than the Spanish. Once again, the presence of expletive *ne*, acting as a marker of comparison and providing an extra contrast in the subordinate clause, results in differences in the structural possibilities of French and Spanish.

Notions of parallelism play an important part in determining the acceptability of such comparisons. Any decrease in the parallelism of contrasts will have a marked effect on the sentence's acceptability:

(105) Les hommes de l'usine du coin lisent moins de livres que les femmes du bureau de la place n'écrivent de lettres
The men in the factory on the corner read less books than the women in the office on the square write letters

(106) ?Les hommes de l'usine du coin lisent moins de livres que les femmes du bureau de la place ne mangent de sandwichs
The men in the factory on the corner read less books than the women in the office on the square eat sandwiches

In (105) there are five separate and parallel contrasts; in (106) there are also five contrasts, but two of them (*lisent/mangent, livres/sandwichs*) are not parallel, hence the sentence's lowered acceptability.

Comparison over an unbounded context

As with expressions of full comparison, constructions expressing partial comparison may also contain more than one subordinate clause, the second object of comparison being embedded indefinitely far down, subject to processing/perceptual constraints. Also, as for expressions of full comparison, the position of *ne* appears to be flexible:

(107) a. Marie est plus déprimée que Jean ne m'a dit que Pierre lui avait expliqué qu'elle paraissait triste auparavant
b. Marie est plus déprimée que Jean m'a dit que Pierre lui avait expliqué qu'elle ne paraissait triste auparavant
c. Marie est plus déprimée que Jean ne m'a dit que Pierre lui avait expliqué qu'elle ne paraissait triste auparavant
Marie is more depressed than Jean told me that Pierre had explained to him that she seemed sad before

Each version seems to be equally acceptable to most native speakers, though multi-clause examples may be considered less acceptable as complexity increases.[30] Sentence (107) is exactly parallel to (32–4), earlier. The role of *ne* appears, therefore, to be the same for constructions expressing either partial or full comparison.

The following set of examples,[31] parallel to (35–40), are more complex illustrations of partial comparison, involving nouns as the compared objects, over an (in theory) unbounded context:

(108) Evidemment, ils peuvent employer plus de femmes qu'ils n'employaient d'hommes auparavant
(109) Evidemment, ils peuvent employer plus de femmes que le gouvernement ne leur permettait d'employer d'hommes auparavant.
(110) Evidemment, ils peuvent employer plus de femmes que le gouvernement ne pensait à leur permettre d'employer d'hommes auparavant
(111) Evidemment, ils peuvent employer plus de femmes que le gouvernement ne consentait à penser à leur permettre d'employer d'hommes auparavant
(112) Evidemment, ils peuvent employer plus de femmes qu'il ne paraissait que le gouvernement consentît à penser à leur permettre d'employer d'hommes auparavant
(113) Evidemment, ils peuvent employer plus de femmes que le gouvernement ne voulait qu'il parût qu'il consentît à penser à leur permettre d'employer d'hommes auparavant
Obviously, they can employ more women than the government wanted it to seem that it agreed to think of allowing them to employ men before

In each of the above, expletive *ne* appears before the first tensed subordinate verb, i.e. in the preferred position, though it could appear with any of the other tensed verbs.

The topicalized sentential construction

The example of a topicalized construction given above, (92) (repeated), involves the adjective as the compared category:

(92) Le travail est plus difficile que détaillé est le contrat

Here the adjective *détaillé* has been topicalized, i.e. it occupies clause-initial position. As noted in Chapter 1, this construction is very limited, due to the relatively fixed word order of French. This contrasts with the situation in Spanish, where most categories topicalize quite freely.

Sentence (92) seems fairly acceptable to most native speakers, though they prefer the sentential construction in (114):

(114) Le travail est plus difficile que le contrat n'est détaillé.

In fact, the acceptability of such constructions, which are only marginal at best, seems to vary depending on the category fronted. The following examples involve topicalization of the noun, adverb, prepositional phrase and verb:

(115) a. *Jean vend plus de bicyclettes que de voitures achète Pierre
 b. *Jean vend plus de bicyclettes que de voitures Pierre achète
 Jean sells more bicycles than Pierre buys cars

(116) a. ??Le bébé rampe plus soigneusement que négligemment marche son frère
 b. *Le bébé rampe plus soigneusement que négligemment son frère marche
 The baby crawls more carefully than his brother walks carelessly

(117) a. ?La cruauté est moins dans nos têtes que dans nos coeurs est la générosité
 b. *La cruauté est moins dans nos têtes que dans nos coeurs la générosité est
 Cruelty is less in our heads than generosity is in our hearts

(118) ?L'athlète nage moins que courent ses amis
 The athlete swims less than his friends run

Example (115), involving topicalization of the noun phrase, is unacceptable with or without subject–verb inversion. Example (116), with adverb topicalization, is marginally acceptable with subject–verb inversion. The same judgements apply to (117), with the prepositional phrase in clause-initial position. Example (118), involving the verb as the category of comparison, is marginally acceptable, though it is possible that this is interpreted as an example of normal stylistic subject–verb inversion, its marginal status deriving from the omission of expletive *ne*. In general, these constructions are felt to be, if not entirely unacceptable, then certainly marginal, described by some native speakers as sounding rather dated, or literary, in style. This is unsurprising for two reasons: firstly, as stated, word order in French is relatively fixed and topicalization is an unusual phenomenon; secondly, the topicalized construction is not actually required by French, as it is in Spanish, as a means of escaping from the tensed verb constraint applying in comparatives of inequality. Recall that topicalization in Spanish places the fronted category in a position of strong focus. In French, on the other hand, the expletive particle *ne* is available to act as a marker of comparison and therefore 'disambiguates' the comparative particle *que*, allowing a tensed verb to follow unproblematically. For this reason, in each case, the full sentential version of (115–18), including expletive *ne* before the verb, will be the only fully acceptable version.[32]

As further support for this analysis, it is interesting to note that for most native speakers such topicalization structures actually become more unacceptable if *ne* is inserted. Thus (119) is felt to be worse than (92), (120) worse than (116) and (121) worse than (117):

(119) *Le travail est plus difficile que détaillé n'est le contrat
(120) *Le bébé rampe plus soigneusement que négligemment ne marche son frère
(121) *La cruauté est moins dans nos têtes que dans nos coeurs n'est la générosité

This is predictable under an analysis of *ne* as a marker of comparison within a comparative clause. Topicalized structures have an element in a position of strong focus immediately following comparative *que*, therefore the comparison marker *ne* would not be required, as it can be argued that the clause following the topic position is semantically defocussed and therefore outside the scope of the comparison proper; from the syntactic point of view, this clause can be seen as separate from the comparative clause proper, which contains only the topicalized category (see section 2.5). Obviously, judgements requiring an appreciation of the extent of a given sentence's unacceptability are very difficult to make, even for native speakers. Nevertheless, within these limitations it seems possible to state that topicalized structures do not require the presence of expletive *ne* and that, however marginal they may be, their unacceptability is accentuated by the presence of *ne*.

The phrasal construction involving que ce que

The relativized phrasal construction expressing partial comparison is exemplified in (93) (repeated):

(93) Le travail est plus difficile que ce que le contrat est détaillé

As was the case for phrasal constructions expressing full comparison, these constructions are somewhat marginal, their acceptability varying considerably. The following are examples of phrasal comparatives expressing partial comparison of the noun, adjective, verb, adverb and prepositional phrase:

(122) ?Je rencontre moins d'ennemis que ce que je rencontre d'amis
I meet less enemies than I meet friends
(123) ?Il paraît plus triste maintenant que ce qu'il paraissait tragique auparavant
He seems more sad now than he seemed tragic before
(124) Mon père travaille moins que ce qu'il travaillait
My father works less than he worked
(125) *Il court plus énergiquement que ce qu'il court rapidement
He runs more energetically than he runs fast
(126) ?La cruauté est moins dans nos têtes que ce que la générosité est dans nos coeurs
Cruelty is less in our heads than generosity is in our hearts

Sentence (124), involving the verb, seems more acceptable than (122), (123) and (126), involving the noun, adjective and prepositional phrase. However, only (125), involving the adverb, seems totally unacceptable. This may be a reflex of the lack of a proform for this category.

Once again, it is unsurprising that the relativized phrasal construction is much less acceptable in French than its *de lo que* equivalent is in Spanish. The phrasal construction is simply not required in French, where a full sentential construction, with expletive *ne*, is always available. Expletive *ne* does not appear in these phrasal constructions for reasons stated in detail earlier: these are relativized constructions with *ce* as the head. They do not contain comparative subordinate clauses, so no marker of comparison is required. Where native speakers do accept *ne* in *que ce que* constructions, this is by analogy with the ordinary sentential construction and constitutes an attempt to improve the phrasal structure's acceptability, making it look more like a 'normal' comparative. What is surprising is that the relativized phrasal construction is acceptable at all, given its redundancy.

Muller (1983: 288) appears to find the following sentences, involving the noun phrase as the compared category, completely acceptable:

(127) Luc a vendu plus de limonade que ce que tu as prétendu avoir vendu de bière
Luc has sold more lemonade than you claimed to have sold beer
(128) Luc a vendu plus de pain que ce que tu sais avoir vendu de bière
Luc has sold more bread than you know you sold beer

He contrasts this with the unacceptability of (129):

(129) *Luc a vendu plus de pain que tu ne sais avoir vendu de bière

(This is problematic for his analysis since he wishes to defend the hypothesis that (129) is derived from (128). This is clearly impossible as the two are unrelated.)

Native speakers I have consulted, however, find both (127) and (128) marginal and, specifically, find (128) very much less acceptable than (127). The supposed contrast in acceptability between (128) and (129) is not, then, as strong as Muller claims and is partly influenced by the embedding of the second compared constituent, which always lowers acceptability. Muller draws the conclusion that if (128) and (129) are not equivalent, then the structure of (128) must add something to the meaning. In fact, the root of the problem has nothing to do with the structure, but rather the semantics of the verb *savoir*. Notice that if *savoir* is replaced by, for example, *croire*, acceptability is restored:

(130) Luc a vendu plus de pain que tu ne crois avoir vendu de bière
 Luc has sold more bread than you believe you sold beer

What is different about the structures of (128) and (129) is that (129) contains a quantifier gap before *de bière* and (128) does not. In (128) the relativized head *ce* is a proform representing this quantifier and bound, hence precisely defined, by its following restrictive relative clause. A verb of certainty like *savoir*, then, cannot appear in (129) precisely because of the 'semantic gap', the quantifier which must be inferred. After all, how can something be 'known' which has to be inferred? *Savoir* may, however, appear in (128) because the quantifier does not need to be inferred, but is actually present, pronominalized as *ce*. Thus in relativized comparatives the definite relative clause head *ce* may combine acceptably with a verb of certainty, since what is 'known' is explicit in such constructions, but only inferable in sentential constructions. To draw the conclusion, as Muller does, that (128) means something different from (129) is, therefore, mistaken.

3.2.2 The comparative of equality

Unlike the case in Spanish, exactly the same number of structural possibilities exist for the expression of partial comparison involving the equative construction as for the comparatives of inequality:

1 a reduced sentential construction:

(131) La vie est aussi dure que transitoire
   Life is as hard as (it is) transitory

2 a full sentential construction with declarative word order in the second clause:

(132) La vie est aussi transitoire que la mort est permanente
   Life is as transitory as death is permanent

3 a topicalized sentential construction:

(133) La vie est aussi transitoire que permanente est la mort
   Life is as transitory as death is permanent

4 a relativized phrasal construction

(134) La vie est aussi transitoire que ce que la mort est permanente
   Life is as transitory as death is permanent

The reduced sentential construction

The following set of (simple) sentences illustrate partial comparison involving the categories of noun, adjective, adverb and prepositional phrase:

(135) Il n'y a pas toujours autant de solutions que de problèmes
   There are not always as many solutions as problems
(136) Cette technique est aussi sophistiquée que compliquée
   This technique is as sophisticated as complicated
(137) L'athlète court aussi énergiquement que rapidement
   The athlete runs as energetically as quickly
(138) La cruauté est autant dans nos têtes que dans nos coeurs
   Cruelty is as much in our heads as in our hearts

The full sentential construction

Alongside the reduced construction there is also the possibility of a full sentential construction, e.g.:

(139) Il boit autant de vin qu'il buvait de bière
   He drinks as much wine as he drank beer
(140) Cet homme est aussi beau que ces femmes sont élégantes
   This man is as handsome as these women are elegant

(141) L'athlète court aussi rapidement qu'il nage énergiquement
The athlete runs as quickly as he swims energetically
(142) La cruauté est autant dans nos têtes que la générosité est dans nos coeurs
Cruelty is as much in our heads as generosity is in our hearts
(143) Je ris autant que je pleure
I laugh as much as I cry

Examples (139–43) involve comparison of the noun, adjective, adverb, prepositional phrase and verb, respectively.

Comparison over an unbounded context

As for the comparatives of inequality, it is possible for equative constructions expressing partial comparison to contain multiple subordinate clauses, with subsequent embedding of the second compared item, subject to the usual performance constraints. Equative constructions exactly parallel to the set of examples (108–13) on pages 92–3 can easily be constructed simply by replacing *plus* with *autant*. The acceptability of such constructions does, however, tend to decrease as embedding increases.

Expletive *ne*

So far, none of the sentential equative examples illustrated have included expletive *ne*. Nevertheless, they may include this element and for some speakers may be preferred with *ne*:

(144) Il boit autant de vin qu'il ne buvait de bière
(145) Cet homme est aussi beau que ces femmes ne sont élégantes
(146) L'athlète court aussi rapidement qu'il ne nage énergiquement
(147) La cruauté est autant dans nos têtes que la générosité n'est dans nos coeurs
(148) Je ris autant que je ne pleure

When there is embedding after *que*, the position of *ne* is variable:

(149) a. Cette politique a été aussi préjudiciable à nos intérêts qu'on ne croyait que Jean avait déclaré qu'elle serait avantageuse
  b. Cette politique a été aussi préjudiciable à nos intérêts qu'on croyait que Jean avait déclaré qu'elle ne serait avantageuse
  c. Cette politique a été aussi préjudiciable à nos intérêts

qu'on ne croyait que Jean avait déclaré qu'elle ne serait avantageuse
This policy has been as harmful to our interests as one believed that Jean had stated that it would be advantageous

All three versions of (149) appear to be acceptable (as, of course, would a version excluding *ne*). The reasons behind the appearance of *ne* in equatives and its flexible positioning in multiple-clause comparatives have already been alluded to in the discussion of full comparison and will be considered in greater detail in section 3.3.9.

The topicalized sentential construction

In the topicalized equative construction exemplified earlier the adjective is the compared category:

(133) ?La vie est aussi transitoire que permanente est la mort
Life is as transitory as death is permanent

As already mentioned, the relatively fixed word order of French makes such constructions marginal. Although (133) seems fairly acceptable to most native speakers, the sentential version in (150) is preferred:

(150) La vie est aussi transitoire que la mort (n')est permanente

The following examples involve topicalization of the noun, adverb, prepositional phrase and verb:

(151) *Mon père vend autant de livres que de disques achète mon oncle
My father sells as many books as my uncle buys records
(152) ?Le bébé rampe aussi soigneusement que négligemment marche son frère
The baby crawls as carefully as his brother walks carelessly
(153) ?La cruauté est autant dans nos têtes que dans nos coeurs est la générosité
Cruelty is as much in our heads as generosity is in our hearts
(154) Marie sourit autant que se renfrogne Jean
Marie smiles as much as Jean frowns

Sentence (151), involving topicalization of the noun phrase, is completely unacceptable, while topicalization of the adjective, adverb, prepositional phrase and verb (133, 152, 153, 154) seems more acceptable, though still not completely so (except for (154[33])). Reasons why topicalization structures should be marginal in French have already been discussed.

In each case, the addition of expletive *ne* substantially lowers the level of acceptability. This is for the reasons already stated.

The phrasal construction involving que ce que

The equative relativized phrasal construction expressing partial comparison is exemplified in (134) (repeated), where the adjective is the compared category:

(134) ?La vie est aussi transitoire que ce que la mort est permanente

Once again, phrasal comparatives are seen to be only marginally acceptable. The following examples involve the noun, verb, adverb and prepositional phrase as the objects of comparison:

(155) ?Je possède autant de chiens que ce que je possède de chats
I own as many dogs as I own cats
(156) ?L'enfant sanglote autant que ce qu'il pleure
The child sobs as much as he cries
(157) *Elle voit son fils aussi fréquemment maintenant que ce qu'elle le voyait rarement auparavant
She sees her son as frequently now as she saw him rarely before
(158) ??La cruauté est autant dans nos têtes que ce que la générosité se trouve dans nos coeurs
Cruelty is as much in our heads as generosity is found in our hearts

Acceptability judgements are much the same as for the equivalent comparative of inequality constructions, though the equatives are perhaps judged to be slightly worse; as before, the example involving the adverb appears least acceptable. Expletive *ne* does not appear in such constructions for reasons stated earlier (see pages 79–83).

Why phrasal constructions should be so marginal in French has already been discussed. The fact that they are even less acceptable for the expression of a comparative of equality than for that of a comparative of inequality is nevertheless interesting, since it mirrors the fact that although the *de lo que* construction in Spanish is fully grammatical, it is also judged to be less acceptable for a comparative of equality construction than for a comparative of inequality.

At this stage it might be interesting to recall a point made in the preceding chapter regarding the differing acceptability of comparatives of inequality and the comparative of equality in Spanish where comparison involved transitive and intransitive verbs. The relevant examples are repeated below:

(2:16) Vende menos que compra
(2:17) *Vende menos que tiene
(2:18) Vende menos de lo que tiene
(2:19) Vende menos de lo que compra
(2:54) Vende tanto como compra
(2:55) Vende tanto como tiene
(2:56) Vende tanto como lo que tiene
(2:57) Vende tanto como lo que compra

The set of examples illustrating the comparative of inequality contains one ungrammatical member, (2:17). A detailed analysis of this can be found on pages 28–31, but the basic reason for the unacceptability of (2:17) compared to (2:55), its equative equivalent, was the inability of a tensed verb to follow *más/menos . . . que*, except in an expression of partial comparison (e.g. (2:16)). It is to be expected, then, that the French equivalents of this set would all be equally grammatical, given the apparent lack of such a constraint:

(159) Il vend moins qu'il n'achète

Sentence (159) is equivalent to (2:16), both verbs intransitive.

(160) Il en vend moins qu'il n'en a

Sentence (160) is equivalent to (2:17), both verbs transitive. The existence of the proform *en* indicates clearly that it is the lexically unspecified objects of the verb which are being compared. This makes (160) also equivalent to (2:18), the Spanish phrasal construction.

(161) Il en vend moins qu'il n'en achète

Sentence (161) is equivalent to (2:19), both verbs transitive.

(162) Il vend autant qu'il (n')achète
(163) Il en vend autant qu'il (n')en achète

Both (162), both verbs intransitive, and (163), both verbs transitive, are equivalent to (2:54), which allows both readings in Spanish. Sentence (163) is also equivalent to the Spanish phrasal construction (2:57), both verbs transitive.

(164) Il en vend autant qu'il (n')en a

Sentence (164) is equivalent to (2:55) and also to (2:56), both verbs transitive.
Six French sentences cover the range of meanings of eight Spanish sentences. The French phrasal construction is also possible, e.g.:

(165) Il vend moins que ce qu'il a

However, (165) is simply an alternative to (160), which is preferred. It is not a necessary alternative, unlike Spanish (2:18). The difference in the range of constructions can be ascribed to the lack of a tensed verb constraint in French (linked to expletive *ne*) and the existence of the proform *en*, clearly distinguishing between transitive and intransitive verbs in such contexts.

Equally, the lack of major differences between the structural possibilities for the comparatives of inequality and the comparative of equality in French, amply illustrated above, may be ascribed to the presence of the marker of comparison *ne*.

3.3 EXPLETIVE *NE*

3.3.1 Other instances of expletive *ne*

The presence of an expletive[34] element in comparative constructions has been illustrated. However, expletive *ne* may also occur in a number of other construction types. These include subordinate clauses after verbs of fear, verbs of prevention, of precaution, negative or interrogative verbs of doubt or denial, after the conjunctions *avant que*, *à moins que* and *sans que* and after phrases like *il s'en faut que* (listed in Grevisse 1969: 872–80). The expletive *ne* which appears in comparatives is frequently linked with these other occurrences. Yet *ne* appears to be very unstable in such constructions: 'L'emploi de ce ne explétif . . . n'a jamais été bien fixé et tend même à disparaître . . . il est le plus souvent facultatif; la langue parlée, en tout cas, se débarrasse de plus en plus de cette particule parasite' (Grevisse 1969: 872). Harris (1978: 224) agrees with this assertion: 'In popular French . . . this pleonastic negative has been virtually abandoned.' This tendency is diametrically opposed to the tendency observed in comparative constructions, which is not only for comparatives of inequality to be preferred with expletive *ne*, but for the use of this element to spread to the equative construction, thus actually increasing the frequency of its occurrence.

Damourette and Pichon (1928) also categorize the *ne* appearing in comparatives with the expletive element appearing in the other constructions mentioned, calling it 'discordantiel' (p. 232). Their definition of *ne discordantiel* being that *ne* 'marque une inadéquation du fait qu'il suspecte avec le milieu' (p. 250):

> dans la crainte, il y a discordance entre le désir du sujet de la principale et la possibilité qu'il envisage . . . dans la précaution, il y a discordance entre les efforts que fait le sujet et le danger qui subsiste en dépit d'eux . . . dans l'empêchement, il y a discordance entre le phénomène qui devrait se produire et la force qui l'empêche.
> (p. 234)

> Ne pas douter implique précisément un doute . . . il y a discordance entre ce doute réel . . . et l'affirmation principale, qui vient prétendre qu'on ne doute pas.
> (p. 236)

Their definition of *ne discordantiel* is vague at best, relying as it does on notions of non-matching of premises, and can be applied only with some difficulty to the range of constructions they wish to bring under its umbrella. Comparative *ne* is considered 'le cas le plus clair . . . il y a . . . une discordance entre la qualité envisagée et l'étalon auquel on la rapporte' (pp. 232–3). Yet, as has already been pointed out, comparative *ne* may appear in equatives, where there cannot be said to be any '*discordance*', and is generally not optional, unlike *ne* in the other construction types listed.

In his study of expletive *ne* Muller (1978: 85) describes *ne* as 'effaçable, mais nous éviterons de dire qu'à cela ne correspond jamais un changement de sens', and, despite the fact that it may not usually be omitted in comparatives, wishes to include comparative *ne* in the same category as *ne* appearing in other constructions. Surprisingly, although he mentions comparative *ne*, he does not deal with it, in an otherwise exhaustive treatment: 'Pour des raisons de commodité, nous exclurons de cette étude l'examen des constructions comparatives, nous limitant à l'examen de *ne* conditionné par un verbe, un nom à complétive, ou une conjonction' (p. 78). Less surprisingly, several of the critieria he mentions for this expletive element could not apply to comparative *ne*. The fact that it is not 'effaçable' has already been mentioned; he also states that 'les compléments de comparatifs sont à l'indicatif avec *ne*. Les constructions verbales étudiées ici sont au subjonctif' (p. 91), and 'il me semble donc que *ne* soit utilisé comme négation du subjonctif' (p. 99). There is no link whatsoever between expletive *ne* in comparatives and the subjunctive mood.³⁵ The omission of comparative *ne* from this study enables Muller to circumvent the obvious problems entailed by attempting a universally valid analysis of expletive *ne*, while allowing him to simply assert, without proof, that his analysis can account for the occurrence and function of *ne* in comparatives; in this he is implicitly admitting that comparative *ne* is a very different element.

Moignet (1981: 205) also speaks of expletive *ne* as being an optional element: 'sa présence est facultative ... il signifie minimalement et subtilement.' Leaving aside the non-explanatory nature of such a definition, it must be repeated once again that *ne* is optional only in constructions other than the comparative.

For Gougenheim (1939: 264) expletive *ne* is 'une variation stylistique'; in other words, it is optional. He includes its use in comparatives within this definition, despite its non-optional nature. However, he also points out that this expletive *ne* may sometimes be replaced by *ne ... pas*, with truly negative import, e.g. *Je crains qu'il ne vienne* versus *Je crains qu'il ne vienne pas* (p. 269). Again, comparatives differ; it is impossible to replace comparative *ne* with *ne ... pas*. The insertion of *pas* would not change the meaning, but simply render the comparison unintelligible, e.g.:

(166) *J'ai plus d'amis que je n'en avais pas

Gaatone (1971a), in his perceptive study of negation in French, also lists comparative *ne* as an instance of the expletive element appearing elsewhere. Nonetheless, having stated that this element is usually optional, he admits that in comparatives of inequality its omission is 'rarissime' (p. 94) and that 'l'emploi de *ne* est la règle ... les cas de non-emploi sont exceptionnels' (p. 98). This is in stark contrast to its unpredictable occurrence in other constructions: with verbs of fear 'le non-emploi reste très fréquent'; with verbs of preventing 'le non-emploi de *ne* est de loin le plus fréquent'; with negated verbs of doubt and denial 'Le non-emploi de *ne* est beaucoup plus fréquent que son emploi'; after *à moins que* 'Les cas d'omission ne sont pas rares'; after *avant que* 'le non-emploi de *ne* est de loin plus fréquent' (p. 98). He also mentions the general occurrence of the subjunctive mood with expletive *ne*: '*Ne* explétif se rencontre dans des propositions subordonnées conjonctives introduites par *que* . . . et est appelé par des mots qui régissent, en règle générale, l'emploi du subjonctif (sauf pour les subordonnées de comparaison)' (p. 81).

There is, then, general agreement that the expletive *ne* found in comparatives is the same element that turns up in a number of other disparate construction types. This is despite the fact that there is no particular evidence to support such an analysis. On the contrary, the two features of the expletive element most frequently mentioned, first, that it is optional and second, that it may trigger the subjunctive, are both untrue of comparative *ne*. It seems the motivation for this analysis of expletive *ne* does not derive from any actual evidence, but is rather a reflection of a natural desire to include all occurrences of this item under a single definition. I contend, however, that this is neither possible nor desirable in this case. Whatever the correct analysis of other occurrences of *ne*, the expletive element appearing in comparatives has sufficient distinctive features to warrant a separate analysis.

3.3.2 The negativity of comparison

General studies of comparison frequently stress the fact that such constructions involve some notion of negativity, though they almost always deal only with the comparatives of inequality. Seuren (1973: 530) quotes Jespersen (1917: 80) as having 'intuited the presence of a negation element in comparatives' and goes on to claim that we therefore have 'a natural explanation for the so-called "*ne explétif*" in French comparatives' (p. 535). Seuren (1984: 109) returns to the same theme: 'there is an intimate relationship of the comparative in English and most other European languages with negation.' He also states that in Romance 'the negation has not been lexicalized into *que* but crops up again in the comparative clause' (p. 123). This is certainly not true of Spanish and represents an unjustified generalization. Stassen (1985: 216–17) makes a more modest claim: 'In some languages with a Particle Comparative, there are grounds to assume the presence of *an underlying negative element*.'

Both Stassen and Seuren base their analysis on two separate premises, the first etymological and the second connected with the appearance of so-called 'negative polarity' items in the subordinate clause of comparatives of inequality. The etymological grounds are less strong than might be supposed: 'although many, perhaps even most, historical details are shrouded in mystery and may even remain that way forever, enough is known to assert with some confidence that the European *than*-comparatives derive historically from semantically more transparent constructions' (Seuren 1984: 123). In fact, the evidence for such an assertion in Romance is weak and depends largely on a generalization from the historical evidence relating to non-Romance languages. In any case, what is true from a diachronic perspective may have little relation to a synchronic description, as Seuren (1984: 124–5) himself admits:

> Against this partially fuzzy and blurred background of historical development, the question now arises what historical reanalysis means in terms of synchronic description. What exactly happens when a semantically transparent construction jells into a new category or is shaped into the form of an existing category thereby affecting the semantic transparency of the latter? This question . . . is not easy to answer . . . I would be inclined to say that reanalysis in the case of comparative constructions in the European languages means that the lexicon has been enriched . . . so that it is no longer necessary, psycholinguistically, to go through the whole semantic computation of the comparative . . . . Computationally there is an advantage in that a system with a large inventory of ready-made but semantically more complex building blocks for sentences is more efficient in terms of processing . . . single lexical items are grammatically easy to handle, and can still carry a considerable load of semantic information. Such storing of semantic information into ready-made lexical items occurs generally when the semantic information in question is of a typical, recurring nature.

The semantic information in comparative constructions is without doubt of a typical recurring nature and I would suggest that expletive *ne*, so closely associated with comparatives, is an excellent candidate for the definition above: it is a 'ready-made lexical item' in which the semantic notion of comparison is 'stored', whence its ability to act as a marker of comparison. It does not, however, at least synchronically, appear to 'store' any notion of negativity.

Turning now to the second premise, relating to the occurrence of 'negative polarity' items in the comparative clause, both Stassen and Seuren, as well as Bergmans (1982: 84), give various examples, though only in English, to demonstrate that some items, normally associated with the presence of negativity, can occur after comparatives; however, the examples illustrate almost exclusively the comparative of superiority. The following examples are taken from Seuren (1973: 534):

(167) That stuff was more than I could **be bothered** reading
(168) The fifth glass was more than I **cared** to drink
(169) I've solved lots of more difficult problems than he has got very **far** in even understanding
(170) He was a greater bore than I **could possibly** put up with
(171) The sound of her voice was more than I **could stand/bear**

The words in bold print are the negative polarity items. These sentences are all given as fully acceptable, though I find (169) decidedly strange. A closer examination of these sentences, however, reveals some odd facts. If *more* is replaced by *less*, we find that all five sentences become much less acceptable. This is hardly expected if the presence of negative polarity items is linked to comparison. Even more interestingly, (167), (168), (170) and (171) actually sound better as equatives:[36]

(172) a. ?That stuff was less than I could be bothered reading
     b. That stuff was as much as I could be bothered reading
(173) a. ?The fifth glass was less than I cared to drink
     b. The fifth glass was as much as I cared to drink
(174) a. ?He was a lesser bore than I could possibly put up with
     b. He was as much of a bore as I could possibly put up with
(175) a. ?The sound of her voice was less than I could stand/bear
     b. The sound of her voice was as much as I could stand/bear

Equatives, however, are never analysed as containing underlying negation. This implies strongly that the reasons why such negative polarity items are sometimes acceptable and sometimes not are much more complex and not directly linked to the notion of comparison of inequality.

Stassen (1985: 218) also makes the opposite point, that 'positive polarity' items may not occur in comparative clauses, e.g.:

(176) *He has got more support than you already have

Again, the equative version of this seems to me to be equally unacceptable:

(177) *He has got as much support as you already have

What is true of comparatives of inequality is just as true of the comparative of equality. Since no-one wishes to propoose underlying negativity in the comparative of equality, such examples, however interesting, do not bear on the issue of negativity in comparison. Nonetheless, Napoli (1983: 683) also insists that 'comparatives involve implicit negation', relying, at least in part, on similar considerations.

In the same vein, the point is sometimes made that indefinite terms like *jamais, personne*, may appear in the subordinate clause of a comparative in French. The following example is taken from Muller (1983: 290):

(178) Paul est plus riche que personne ne le sera jamais
Paul is richer than anyone will ever be

Sentence (178) is contrasted with the following:

(179) Paul est riche comme personne ne le sera jamais
Paul is rich as no-one will ever be

The subordinate clauses of (178) and (179) appear identical. Muller takes this as proof that the comparative subordinate clause contains a negative. In (179) the subordinate clause does contain a negative; in (178), however, although the subordinate clause looks identical, it does not contain a negative, as indicated by the English gloss. This is precisely because *ne* in (178) is not a marker of negation, but of comparison, whereas the *ne* appearing in (179) is the negative particle. The appearance of indefinite items in the subordinate clause does not prove the negativity of expletive *ne*. On the contrary, it is the fact that *ne* is not negative which allows such terms to occur, as Gaatone (1971: 95) states: 'en effet, la neutralisation de l'opposition positif/négatif dans le terme subordonné d'une comparaison d'inégalité permet à *ne* explétif d'être employé côte à côte avec des termes tels que *jamais, personne*, etc. . . . sans risque de confusion.'

There is an element of circularity in the argumentation based on the acceptability/non-acceptability of negative/positive polarity items in comparatives, as Von Stechow (1984b: 188–9) notes:

> Seuren's . . . analysis strongly relies on the fact that *than* is historically derived from . . . [a form meaning] 'by which not'. What worries me about this argumentation is this: How should the speaker know that *than* is derived in this way and has the meaning *and + not*? You can of course say that there is indirect evidence for this decompositon, viz the presence of NPIs

[negative polarity items] in the *than*-S. But this would be a circular argument, since the point at issue is precisely whether NPIs are conditioned by a negation or by a more general feature of operators . . . . It is not even clear to me that a language with an . . . overt negation *has* to be analyzed along Seuren's lines . . . I am not sure that the negation has much to do with the comparative. The . . . negation somehow marks the unexpected.

This seems a much more reasoned approach to a description of negativity in comparison and one which could apply to French expletive *ne*, though I would not agree that what it marks is unexpected; rather, it simply marks the structure as expressing comparison. Von Stechow also dismisses the idea that historical evidence about the role of negation in comparison can be adduced to explain the nature of the construction now:

> Another argument would be to say that the semantics for the comparative was fixed at a time when the construction was transparent and that it has been fossilized since. I think that no one holds such a view, because it would make the sense of the construction practically unlearnable.
>
> (188–9)

'Mental' negativity

The idea that comparison involves the notion of negativity is usually based on assumed mental processes. Harris (1978: 247) speaks of Romance languages which 'mark this negative idea overtly, either by the use of a pleonastic negative, or modally, or both'. Bergmans (1982: 192) describes comparative relations as 'set/sub-set' relations, though this can clearly apply only to the comparative of superiority. For Le Bidois and Le Bidois (1938: 283) there is 'une valeur négative inhérente à l'échantil'; 'la présence ou l'absence dans l'esprit d'une idée négative . . . détermine l'emploi . . . de *ne*; et là où il paraît, il est loin d'y paraître pour rien' (p. 285). Small (1924: 16) states 'This use of the negative may be explained on psychological grounds. The speaker probably has in mind a negative conception when he thinks of inequality' and 'the primitive idea of opposition seems to remain, as shown by the frequent use of the negative in the second member of comparison and by a strong adversative element in the concept of comparison in the mind of the speaker' (p. 18). Somewhat bizarrely, he equates the idea of opposition with 'primitive' languages:

The comparative in the speech of uncivilized or savage peoples is nothing more than the paratactical construction; simply *A has the quality, B has not* . . . more advanced languages leave behind the simplest conception of separation or opposition and seem to lean toward the idea of composition or bringing together.

(1924: 18)

He goes on to claim that the construction 'with negative in the second member is the regular one in Romance when the verb is expressed' (19), quite excluding Spanish and several other Romance languages from his analysis.

Moignet (1981: 201), on the other hand, speaks of *plus/moins* as being 'des termes signifiant des mouvements de pensée de majoration ou de minoration'; despite this inclusion of the comparative of inferiority, he goes on to explain the presence of expletive *ne* in comparatives of inequality in a way which explicitly excludes those constructed with *moins*: '*Ne* . . . traduit le signe "−" dont est affecté le second terme de la comparaison quand le premier est affecté du signe "+"' (p. 205). For Grevisse (1969: 872) the use of expletive *ne* 'se fonde sur le fait que la subordonnée contient une idée négative'; for Wagner and Pinchon (1962: 396) comparative *ne* 'évoque, à n'en pas douter, une négation implicite'. Moignet (1970: 109) speaks confidently of 'L'orientation en direction de la négativité signifiée par *ne*'.

Attempts at explaining the presence of *ne* on the basis that the second category of comparison is marked mentally with a minus sign and overtly by a negative element signifying its relation of inequality with the category of comparison in the matrix are clearly dubious on semantic grounds, but, more seriously, they automatically exclude the comparative of equality and, in fact, have great difficulty in accounting for the comparative of inferiority. Here one would be forced to assume that any cognitive minus sign would belong to the category modified by *moins*, a plus sign being assigned to the second category. But then how could expletive *ne* be the overt manifestation of a plus sign? Muller (1983: 295) realizes this and attempts to circumvent the problem as follows:

> de fait, *moins* peut être considéré comme une variante de *plus*, peut-être comme le comparatif 'synthétique' de *peu*: **plus peu* . . . la phrase *Pierre est moins riche que Paul ne l'est* sera donc analysée comme une comparative d'inégalité de *peu riche* ce qui implique que l'échelle de quantification soit orientée négativement (le maximum de la propriété *peu riche* est zéro).

It is more than slightly surprising that a supposedly 'natural' explanation of the occurrence of comparative *ne* in terms of mental processes should have recourse to such a highly artificial and counter-intuitive device. Moreover, no amount of similar linguistic gymnastics could allow *aussi/autant* to be analysed thus. The fact that expletive *ne* also appears in equatives must, then, be an inexplicable oddity for such analyses.

At this point it seems appropriate to quote the warning words of Damourette and Pichon (1928: 228):

> Partir des cadres d'une logique *a priori* et essayer de trouver comment la langue remplit ces cadres, c'est peut-être faire une bonne oeuvre didactique, mais ce n'est pas faire avancer la question du fonctionnement psychique réel du langage. C'est à la langue elle-même qu'il faut aller demander les secrets de sa structure psychologique interne.

In fact, though a diachronic analysis of the particle's role, which is beyond the scope of this synchronic study, would no doubt be an interesting line of enquiry, there is little synchronic basis for an analysis of comparison as involving negativity. Pottier (1982: 41) describes comparison as being 'un double mouvement: I Rapprochement de deux Entités ou de deux Propositions, dans la mesure où elles sont comparables (un minimum de traits communs est donc nécessaire). II Distinction, à partir d'un acquis, entre des Entités ou des Propositions'; and Huttenlocher and Higgins (1971: 495) report evidence to suggest that people 'tend to think about "more" and "less" in terms of directional movement, with "more" being a movement in an upward direction and "less" a movement in a downward direction'.

It has been stated and illustrated that expletive *ne* may occur in the equative construction. This fact is explained by Gaatone (1971: 97) as a case of attraction. It seems probable that *ne* appears in the equative construction by analogy with the comparatives of inequality. An equative construction with a negative matrix is, of course, semantically equivalent to a comparative of inferiority, e.g.:

(180) Il n'est pas aussi/si triste qu'il (ne) l'était
    He is not as sad as he was
(181) Il est moins triste qu'il ne l'était
    He is less sad than he was

This semantic equivalence cannot, however, be the basis for the appearance of *ne* in equatives, since the non-negative version of (180) is at least equally acceptable:

(182) Il est aussi triste qu'il (ne) l'était

If *ne* is seen simply as a marker of comparison, it is natural that it should spread from the comparatives of inequality to the comparative of equality. As proof that *ne* is seen as a marker of comparison rather than a marker of negativity, notice that when the only focus of comparison in the subordinate clause is tense, the equative may actually be preferred with *ne*:

(183) ?Mon père dort autant qu'il dormait
(184) Mon père dort autant qu'il ne dormait
My father sleeps as much as he used to sleep

For many speakers I have consulted (184) is felt to be totally acceptable, while (183) is not. There is no relation of negativity between the matrix and the subordinate clause here. Example (183) should be completely acceptable. The reason it is not is simply that tense alone (as has been shown to be the case in Spanish, with important consequences for the syntax of these constructions) does not constitute an adequate focus of comparison. In (184) the inclusion of *ne* retrieves the sentence by adding an extra element acting as a focus of contrast. This analysis is further supported by the fact that (185) is fully acceptable:

(185) Mon père dort autant qu'il dormait il y a deux ans
My father sleeps as much as he used to sleep two years ago

Example (185) is much better than (183) because of the inclusion of *il y a deux ans*. This provides an extra contrast with the matrix, tense no longer being the only focus element. While expletive *ne* could appear in (185) also, its presence is less strongly required than in (184) due to the additional focus of contrast constituted by *il y a deux ans*. As a result, it may appear in (185), but must appear in (184). The concept of negativity does not enter into this argumentation.[37]

3.3.3 *Ne* after a negative matrix

It is frequently claimed that *ne* may not appear after a negative matrix, this being held as proof that it is itself negative. As has just been shown, quite the opposite is true of the comparative of equality. In fact, this is also untrue of the comparatives of inequality. Moignet (1970: 109) claims that the subordinate clause of a comparative construction 'n'admet pas la particule *ne*' when the main clause verb is negative. Similarly, Jonas (1971: 285) states categorically 'Si le premier terme d'un système comportant une marque de disparité est négatif, l'adverbe de négation *ne* n'apparaît jamais devant le verbe du deuxième terme', and again, 'Du moment que le premier terme est affecté, dans le domaine de la signification, par cette négation, *ne* n'apparaît pas devant le verbe du deuxième terme' (p. 293). Gougenheim (1939: 263) also argues that *ne* may appear only 'dans les subordonnées comparatives (d'infériorité ou de supériorité) dépendant d'une principale positive'. Muller (1983: 307) too gives an example of a comparative with a negative matrix clause with *ne* absent from the subordinate clause:

(186) Luc n'est pas plus riche que Max l'est
    Luc is not richer than Max is

However, it seems to me that (186) is acceptable, not because *ne* is not present, but rather because *le* is. Example (187) is not ungrammatical, but it is difficult to process due to the (superficial) appearance of too many negatives:

(187) Luc n'est pas plus riche que Max ne l'est

In (186) *le* acts as a focus of comparison, representing the second compared category. Notice that if a similarly negative sentence is constructed with the adverb as the compared element, it is much less acceptable without *ne*:

(188) ?Luc ne danse pas plus élégamment que Max danse
    Luc does not dance more elegantly than Max dances

Sentence (189) is preferred:

(189) Luc ne danse pas plus élégamment que Max ne danse

This is because there is no proform available for the adverb in the subordinate clause and hence no available focus item. Without this overt focus of comparison, the clause is not overtly marked as a comparative clause. Hence the marker of comparison, *ne*, must be included despite the negative matrix clause if the clause introduced by *que* is not to appear superficially to be an ordinary tensed subordinate clause. If there is a rule in operation here, it is not that a negative matrix may not be followed by expletive *ne*, but rather that, like all other comparatives, it must be followed by a recognizably comparative subordinate clause. If *le* (or *en*, in the case of a comparative involving the noun) is available, they may be sufficient, as foci of comparison, to mark the clause as a comparative and be preferred in this context as being easier to process than *ne* after *ne . . . pas*. When a proform is not available, *ne* must appear.

Grevisse (1969: 876) makes a more modest claim: 'Quand la principale est négative . . . ordinairement on ne met pas *ne* dans la subordonnée . . . . Mais on peut aussi mettre *ne*.' Examples of *ne* appearing after a negative matrix clause are also given in Napoli and Nespor (1977: 89). Gaatone (1971: 96) states:

> l'emploi de *ne* dans les subordonnées dépendant d'un terme de comparaison négatif n'est pas moins fréquent que dans celles qui dépendent d'un terme de comparaison positif. Ce fait nous paraît prouver suffisamment que l'emploi de *ne* est lié à une certaine structure syntaxique plutôt qu'appelé par une discordance entre deux parties de l'énoncé. La discordance en question devrait normalement disparaître, et avec elle le *ne* discordantiel, lorsque le mot introduisant une comparaison d'inégalité est lui-même nié. Mais il n'en est rien.[38]

It is untrue, then, that expletive *ne* may not appear after a negative matrix verb; it frequently does appear and indeed sometimes must (see (189)). What seems rather more plausible is that it is less likely to occur after a negative matrix simply because the sequence *ne . . . pas . . . ne* may be initially difficult to interpret. While I am arguing that synchronically expletive *ne* has no negative import, it is nonetheless true that it has the form of a negative. It is therefore unsurprising that its appearance in close proximity to *ne . . . pas* may be undesirable. In addition, the availability of proforms acting as foci of comparison means that it is possible for the subordinate clause to be marked as a comparative, via these foci, when the presence of the standard marker of comparison, *ne*, might lead to ambiguity.

3.3.4 Negation in the subordinate clause

In a similar way, it is sometimes asserted that ordinary negation may not appear in the subordinate clause of a comparative construction because of this 'comparative negation', since a constraint against double negatives will apply, e.g. Bergmans (1982: 89): 'It is the

COMPARATIVE NEGATION which causes other negation to be banned from the second clause of THAN-sentences'. Muller (1978: 90) also feels that 'la négation semble exclue dans les subordonnées comparatives', a view repeated in Muller (1983: 308):[39] 'le terme introducteur de la comparative d'inégalité forme une association négative avec *ne*, qui explique que *pas* soit exclu.' In fact, negation is generally excluded in the second half of comparative constructions for purely logical reasons. Without an appropriate context, they are simply difficult to interpret. Notice that if an appropriate context is set up, they become acceptable, e.g. in English:

(190) Neither Peter nor Mary works, but he doesn't work more than she doesn't!

Example (190) is ironic and implies that Peter is lazier than Mary, as the extent to which it is true of Peter that he does not work is greater than the extent to which the same thing is true of Mary. A sentence like (190) is not immediately interpretable, but this need not be the result of some extra underlying negativity 'lurking' in the *than*-clause and interfering with the overt negation.

The French version of (190) seems less acceptable:

(191) ?Ni Pierre ni Marie ne travaille, mais il ne travaille pas plus qu'elle ne travaille pas

The lower acceptablity of (191) is predictable. The marker of comparison, expletive *ne*, is missing. It is not possible to insert expletive *ne* as we would then have the unacceptable sequence *ne ne*:

(192) *Ni Pierre ni Marie ne travaille, mais il ne travaille pas plus qu'elle ne ne travaille pas

Rather than supporting an analysis of expletive *ne* as a negative element and requiring a double negation constraint to be invoked, this supports an analysis of comparative *ne* as a marker of comparison unrelated to negation. Comparatives of inequality without *ne* in the subordinate clause are rare and generally unacceptable. Therefore, any comparison involving a negative subordinate clause will be both logically difficult to interpret, as in English, and unacceptable because of the (forced) absence of expletive *ne*. It is not surprising then, that such negative clauses are rare. In fact, sentences such as (193) and (194) are, from the syntactic point of view, equally marginal for exactly the same reason, the lack of expletive *ne*:

(193) ??Il travaille plus qu'elle ne travaille pas
He works more than she doesn't work
(194) ??Il travaille plus qu'elle travaille
He works more than she works

The difference between them is that (194) can be saved by the insertion of *ne* in the subordinate clause, while (193) cannot. This predicts that the Spanish equivalent of (193) would be more acceptable than the French (and about as acceptable as the English) as the only constraint is logical (there being no expletive negation in either language):

(195) El trabaja más que no trabaja ella
(196) He works more than she doesn't work

Both (195) and (196) are fully grammatical, if odd. Example (193) is both odd and ungrammatical. This answers a question posed by Bergmans (1982: 220): 'Can the negation be considered hidden in: *Elle est plus riche que vous ne croyez*?' Bergmans' preferred answer is no, because the negation is overt, expressed by *ne*. In fact, the question is irrelevant: there is no negation in such a sentence.

Muller (1983: 306) points out the contrast between the following two sentences:

(197) Max est plus heureux qu'il n'est décent de l'être
       Max is happier than it is decent to be
(198) *Max est plus heureux qu'il est indécent de l'être
       Max is happier than it is indecent to be

He explains the different levels of acceptability here in terms of where the negativity lies. For him, in (197) *ne* is negative, but is 'associé au terme introducteur'. This is why it cannot be replaced by a negative affix, as in (198). In fact, (198) is ungrammatical simply because of the absence of expletive *ne*, while (197) is grammatical because of its presence. They have totally opposing meanings. Sentence (199), with *ne*, is grammatical:

(199) Max est plus heureux qu'il n'est indécent de l'être

Any oddity here is due to the strangeness of suggesting that it is indecent to be happy. The difference between (197) and (198), then, is not where the negativity is expressed, as Muller believes. There is no negativity in (197). Rather, one sentence contains the required marker of comparison *ne*, while the other lacks it.

Muller (1983: 287) notes that in the *que ce que* construction full negation is possible in the subordinate clause:

(200) Pierre a bu moins de vin que ce que Paul n'avait pas bu hier
Pierre drank less wine than Paul had not drunk yesterday

He contrasts this with (201):

(201) *Pierre a bu moins de vin que Paul n'en avait pas bu hier

The interpretation of (200) and (201) is exactly the same and they are equally difficult to process initially. The ungrammaticality of (201) stems not from this, but rather from the unavoidable absence of the comparative marker *ne* in a negated subordinate clause, as explained above. Why, then, is (200) grammatical? Example (200) is a phrasal construction. In phrasal constructions we do not have a comparative subordinate clause, but rather a restrictive relative clause headed by *ce*; the only element involved in the comparison proper is the pronoun *ce*. The structure of this means of expressing comparison has been discussed on pages 79–83: as there is no comparative subordinate clause, expletive *ne* does not occur in phrasal comparatives (just as in Spanish, in parallel fashion, the tensed verb constraint, which expletive *ne* enables French to avoid, does not apply to phrasal comparatives). Because expletive *ne* does not occur in the relative clause of phrasal comparatives, full sentential negation can appear unproblematically and (200) is fully acceptable. Nothing is 'missing', unlike the case of (201), where expletive *ne* is missing. This situation is exactly what my analysis would predict, but is problematic for Muller.

3.3.5 Expression of negation in modern French

A number of studies of negativity in French, e.g. Pohl (1970, 1975), Ashby (1976, 1981), Sankoff and Vincent (1977), Muller (1984), contain convincing evidence of the fact that the standard negative particle *ne* is disappearing in French, replaced in many contexts by *pas* alone. Pohl (1970: 43) states that 'L'évolution générale de la langue tend en effet . . . à l'élimination de *ne*.' Ashby (1976: 119) sees 'the deletion of *ne* in Modern French as part of an on-going linguistic change, whereby this now redundant first negative may ultimately disappear from the language' and feels that 'Its eventual disappearance from the language would mean, of course, the elimination of a redundancy' (p. 136). The same conclusions are reiterated in a later study by Ashby (1981: 674–5): 'Speakers of modern French now show a strong tendency to dispense with *ne*';

'*Ne* . . . may be progressively squeezed out. And since it has become only a redundant mark of negation in modern French, *ne* can be easily dispensed with' (p. 681).

None of these studies of the distribution of *ne* considers the expletive element in comparatives. Clearly, the evidence here is of a very different nature. *Ne* not only shows no sign of disappearing in such constructions but appears, rather, to be spreading to the equative construction. This does not, however, constitute counter-evidence to the position that the redundant negative particle is disappearing in French once it is accepted that comparative *ne* is not a negative element. Nor is it redundant: quite the contrary. Expletive *ne* shows no sign of disappearing from comparative constructions precisely because it is a marker of comparison; therefore, changes affecting the negative item *ne* in French are of no relevance. Indeed, the elimination of truly negative *ne* might be expected to favour the spread of a non-negative *ne*, freeing it to take on other functions. An analysis of comparative *ne* which precludes negativity supports the thesis that negative *ne* is disappearing and, conversely, since the *ne* in comparatives is most certainly not disappearing, the fact that the negative particle is being eliminated from the language supports the thesis that comparative *ne* is not a negative.

The stability of expletive *ne* in comparatives might be thought to have been artificially supported by the influence of teaching. However, Muller (1983: 313) refutes this:

> Contrairement à ce qu'on pense souvent, *ne* . . . dans les comparatives ne se maintient pas à cause de l'action conservatrice de l'école et des grammairiens: les emplois . . . ont longtemps subsisté dans la langue populaire, et ont été critiqués par les grammairiens.

In fact, as Harris (1978: 249) states, 'The use of pleonastic negatives in comparative structures seems to be a Romance rather than Latin development' and they may never have been interpreted as true negatives at all. The following statement in Jonas (1971: 309) gives some support to this hypothesis: 'On remarquera enfin . . . qu'en ancien français, un nouveau système de négation s'instaure, celui de la négation à deux termes (*ne* . . . *mie*, *ne* . . . *pas*) et que ce système n'apparaît pas . . . dans le deuxième terme des comparatives de disparité.'

Whatever the historical facts, a synchronic description of expletive *ne* in comparatives leads inexorably to the conclusion that it is not now a negative particle. It may look like a negative item, but its behaviour belies such an analysis. On the contrary, it is a marker of the comparative construction.

3.3.6 Interpretation of expletive *ne*

Despite what I consider to be the wealth of evidence that this expletive *ne* is not a negative, most descriptions of the comparative constructions of French cling to the notion that this is precisely what it is. This leads on occasion to some complex definitions of what actually constitutes negation. Le Bidois and Le Bidois (1938: 284), for example, claim that '*Ne* . . . décèle . . . l'existence d'un point de vue négatif dans la pensée du locuteur.' Jonas (1971: 307-8) states that

> Il est évident que ce *ne* n'est pas une négation qui porte sur ce qui est formulé dans le deuxième terme, et seulement dans le deuxième terme, du système comparatif, mais qu'il est une négation située dans le deuxième terme qui avec le premier forme un tout et que la valeur de ce *ne* doit se découvrir dans ce tout et non dans une partie de ce tout . . . . Le rôle de ce *ne* est donc de marquer, dans le deuxième terme de la structure, une différence . . . à un certain point de vue, . . . entre les deux termes du système comparatif.

When comparative *ne* occurs in contexts where, as a truly negative element, it could not occur, this is not considered worthy of note and is summarily dismissed as the result of speakers' caprice: 'La notion de discordance est tellement puissante, tellement ancrée dans les profondeurs de l'esprit de l'usager, que ce dernier en arrive parfois à l'exprimer là où il ne faudrait pas' (p. 317). It is unsurprising for a marker element to spread to other comparative contexts, but the same behaviour on the part of a negative would be difficult to explain.

Zaslawsky (1977: 74), discussing his example (23) – *Pierre est plus intelligent que Jacques ne l'est* – explains the occurrence of *ne* by stating that *Pierre* and *Jacques* are

> en concurrence pour la possession de la plus grande intelligence . . . [cet énoncé] introduit un dilemme tout à fait analogue à celui qui oppose tel ou tel prédicat et sa négation puisque, étant donné deux individus d'intelligence inégale, il y en a nécessairement un qui est plus intelligent que l'autre . . . cette analyse contribuerait à expliquer . . . le morphème négatif *ne*.

For him the negative status of *ne* is beyond doubt.

Bergmans (1982) cites Huttenlocher, Higgins, Milligan, and Kauffman's (1970: 341) claim that explicitly negative sentences are harder to understand than non-negative sentences. If *ne* were a negative item, then it follows that comparatives including *ne* would be harder to understand than those excluding *ne*. As I have shown, the opposite holds true. Bergmans also cites (p. 205) Leys' (1980) claim that negative particles in comparative clauses may take on new functions, though their negative import remains, and appears to believe that, for English, 'No ordinary native speaker will consciously connect comparison and negation on the basis of *than*' (p. 206), while, for languages which do have a surface marker of negation in comparatives (like French, under his analysis), this conscious connection will be made: 'as regards a native speaker's *conscious* knowledge, this will be guided and supported by surface forms' (p. 207). Even if one were willing to accept that some connection between comparison and negation could be felt unconsciously by certain groups of speakers and consciously by others, determined solely by language-specific details of the constructions involved, it is not the case that in French the comparatives do contain a surface marker of negation. As the studies cited in section 3.3.5 illustrate conclusively, such a surface negation would be more likely to be realized by *pas* than by *ne*.

Muller's (1983) analysis of the link between negation and comparatives in French is equally convinced of the negativity of *ne*, and although he admits that 'On ne peut . . . traiter *ne* explétif comme un épiphénomène marginal', he dismisses its problematic interaction with true negation as being the result of 'une sorte de saturation par la négation . . . les négations multiples sont généralement mal acceptées' (p. 287). He concedes that *ne*, as a marker of negation, is redundant:

> On peut imaginer qu'il y a donc redondance, l'inégalité étant signifié à la fois par le terme introducteur (*plus, moins* . . .) et par l'orientation négative de la subordonnée, cette redondance étant à l'origine de la neutralisation de la négation (qui devient à son tour explétive).
>
> (p. 292)

However, he seems unaware of the circularity of this argument: it is the so-called 'orientation négative' of the subordinate clause which is being held to account for the appearance of *ne* in the first place. It cannot both cause *ne* to appear and make it redundant at one and the same time.

Muller attributes the fact that '*ne*, contrairement à la négation pleine, peut apparaître avec des expressions incompatibles avec la négation' to 'l'absence de *pas*' (p. 299), rather than to the more obvious fact that it is not negative. He later (p. 301) cites two sentences in which he feels the appearance of *ne* to be problematic:

(202) Ils sont moins fermés au progrès que certains (?*n')ont pu l'affirmer
They are less closed to progress than certain people have been able to claim

(203) Les bonapartistes sont plus nombreux qu'on (?*ne) pourrait le supposer
The Bonapartists are more numerous than one might suppose

Since, for him, *ne* is negative, he puts its low acceptability here down to 'des difficultés d'interprétation négative de la subordonnée'. A more natural explanation might rest on the choice of verb in the subordinate clause. *Pouvoir* is one of a small number of verbs in French with which *ne* may appear alone as the marker of negation, *pas* being optional. This being the case, it might be expected that comparative *ne* would be virtually excluded with *pouvoir* as there is a clear risk of confusion between expletive *ne* and the true negative. It is a simple matter to prove that this is the case. If *pouvoir* in (202) and (203) is replaced by another verb the problem disappears:

(204) Ils sont moins fermés au progrès que certains n'ont essayé de l'affirmer
They are less closed to progress than certain people have tried to claim

(205) Les bonapartistes sont plus nombreux qu'on ne voudrait le supposer
The Bonapartists are more numerous than one would wish to suppose

Muller's analysis, insisting as it does on the fact that *ne* is a negative element, meets a number of problems which would disappear if the idea were abandoned that *ne* in comparatives has negative import.

Non-negative ne

There are, in fact, studies which appear to reject the view that comparative *ne* is a true negative. Gougenheim (1939: 262) regards it as syntactically conditioned, a 'servitude grammaticale'. Ferrar (1984: 179) mentions, though only in a footnote, that *ne* is 'without negative force'. For Gaatone (1971: 80) '*ne* n'a aucun sens . . . toutes les valeurs qu'on a pu attribuer à *ne* se trouvent non dans *ne* même, mais dans les mots qui le conditionnent.' Gaatone sees expletive *ne* as a syntactically conditioned item devoid of meaning. While this may be generally true, comparative *ne*, unlike other occurrences, does have a vital role to play. Pinkham (1982:29) states, again in a footnote, that 'Use of *ne* (which is not a negative) is obligatory except in comparisons of equality.' Apart from this, unjustifiably clear-cut, aside as to the nature of *ne*, its occurrence and function are not discussed.

There is, then, an unwillingness to consider the true function of expletive *ne* in comparatives even, or perhaps especially, amongst those who reject the notion that it has negative import. In other words, while they may be happy to state what *ne* is not, they stop a long way short of grappling with the question of what *ne* actually is. I have claimed that the role of expletive *ne* in comparative structures is that of a marker of comparison. To insist that it has negative force leads to what Leys (1980: 102), quoted in Bergmans (1982: 185), calls 'the highly counter-intuitive conclusion that the meaning of a construction may be hidden from ordinary speakers and be only accessible to trained linguists'.

3.3.7 Interaction of *ne* with foci of comparison

It was mentioned on page 76 that there is a certain amount of interaction between *ne* and the proforms *le/en* in comparatives. To exemplify this, a scale of acceptability was given for the sentences in (29) (repeated):

(29) a. *??Il est plus riche qu'il était
    b. ??Il est plus riche qu'il l'était
    c. ?Il est plus riche qu'il n'était
    d. Il est plus riche qu'il ne l'était
        He is richer than he use to be

A similar range of judgements is found for comparatives involving the noun as the compared category, e.g.:

(206) a. *Il a plus d'argent qu'il avait

b. ??Il a plus d'argent qu'il en avait
c. ?Il a plus d'argent qu'il n'avait
d. Il a plus d'argent qu'il n'en avait
He has more money than he had

These acceptability judgements seem generally valid, particularly for (29/206a) and (d); there is some variation in the acceptability of (b) and (c), but on the whole (c) is judged better than (b).

The fact that the proforms *le* and *en* are available for certain types of comparison (usually, those involving adjective and noun, respectively) marks a further difference between French and Spanish, where equivalent proforms are not available in such constructions. Clearly, proforms representing the gapped category (that is, the quantified category to be inferred) act as foci of comparison: they represent the second compared category. Therefore, the degree of acceptability exhibited by the (b) version is unsurprising; even though the marker of comparison *ne* is missing, which would ordinarily result in ungrammaticality, the occurrence of *le/en* 'saves' the sentences to a certain extent as their status as foci of comparison may also mark the construction as a comparative. Their unavailability in Spanish is yet another reason why the tensed verb constraint holds so strongly in that language. Notice, however, that the version in (c), with expletive *ne*, the standard marker element in comparatives, is preferred and for some speakers is perfectly acceptable. The role of *ne* as a marker element is, then, more important in terms of marking the construction as a comparative, by virtue of disambiguating the comparative particle *que*, than that of *le/en*, as my analysis would predict. The version in (a) lacks either a focus of comparison or a marker of comparison and is therefore ungrammatical, as the comparative clause does not differ overtly from an ordinary tensed subordinate clause.

It follows from this that for those categories for which a proform does not exist, e.g. the adverb, there will be only two possibilities, either including or omitting *ne*, and the requirement for *ne* will be, if anything, even stronger:

(207) a. *??Il court moins vite qu'il courait
b. Il court moins vite qu'il ne courait
He runs less fast than he used to run

Example (207a) is unacceptable because the required marker of comparison, *ne*, is absent and there is no focus of comparison available either. As *ne* is the marker of comparison, its absence will result in an overt focus of comparison being required; in the case of the adverb, however, there is no such proform available.

If this analysis is valid and the problem with the (a) examples really is the lack of either an overt focus item or a comparison marker, it might be expected that the addition of an extra contrasting item in the subordinate clause could improve the sentences:

(208) ??Il est plus riche qu'il était dans le passé
 He is richer than he was in the past
(209) ??Il a plus d'argent qu'il avait la semaine dernière
 He has more money than he had last week
(210) ??Il court moins vite qu'il courait quand il était jeune
 He runs less fast than he ran when he was young

Native speakers do consider (208–10) to be significantly better than (29a), (206a) and (207a). Clearly, these sentences are still some way from being fully acceptable, but the fact that they are felt to be improved by the addition of extra contrasting information proves that at least part of the problem with the (a) sentences is the lack of overt focus elements, whether of comparison or of contrast. The availability of *ne* as a marker of comparison in French, however, prevents this from being problematic, unlike the case in Spanish, where the lack of such an unambiguous marker element has noticeable effects on the syntax of comparative constructions.

The interaction of the proforms *le/en* and expletive *ne* is not noted in descriptions of comparison in French, yet frequently examples which are adduced to show that *ne* need not appear in the subordinate clause of a comparative do contain an anaphoric proform, e.g. Le Bidois and Le Bidois (1939: 284–5), where the following examples (from Racine and Saint Evremond) are cited:

(211) Jamais père ne fut plus heureux que vous l'êtes
 Never was a father happier than you are
(212) Il n'y a personne qui ait plus d'admiration que j'en ai pour les ouvrages des anciens
 There is no one who has greater admiration than I have for the works of the ancients

Le Bidois and Le Bidois explain the omission of *ne* here as being a result of the writers' not seeing 'l'image au négatif'. Whether or not this is so, the reason these sentences appear acceptable is precisely because they contain a proform capable of marking the construction as a comparative by virtue of constituting an overt focus of comparison in the absence of *ne*. Le Bidois and Le Bidois give a number of other examples where *ne* is omitted, and in each case there is a proform, *le* or *en*, in the subordinate clause. Not a single example omits both *ne* and the proform. They conclude:

> Les deux tours: 'Il est plus grand *qu'il l'était*', 'Il est plus grand *qu'il ne l'était*' sont en soi également acceptables; mais ce qui doit régler la préférence, c'est le sens, c'est la façon (positive ou négative) dont se pense la seconde idée.

In fact, they are not equally acceptable, the first being possible only because of the inclusion of *le*, acting as a focus of comparison. The difference between them is not, as Le Bidois and Le Bidois claim, that for the version including *ne* to be acceptable it must be the case that 'he' was not very tall before. This is easily demonstrated:

(213) Il est plus grand qu'il n'était et il a toujours été assez grand
      He is taller than he was and he has always been rather tall

Sentence (213) is not contradictory, disproving the suggested implication.

Gaatone (1971: 95), although he feels omission of comparative *ne* is rare, gives three examples where it is omitted. Again, in each of these, a proform occurs, thus licensing the omission of *ne*:

(214) Ce fut plus rapide qu'elle l'eût cru
      It was faster than she would have thought
(215) Tout est toujours un peu pire qu'on l'attend
      Everything is always a little worse than one expects
(216) Elle était douce, mais aussi comme elle était triste, d'abord à cause de sa douceur même presque décantée, plus que peu de voix humaines ont jamais dû l'être, de toute dureté . . .
      She was sweet, but how sad she was also, firstly because of her very sweetness, almost devoid, more than few human voices must ever have been, of all harshness . . .

Gaatone also fails to make the obvious connection here: it is the presence of the proform *le* which allows the (rare) absence of *ne*.

When the possibility for *ne* to be absent is noted, mistaken conclusions are often drawn. Grevisse (1969: 876) offers the following three possibilities:

(217) a. Vous êtes plus grand que vous croyez[40]
      b. Vous êtes plus grand que vous ne croyez

c. Vous êtes plus grand que vous ne le croyez
You are taller than you think

He notes that, according to *L'office de la langue française*, these

présentent des nuances délicates. Le *ne* de la deuxième insiste sur le fait ('vous croyez n'être pas grand'). Le *le* de la troisième apporte plus d'insistance. L'idée générale reste la même dans les trois phrases, mais de la première à la troisième, il y a progression ascendante.

It is not the case that the (b) example is more 'negative' than the others, as has already been demonstrated (see (213)). It is also not the case that (a) is fully acceptable: for most speakers it is not, since it lacks either a focus element or a comparison marker. It is, however, true that (c) is felt to be more emphatic than (b). This is precisely because (c) contains both a marker of comparison and a focus element (*ne* + *le*), while (b) contains only a marker of comparison (*ne*).

De Boer (1954: 17–18), on the other hand, discussing similar examples, rejects the notion that the presence or absence of *ne* (which he considers 'plus ou moins obligatoire') can reflect any negativity in the subordinate clause, and reaches a conclusion with which it would be difficult to disagree: 'On a l'impression que M. Frei n'a pas tort de dénoncer "la manie des puristes et des grammairiens de chercher dans certaines fluctuations de l'usage des nuances sémantiques subtiles".'

The proforms *le* and *en*, then, act as foci of comparison additional to the marker *ne* in comparison involving certain categories. As such, in the absence of *ne* they enhance a construction's acceptability. The requirement for *ne* is still strong in such comparatives, but is clearly even stronger in expressions of comparison involving categories for which there is no proform. The difference between a comparative construction involving *ne* and a proform and one in which only a proform occurs is not related to any notion of negativity; rather, it is a difference in acceptability, for most speakers, and of emphasis, for all.

There is another context in which *ne* does not occur and which has already been mentioned: the relativized phrasal comparative involving *que ce que*. In such expressions of comparison only the head of the relative clause, *ce*, is involved in the comparison proper, e.g. (218):

(218) Il a plus d'argent que ce qu'il avait
He has more money than he had

These phrasal comparatives are really like reduced sentential comparatives with *ce* the complement of *que*; there is no comparative subordinate clause, only a relative clause binding the pronoun *ce* (here, *qu'il avait*), which represents the second object of comparison. Equally, there is no quantifier 'gap' here: the restrictive relative clause acts as an operator binding its head and therefore parallels the binding relation holding between the 'gapped' quantifier and proform *en* in (219), the full sentential version of (218):

(219) Il a plus d'argent qu'il n'en avait

It is precisely because phrasal comparatives do not involve a comparative subordinate clause that *ne* may not appear (except, very infrequently, by analogy: see pp. 79–83). Its role is as a marker of comparison, which also saves the comparative subordinate clause containing a tensed verb from falling foul of the tensed verb constraint outlined in Chapter 2 by distinguishing comparative *que* from the tensed clause complementizer *que*. It is therefore not required in phrasal comparatives where, I repeat, there is no comparative subordinate clause and the pronoun *ce* is the focus of comparison, the ensuing relative clause being defocussed. As a result, a tensed verb is free to appear in the relative clause; it does not need to be licensed by *ne*. This is exactly parallel to the case of relativized phrasal *de lo que* comparatives in Spanish, where *lo* (in some form) is the focus of comparison and the ensuing relative clause is defocussed, allowing a tensed verb to appear. The difference between the two languages lies not here, but in the lack of a comparison marker equivalent to *ne* in Spanish to save the subordinate clause in sentential comparatives from the tensed verb constraint. It has been suggested that such a comparison marker is not required in Spanish since *que*, distinct from the equative particle *como*, may serve this purpose; nonetheless, the fact that comparative *que* and the tensed clause complementizer are homonyms leads as a consequence to the constraint against tensed verbs in comparative clauses.

The fact that expletive *ne* may not occur in French phrasal comparatives, because the tensed verb is in a relative clause and hence may appear 'legitimately', lends further support to my claim that while *ne* is a marker of comparison in French comparatives, it also allows them to escape the tensed verb constraint by distinguishing clearly between comparative *que* and the complementizer *que*. This draws a sharp distinction between this language and Spanish.

3.3.8 Expletive *ne* versus expletive *no*

The existence of an expletive element in Spanish, *no*, was mentioned in Chapter 2. It might be thought that *no* in Spanish and *ne* in French were equivalent. In fact, they are completely dissimilar. As has been shown, Spanish *no* is only marginally acceptable for a few speakers; French expletive *ne* is virtually obligatory for all speakers. *No*, for those speakers who accept it, may appear only in comparatives of inequality; *ne* may appear in the equative construction in French. *No* may appear only when there is no tensed verb, in other words, in a reduced clause; *ne* appears only when a tensed verb does occur, in a non-reduced subordinate clause. Spanish *no* is a marginally acceptable epiphenomenon; French expletive *ne* is a marker of comparison.

No in Spanish does not have the role of *ne* in French: it is not a marker of comparison, nor can it prevent the tensed verb constraint from applying. It was suggested in Chapter 2 that the reason why expletive *no* does not appear in comparative subordinate clauses may be because it would be indistinguishable from normal full sentential negation. It is precisely because expletive *ne* in French cannot be thus confused, sentential negation being signified by the disjoint negative *ne . . . pas* or, increasingly, by *pas* alone, that it is free to appear in such contexts, take on the role of comparison marker and thereby prevent the tensed verb constraint from applying.

3.3.9 Concluding remarks

I have claimed that the function of expletive *ne* in comparatives is to act as a marker of comparison and that it prevents the tensed verb constraint which applies in Spanish from applying in French. At the same time, I have also claimed that expletive *ne* in comparatives has no negative force.[41] This runs counter to the usual claim that it is a negative element overtly signifying the covert negation in expressions of comparison. Evidence has been adduced to the effect that *ne* is not a marker of negation, including the following facts: if it were a negative, it should be possible to insert *pas* after the verb and this is not possible; if it represented some idea of 'mental' negativity this would apply only to positive *plus . . . que* comparatives, but expletive *ne* also appears after negative comparatives of superiority, after *moins* and, increasingly, after *aussi/autant*; it is unlike other examples of expletive negation, which are optional and linked to the subjunctive mood, while comparative *ne* is neither of these; it may appear after a negative matrix clause; it never appears in a reduced sentential comparative, as might be expected if it marked a mental concept of oppositon, but is eliminated along with the verb, pointing to its secondary role as a 'licenser' of the tensed verb; so-called 'negative polarity' items occur freely in the comparative of equality as well as in the comparatives of inequality, which does not support the idea that there is any connection between their acceptability and the existence of negativity; there is little or no historical evidence to support the idea that comparatives once involved negation in Romance (they did not in Latin); the negative particle *ne* is disappearing in Modern French, while the expletive *ne* is strongly required in comparatives of inequality and actually spreading into the equative construction.

It seems clear that there is more than enough evidence to justify a treatment of expletive *ne* in comparatives as a distinctive item. I have argued that this distinctiveness lies in its role as a marker of comparison. There is support for this analysis, both language-internal and language-external, as I hope to have shown. The language-internal evidence concerns its behaviour and distribution in the French constructions, amply illustrated. The language-external evidence concerns the relatively restricted range of constructions available in Spanish for the expression of comparison, particularly of inequality, in contrast to the situation in French. My analysis of *ne* as a marker element, unavailable in Spanish and not required by this language, but available in French, is capable of explaining why a tensed verb constraint operates in Spanish but not in French. I have demonstrated that this constraint is as true of French as it is of Spanish. The reason it does not lead to ungrammaticality in French sentential comparatives, but does have this consequence in Spanish, is solely due to the existence of the comparison marker, expletive *ne*, of French.

3.4 THE CLAUSE INTRODUCER

It has been shown that the range of constructions available for the expression of comparison is the same for both the comparatives of inequality and the comparative of equality. This is unlike the situation in Spanish, where the equative construction allows a greater range of structural possibilites than the comparatives of inequality. I have argued that this is related to the fact that the two types of comparatives do not share the same clause introducer or 'comparative particle'. In the same way, the homogeneous range of constructions in French is a natural consequence of the fact that there is only one 'comparative particle' in French, *que*.[42] Thus both types of comparative, along with the comparatives of Russian and Finnish, belong to Stassen's (1985: 195–6) seventh group of particle comparatives, whereas the Spanish constructions must belong to two separate groups (see section 1.5.3). Additionally, the fact that French has only one comparative particle means that *que* cannot act as a marker of comparison, unlike Spanish *que*. Hence another marker is required (see section 1.8).

In the description of the Spanish constructions it was claimed that the 'comparative particle' *que*, although isomorphic with the complementizer *que*, is a separate lexical item. The arguments adduced in support of this claim are equally valid for French *que*: comparative *que* may be followed by a pronoun, as, for example, in the *que ce que* phrasal construction, and it may be followed by an infinitive. The complementizer *que* may not appear in just these contexts. If there is general agreement that comparative *que* is not the standard tensed clause subordinator, there is no consensus as to what it actually is.

Moignet (1970: 107–8) relates it to the use of *que* in exclamations:

Il s'impose de rapprocher cet emploi de *que* de celui de la phrase exclamative nominalisée: *Que tu travailles!*, où *que* s'interprète aussi en degré d'intensité de l'action . . . . *Que* . . . fonctionne comme une sorte d'adverbe relatif qui évoque, non pas la substance notionnelle de l'antécédent . . . mais une abstraction de cette sémantèse, l'idée de degré qu'elle implique.

Yet he also feels that 'dans l'emploi comparatif, *que* reste une sorte de pronom'. Moignet (1981) claims that *que* is 'un adverbe relatif' with 'un statut quasi-adverbial' (p. 190) and, apparently at the same time, 'un adverbe quantitatif' which 'véhicule la même idée que son antécédent' (p. 203). He again relates its use in comparatives to its use in exclamations, but he offers no support for this putative link.

Le Bidois and Le Bidois (1938: 281–2) give a convoluted and unconvincing explanation for this use of *que*:

d'où vient à notre *que* . . . la faculté de servir d'outil syntaxique dans la comparaison? Il nous semble que cela peut s'expliquer ainsi. Le système comparatif, *André est plus grand que Paul*, comprend en somme ces deux idées: André est, pour la grandeur, à un degré plus haut, **et** Paul à un degré moins haut (ou, si l'on veut, **et** Paul, à cet égard, vient **après**). Nous avons intentionellement souligné les mots **et** et **après**; c'est qu'ils peuvent nous aider à comprendre le rôle de *que* en phrase comparative. *Que* . . . est un morphème qui ensemble distingue et unit, disons d'un mot, qui confronte. Le *than* de la phrase comparative anglaise nous aide aussi à expliquer notre *que* comparatif. On sait que *than* est une simple variante morphologique de *then*. L'anglais a dit d'abord: A is better *then* B (A est meilleur, et B après); il dit aujourd'hui, sous cette forme à peine changée: A is better *than* B. Ainsi . . . notre *que* comparatif amène un second terme, qui, parce que *postérieur* (d'une postériorité spéciale, qui n'est pas chronologique, mais purement logique), se fait penser comme *inférieur*.

Leaving aside the fact that the suggested link between the English and French constructions here is tenuous at best, it is obvious that the second term of a comparison may only be considered 'inférieur' in a positive comparative of superiority. This analysis of *que* cannot encompass the comparatives of inferiority and equality.

What these analyses have in common is that they attempt to see in comparative *que* a reflection of the semantics of the constructions in which it appears. However, the function of *que* is simply to introduce the second term of the comparison, whether a full clause, a chain of clauses, a reduced clause or a nominal element; its occurrence is syntactically conditioned. Nonetheless, it is not simply a further instance of the standard tensed clause complementizer, as witnessed by its ability to introduce non-clausal elements, for which there may be no tensed clause source, e.g. (220):

(220) Il est plus riche que moi
    He is richer than me

It was argued in Chapter 2 that a partial explanation of the operation of the tensed verb constraint in Spanish might lie in the homonymy of the comparative of inequality clause introducer and the standard subordinator, since the presence of a tensed verb in the second half of the comparison might lead to a preferential interpretation of the clause as an ordinary tensed clause. The French facts might seem to contradict this assertion, since the same situation holds with regard to the 'comparative particle' *que* and the standard subordinator *que*.[43] However, the situation is not the same due to the presence in French of expletive *ne*, which clearly marks the comparative construction as such. It has already been pointed out that marginal expletive *no* in Spanish could not have this function since it is identical to full sentential negation. Its presence after comparative *que* therefore could not mark the construction as comparative and the risk of misinterpretation with a tensed verb would remain unchanged; nor is *no* required as a marker of comparison, a role which Spanish *que* is able to fill by virtue of its not being the universal comparative particle. The availability in French of an expletive item distinct from full sentential negation enables this language to differentiate clearly between clauses following comparative *que* and those following the standard subordinator. This is yet another reason why *ne* is so strongly required in comparative clauses in French. Just as I have argued that in Spanish the tensed verb constraint, while originally syntactic, has a semantic effect in terms of the operation of foci of comparison and contrast in topicalized structures, in a parallel way the requirement for expletive *ne* in French can be seen as a dual requirement, to distinguish between a comparative clause and a standard tensed clause, and to act as the marker of comparison, due to the existence of a universal comparative particle, as I hope to have demonstrated.

3.5 SUMMARY

The comparatives of inequality and the comparative of equality have now been discussed and the range of construction types available for the expression of full and partial comparison exemplified. It has been shown that precisely the same number of structure types are available for both the comparatives of inequality and the equative: three for the expression of full comparison:

1 a reduced sentential construction
2 a full sentential construction
3 two phrasal constructions:

(a) an oblique phrasal construction
(b) a relativized phrasal construction involving *que ce que*;

and four (though one is extremely marginal at best) for the expression of partial comparison:

1 a reduced sentential construction
2 a full sentential construction with declarative word order
3 a topicalized sentential construction
4 a relativized phrasal construction involving *que ce que*.

There is, then, no major distinction between the two types of comparative. The structure types listed above, are not, however, equally acceptable in all contexts. For full comparison, types 1 and 2 are fully acceptable. Type 3(b), on the other hand, enjoys a lower level of acceptability, appearing to be best, and fully acceptable, only when the object of comparison is a noun, and worst when it is an adverb, with the other categories falling somewhere in between. Moreover, all examples of this type seem less acceptable with the equative construction than with the comparatives of inequality, mirroring the situation in Spanish.

For partial comparison, again, types 1 and 2 are fully acceptable. The comments above apply equally to the phrasal construction, type 4 here. Type 3, the topicalized construction, is only rarely acceptable, due to the limited flexibility of word order in French. In all cases, the phrasal construction is more acceptable than the topicalized construction. It is also true of expressions of partial comparison that they are generally less acceptable than expressions of full comparison as a result of the importance of poorly understood notions of parallelism in their interpretation. In other words, the more complex a partial comparison is, that is, the greater the number of contrasts expressed, or the less natural these contrasts are felt to be, the less acceptable it appears to be, as has been illustrated (see pp. 90–3).

The relative unacceptability of the *que ce que* phrasal construction and, particularly, the topicalized construction in French, by comparison with Spanish, is entirely predictable within the analysis proposed here. Recall that Spanish required a phrasal construction and a topicalized construction in order to escape the tensed verb constraint. I have claimed that this constraint disallows a tensed verb in the subordinate clause after comparative *que* in Spanish, unless it is acting as a focus of comparison (topicalized comparatives) or is outside the scope of the comparison proper (relativized phrasal comparatives and topicalized comparatives in which the verb is not in topic position). This was related to the fact that tense alone is never a sufficient focus of comparison. French does not require the phrasal and topicalized constructions as 'escape hatches' from this tensed verb constraint. The expletive *ne* of French comparatives, distinguishing them from their Spanish counterparts, is a comparison marker which also serves to license the appearance of a tensed verb. As proof of this, it has been shown that expletive *ne* does not appear in *que ce que* phrasal comparatives. Note that if its role were anything other than that of comparison marker, this fact could not be explained; the tensed verb of relativized phrasal comparatives does not need to be licensed, nor does the clause need to be marked as being comparative, precisely because it is a relative clause and the tensed verb constraint does not apply to such structures. The tensed verb constraint, therefore, is a restriction which might have applied equally to French and Spanish, but the presence of expletive *ne* in French comparatives marks the clause as a comparative and allows a tensed verb to follow *que* without the risk of ambiguity. Central to this analysis of the role of *ne* is the contention that it is not a negative particle and totally lacks negative force. Language-internal and -external evidence has been adduced in support of the hypothesis that it is a marker element. Equally importantly, it has been shown both that there is no convincing evidence that expletive *ne* functions as any kind of negative, whether as a representation of some proposed negativity involved in the cognitive processes associated with the interpretation of comparatives or otherwise, and that there are reasons in plenty to support a synchronic analysis of *ne* as non-negative. While evidence as to the historical negativity of the expletive particle in comparative constructions has not been considered here, the words of Damourette (1932: 86-7) seem particularly applicable: 'Certes, l'état ancien d'un idiome nous fournit de précieuses indications sur l'évolution des mécanismes linguistiques, mais c'est l'emploi actuel des formes, et non leur origine, qui peut instruire sur leur nature actuelle.' Even if no other evidence existed to support the thesis that expletive *ne* is not a negative, the fact alone that *ne* may appear in positive equative constructions would suffice. This is not to deny that the question of how *ne* has come to play the role it does is an interesting one from a diachronic perspective. This question is, however, beyond the scope of the present, synchronic, study.

Ne, however, is not the only available item capable of marking a construction as a comparative. It has also been shown that the anaphoric proforms *le* and *en*, available in a subset of comparison types (generally, those involving the adjective and noun, respectively, as the objects of comparison), act as foci of comparison, by virtue of representing the second compared category. Expletive *ne*, therefore, may sometimes be omitted in such comparatives, being less strongly required, though its inclusion is preferred by most native speakers. The omission of *ne* where no proform for the compared category exists (for example, in the case of the adverb) is rare. In all cases, inclusion of expletive *ne* is close to being obligatory; only its interaction with focus elements can weaken this. Once again, Spanish lacks equivalent proforms to act as foci and avoid the tensed verb constraint.

The suggestion made in Chapter 1 (section 1.8), that in particle comparatives the particle itself may act as a marker of comparison when it is distinctive (as in Spanish, with *que* and *como*), but that when there is only one available particle a negative element may play this role (as in juxtapositional comparatives), appears to be borne out by the French data. *Ne*, a formally negative particle, is the marker of comparison in this language. The fact that it may also, therefore, disambiguate comparative *que* and the complementizer *que* falls out as a happy consequence and allows a tensed verb to follow the comparative particle. *Ne* is not, despite its form, a negative element, but a syntactically conditioned marker.

A description of the various structures available for the expression of comparison in French, then, shows a less complex picture than the corresponding range of structures in Spanish. This relative simplicity derives almost exclusively from the existence of expletive *ne*. The function this particle fulfils and the role it plays in the expression of comparison in French, however, is not at all simple.

NOTES

1 Both Dubois and Dubois-Charlier (1970: 131) and Muller (1983: 276) explicitly accept that a deletion rule operates to produce the reduced sentential comparative, while Stassen (1985: 196) seems not to acknowledge the existence of reduced sentential comparatives at all, speaking of *que* as preceding 'the standard NP or clause' only. For an interpretive solution see Pinkham (1982).

2 *Davantage* is sometimes mentioned as an alternative to *plus*. However, according to De Boer (1954: 195)

Davantage ne peut ni déterminer un adjectif (*plus grand*), ni être suivi d'un régime substantif (*plus d'argent*), ni être suivi du seconde terme d'une comparaison (*plus que lui*). Le plus souvent il termine la phrase: *Il est riche, mais je le suis davantage*.

Le Bidois and Le Bidois (1938: 282–3) appear to disagree with this, stating, 'L'adverbe *davantage* . . . s'est longtemps fait suivre de *que* comme les autres morphèmes comparatifs . . . malgré . . . les nombreux exemples qu'offre la langue classique de cette construction avec *que*, nos grammairiens . . . s'y sont longtemps opposés.' Gougenheim (1939: 255) agrees: 'Les grammairiens ont voulu interdire l'emploi de *que* après *davantage*; mais *davantage que* est fréquent dans la langue classique . . . et survit dans la langue parlée.' However, according to Grevisse (1969: 834), although '*Davantage* était couramment suivi de *que* à l'époque classique . . . cette construction est proscrite par les grammairiens depuis la fin du XVIIIe siècle.' I will not discuss the use of *davantage*, which is highly restricted and rarely an alternative to *plus*, appearing only in certain constructions other than the types under discussion here.

3 As in Spanish, there exists a small number of morphological comparative adjectives and adverbs:

meilleur	plus bon
pire	plus mauvais
moindre	plus petit
mieux	plus bien
pis	plus mal

The forms on the left have the semantic content of the analytical forms on the right. Both the analytical and synthetic forms of these adjectives and adverbs are found, though *meilleur* and *mieux* are rarely replaced by *plus bon* and *plus bien*.

4 This and the reduced sentential construction above correspond to Muller's (1983: 273) definition of 'une phrase réduite' and 'une phrase', each being a 'complément phrastique'.

5 This, for Muller (1983: 273), is 'ni une phrase, ni une phrase réduite', being a 'complément nominal'.

6 For Muller, this is also a 'comparative nominale' with relativization (p. 284).

7 That *de* is not more widely used as a comparative particle is attributed by Le Bidois and Le Bidois (1938: 281) to the relative force of *que*: 'La valeur de ligature comparative . . . s'est, au cours du temps, révélée bien plus grande, bien plus nette aussi, dans la conjonction que dans la préposition'.

8 *Le* acting as an anaphor here is in fact slightly marginal. This is simply a reflection of the fact that it is generally difficult for prepositional phrases to enter into a comparative construction as the object of comparison, due to their limited suitability for modification.

9 Le Bidois and Le Bidois (1938: 609) speak of *plus* and *moins* in such constructions as having 'une valeur qui tient le milieu entre celle du nom et celle de l'adverbe', a somewhat vague definition.

10 For a detailed analysis of *en* in such constructions see Pinkham (1982: 5–16).

11 See note 8.

12 Strictly speaking, it is the quantifier modifying the verb which is the object of comparison.

13 Muller's (1983: 297) conclusion is that 'le changement de place de *ne* ne correspond pas à un changement de sens, ce qui semble signifier . . . que l'interprétation négative de la subordonnée comparative concerne obligatoirement la première subordonnée.' This is demonstrably false.

14 As in Chapter 2, these examples are adapted from examples given for English in Bresnan (1977).
15 Interestingly, in the following case a change in the construction is felt to effect a change, if not in the meaning, then at least in what is presupposed:

   (a) Il a invité plus de personnes qu'il n'en avait invité l'année dernière
   (b) Il a invité plus de personnes que ce qu'il avait invité l'année dernière
       He has invited more people than he invited last year

   While (b) means only that the number of people invited this year exceeds the number invited last year, (a) has the additional implication that the people invited last year are included amongst those invited this year; this may be because the partitive proform *en* is more directly linked to the partitive *plus de personnes* of the matrix, being semantically parallel, than is the demonstrative *ce*, which is bound, hence quantified, by the ensuing restrictive relative clause and therefore structurally dissimilar from the matrix partitive.
16 It is possible, in phrasal constructions also, for the gap representing the category undergoing comparison with a category in the matrix to be embedded, e.g.:

   Evidemment, ils peuvent employer plus de femmes que ce que le gouvernement consentait à leur permettre d'employer auparavant

   Such constructions are not, however, preferred and acceptability generally becomes lower as the embedding becomes deeper.
17 Where the object of comparison is a noun in a phrasal comparative, the pronoun *ce* does not exhibit number or gender marking, unlike the pronoun *lo* in the Spanish *de lo que* construction.
18 Constructions like this do, however, seem possible in Portuguese, e.g.:

   Pedro bebeu menos vinho do que Pablo
   Pedro drank less wine than Pablo

   Do que is the sequence preposition + pronoun (*de* + *o*, fused) + relative (see Chapter 4, pp. 194–6).
19 Ultimately, Muller abandons this hypothesis in favour of a vaguely formulated indexing solution:

   L'hypothèse qui se présente alors est que la comparative, au lieu d'être construite sur un antécédent effacé ensuite, adopte d'une facon ou d'une autre le terme introducteur comme antécédent: l'indexation de la comparative, par l'intermédiaire de son élément déplacé/effacé, sur un tel antécédent, pourrait expliquer les particularités des comparatives d'inégalité.

   For a more precise description of an indexing solution to the interpretation of comparatives in Spanish, which might be extended to the cases Muller considers, see S. A. Price (1982).
20 Assuming that, as with *más*, *plus* actually has the semantic content equivalent to *plus beaucoup*.
21 When acting as a modifier of the verb, prepositional phrase or noun,

aussi is realized as *autant*, entering into a partitive structure (*autant* + *de* + noun), parallel to *plus/moins*, in the latter case.
22 Another possible version of this sentence is:

   Un président est puissant, autant qu'un roi

   Here *autant* modifies the whole of the preceding verb phrase, not the adjective *puissant*, hence the need normally for a written comma before *autant* or a pronounced pause, in speech.
23 Similarly, another possible version of this sentence is:

   La cruauté est dans nos coeurs, autant que la générosité

   Here *autant* does not modify the prepositional phrase, but the preceding verb phrase.
24 Stylistic inversion in the subordinate clause (see example (15)).
25 See note 14.
26 That such a quantifier must indeed exist is easily demonstrated. In the following two examples *de* appears before the noun being compared in the subordinate clause:

   (a) Pourquoi est-ce qu'il y avait plus de chiens dans la maison que de chats?
       Why were there more dogs in the house than cats?
   (b) L'année prochaine nous admettrons autant de femmes que beaucoup d'universités admettront d'hommes
       Next year we will admit as many women as many universities will admit men

   If there were no underlying quantifier parallel to the noun phrase of the matrix, i.e. *Q de chats*, *Q d'hommes*, there would be no explanation for the appearance of *de*.
27 See note 24.
28 Pinkham (1982: 19) points out that when a subpart of the compared noun phrase in the subordinate clause is identical to a part of the compared element in the main clause, the proform *en* may appear:

   (Pinkham's 55) Il a acheté plus de bouteilles de vin qu'il n'en a acheté de bière
   He bought more bottles of wine than he bought of beer

   However, it need not:

   (Pinkham's 58) Il a acheté plus de bouteilles de vin qu'il n'a acheté de bouteilles de bière
   He bought more bottles of wine than he bought bottles of beer

   While interesting, these are not truly examples of partial comparison in the sense in which the term is being employed in this study, being rather examples of full comparison due to the near identity of the two objects of comparison.
29 See note 24.
30 As noticed by Pinkham (1982: 27), 'there is a decay in acceptability in

French . . . when Comparative Subdeletion [partial comparison] applies in embedded contexts.' A constraint is posited:

> If the compared elements in a comparative construction are not identical, acceptability is reduced as the level of embedding increases. In other words, if two different elements are being compared, the complexity surrounding them cannot be too great. The existence of [this constraint] could be linked either to semantic factors or to perceptual difficulties.

Given the complex parallelism constraints on acceptable expressions of partial comparison, perceptual difficulties provide the most appropriate explanation.

31 See note 14.
32 An exception to this may be more complex sentential constructions expressing partial comparison. It has already been pointed out that such constructions become less acceptable as the level of embedding increases. It seems that the topicalized alternative may sometimes be preferred; for example, (a) may be preferred to (b):

(a) Evidemment, ils peuvent employer plus de femmes que d'hommes le gouvernement consentait à leur permettre d'employer auparavant
(b) Evidemment, ils peuvent employer plus de femmes que le gouvernement ne consentait à leur permettre d'employer d'hommes auparavant

For those speakers for whom this preference holds, the explanation must be linked to the easier availability of the second compared item in (a), making the sentence easier to process than (b), where the same item appears sentence-finally, some way removed from the matrix object of comparison.

33 It is probable that this sentence, involving the verb as the category of comparison, is judged acceptable because it is interpreted, not as an instance of topicalization, but rather of stylistic subject–verb inversion.
34 This element has in fact been given many labels, including 'ne abusif', 'négation implicite', 'ne pléonastique', 'ne redondant', 'ne discordantiel', 'logisch nicht gerechtfertigtes "ne"', 'demi-négation': see Muller (1978: 77) and Jonas (1971: 307). There is no particular significance in the choice of the label 'expletive' here.
35 It is perhaps suggestive that the Spanish equivalents of French constructions involving (optional) *ne* + subjunctive usually involve the subjunctive alone, the distinction between the two languages once again revolving around the role of the expletive element. For an interesting study of the connection between negative polarity and the subjunctive in Romance, see Nathan and Winters Epro (1984).
36 A similar point is made in Von Stechow (1984a: 71)
37 It does seem that *ne* may be more acceptable in equatives where the object of comparison is seen as semantically negative, e.g. (a) is better than (b):

(a) Il est aussi triste qu'il ne l'était
    He is as sad as he used to be
(b) ?Il est aussi heureux qu'il ne l'était

He is as happy as he was

Similarly, (c) is better than (d):

(c) Il la déteste autant qu'il ne la détestait dans le passé
He hates her as much as he hated her in the past

(d) ?Il l'aime autant qu'il ne l'aimait dans le passé
He loves her as much as he loved her in the past

This fact must be related to the relative instability of *ne* in equatives, unlike its position in the comparatives of inequality. It does not confer any negative import on *ne* itself.

38 This straightforwardly contradicts Jonas' (1971: 296) assertion that

si ce premier terme est affirmatif, c'est à dire s'il y a vraiment disparité, l'adverbe de négation *ne* apparaît toujours devant le verbe du deuxième terme; si le premier terme est négatif, il n'y a plus disparité et *ne* n'apparaît jamais devant le verbe du deuxième terme.

39 Muller (1983: 313) gives as fully acceptable:

Luc mange mieux qu'il n'a pas mangé depuis longtemps
Luc eats better than he has not eaten for a long time

Native speakers I have consulted consider this sentence marginal at best. It is possible that *ne* ... *pas* following synthetic *mieux* looks more acceptable than it does when following *plus* + adjective. More plausibly perhaps, the two clauses have a coherent reading when considered separately – *Luc mange mieux/il n'a pas mangé depuis longtemps* – hence the acceptability of the comparative interpreted as ordinary coordination:

Luc mange mieux et il n'a pas mangé depuis longtemps

40 Notice that (217a):

(217) a. ?Vous êtes plus grand que vous croyez

would be expected, under my analysis, to be more acceptable than (29a):

(29) a. ??Il est plus riche qu'il était

This is because, although they both lack expletive *ne*, the first sentence contains an extra focus of contrast, the lexical content of the verb *croyez*, while the second sentence lacks either a focus of comparison or contrast (other than tense) and also lacks the marker of comparison. Native speakers I have consulted confirm that (217a) does seem less unacceptable than (29a).

41 It is obvious that expletive *ne* has the form of a negative particle. Why this should be so is not entirely clear and historical evidence is vague, as mentioned earlier, but the link I am suggesting between particle comparatives including an expletive negative and juxtapositional comparatives (see section 1.8) indicates that the negative particle may originally have signified opposition. While the question of why this particular particle has come to play the role it does is interesting from a diachronic perspective, I feel the synchronic question of what function

expletive *ne* fulfils now may be adequately addressed without reference to the historical facts. Over-concentration on the form of the particle lies behind most descriptions of its role in comparison and is sometimes responsible for conclusions I consider erroneous. Obviously, the synchronic/diachronic dichotomy cannot be total, and the question of why negative elements should so frequently be involved in the expression of comparison is a valid one. However, speakers do not have access to the history of the constructions they use. Moreover, synchronic evidence points to *pas* as the true negative particle of Modern French, not *ne*. This might be expected to free *ne* for other purposes.

42 Le Bidois and Le Bidois (1938: 253) claim that *comme* in the comparative of equality was displaced by *que* from about the middle of the seventeenth century. Muller (1983: 309) agrees, but points out that 'la langue populaire a maintenu longtemps *comme* . . . le francais populaire du Québec conserve partiellement cet usage.'

43 As in Spanish, it is therefore possible for the situation to arise where a sequence *que que* will appear to be required, e.g.:

(a) *Il dit plus souvent que nous nous trompons que que nous n'avons pas raison
He says more often that we are mistaken than that we are wrong

(b) *Il n'y a rien de plus naturel que que les chiens et les chats se haïssent
There is nothing more natural than that dogs and cats should hate one another

De Boer (1954: 135) states that such a sequence may be avoided by omitting one of the *que*s. Le Bidois and Le Bidois (1938: 272) claim this is archaic and mention two further ways of avoiding the sequence: either by interposing the pronoun *ce*, i.e. replacing *que que* with *que ce que*, or by introducing *non pas*, giving *que non pas que*. The first of these they also consider archaic, while the second is 'reléguée maintenant dans la langue populaire'. It is interesting to recall that, as mentioned in the previous chapter, *no* may be inserted in Spanish to avoid the same sequence, giving *que no que*. That French should have inserted *non pas* and not the expletive *ne* found in comparatives indirectly supports my analysis of Spanish *no* here as unrelated to the comparative construction itself.

Native speakers of French prefer to avoid the sequence *que que* by means of rephrasing.

4 Variation between Spanish and French comparative constructions and a consideration of other Romance languages

The comparative constructions of Spanish and French have been discussed in some detail in Chapters 2 and 3. The salient differences in the structural possibilities for the expression of comparison have been highlighted and shown to follow from the general constraints on comparison being proposed here, that some element in the second half of a comparative construction acts as the focus of the comparison and that there exists a marker of comparison, capable of distinguishing between comparatives of inequality and of equality. The data of Spanish indicate that in a comparison of inequality a tensed verb may not follow the marker of comparison, *que*, due to its formal identity with the tensed clause complementizer, a restriction expressed here as a tensed verb constraint. In French, on the other hand, this restriction does not apply due to the existence of the expletive element, *ne*, acting as the marker of comparison and unambiguously identifying such clauses as comparative clauses. While this tensed verb constraint has been shown to be, in theory, equally applicable to both Spanish and French, the effects exhibited in their syntax, as a result of the availability of expletive *ne* in French, differ greatly, leading to a diversity of construction types.

In Spanish, for the expression of a comparison of inequality, it has been shown that there are two construction types (reduced sentential, relativized phrasal) where full comparison is involved, and three construction types (reduced sentential, topicalized sentential, relativized phrasal) when partial comparison is expressed. For the expression of a comparison of equality, on the other hand, there are three construction types (reduced sentential, full sentential, relativized phrasal) where full comparison is involved, and four (reduced sentential, full sentential, topicalized sentential, relativized phrasal) when partial comparison is expressed. The restrictions and preferences which obtain regarding the use of the various construction types have been discussed in section 2.5 of Chapter 2.

In French, by contrast, for the expression of a comparison of inequality, it has been shown that where full comparison is involved there are potentially three construction types (reduced sentential, full sentential, two types of phrasal – relativized and oblique), and for the expression of partial comparison four construction types (reduced sentential, full sentential, topicalized sentential, relativized phrasal). For the expression of a comparison of equality there are also three construction types (reduced sentential, full sentential, two types of phrasal – relativized and oblique) where full comparison is involved, and four (reduced sentential, full sentential, topicalized sentential, relativized phrasal) for the expression of partial comparison. As for Spanish, the actual pattern of usage of the available structures, some of which are quite marginal, is discussed in section 3.5 of Chapter 3.

The salient facts about Spanish comparative constructions are as follows:

1 the use of an expletive negative, *no*, is very limited
2 there are major differences between the structural possibilities for comparatives of inequality and equality, which are related to the different comparative clause introducers, *que* and *como*; *que* acts as the marker of comparison
3 a tensed verb form may not normally follow *más/menos . . . que*
4 the phrasal construction involving *de lo que* is essential to allow a tensed verb to appear in the second half of a comparison of inequality.

The salient facts about French comparative constructions are the following:

1 the use of an expletive negative, *ne*, is widespread; *ne* acts as the marker of comparison
2 there are no major differences between the structural possibilities for the comparatives of inequality and equality, which share the same comparative clause introducer, *que*.

These facts produce the range of structures available for the expression of comparison and account for their diversity. However, disparate and somewhat random though the available structures may superficially appear to be, it has been shown that they can be accounted for in a uniform manner by reference to the general constraints on comparison defended here, which require the presence of both a focus-bearing element in the subordinate clause of expressions of comparison and a marker of comparison in comparatives of inequality.

The existence of a tensed verb constraint is most visible in Spanish, given the general inability of a tensed verb to follow *más/menos* ... *que* (except in topicalized structures, available for the expression of partial comparison only, where the clause-initial topicalized category is in a position of strong focus; see pp. 42–50). The phrasal construction, in which the tensed verb occurs in a relative, rather than comparative, clause is thus essential in Spanish as the sole means of allowing a tensed verb to be expressed in most comparatives of inequality. In such constructions (some form of) *lo*, heading the ensuing relative clause, is the focus of comparison, representing the second compared category.

At first sight the comparative constructions of French do not seem to suffer the effects of such a tensed verb constraint, a tensed verb appearing freely in comparative clauses. However, it has been demonstrated that it is the existence of the expletive particle *ne* which masks the effects of the constraint. The general constraint on comparison would indeed apply, but expletive *ne* constitutes a marker of comparison in the subordinate clause of comparatives of inequality, hence 'licensing' the appearance of a tensed verb inasmuch as it serves to identify the *que*-clause as a comparative, rather than a standard declarative, clause. Hence French, unlike Spanish, has little need of a relativized phrasal construction. This, the role of comparison marker, is the true role of expletive *ne* in French comparatives, and has been shown to be unconnected to notions of negativity.

What is being proposed, then, is that as a result of general constraints on the expression of comparison, that there should be a suitable focus element in the subordinate clause of a comparative, and that there should be a marker of comparison in comparatives of inequality, languages must find an 'escape-hatch' to allow a tensed verb to appear in the second half of a comparative of inequality whenever the comparative 'particle' is homonymic with the tensed clause complementizer. The evidence from Spanish and French suggests that there are at least two possible means of achieving this, either by utilizing a relativized phrasal structure, which places the tensed verb outside the comparison, in a relative clause, or by using an expletive particle as a marker of comparison in the comparative subordinate clause. The following discussion of the means available for the expression of comparison in a number of other Romance languages tests this suggestion against the data of Italian, Portuguese, Rumanian, Catalan, Galician, Friulan, Occitan and Walloon. The order in which these languages will be considered is determined by the level of detail of the analysis; no other significance should be attributed to it. Though the examination of comparative constructions in these languages is necessarily limited, it will suffice to show that the previous assertion is correct and that the striking structural differences found can be accounted for quite simply by these constraints.

4.1 COMPARATIVE CONSTRUCTIONS IN ITALIAN

The comparative constructions of formal Standard Italian seem at first sight to resemble the corresponding constructions of Spanish more closely than those of French in that they display marked differences of structure: the comparatives of inequality and the comparative of equality do not share the same clause introducer and consequently have very different syntactic structures. Equally, as in Spanish, the comparatives of inequality allow both phrasal and sentential constructions. Nonetheless, the comparatives of inequality do share one important feature with their French equivalents: the existence of an expletive negative element in the second half of the comparison. However, in Italian, unlike French, the occurrence of this expletive *non* is closely linked to the subjunctive mood. It is this occurrence of *non* + the subjunctive mood which is the salient feature of Italian comparatives of inequality. The equative construction and the comparatives of inequality are thus distinguished at two levels in Italian in that the latter may involve an expletive negative element, as in French, and the two types of comparison involve different clause introducers (or 'comparative particles'), as in Spanish; Italian appears, then, to utilize two markers of comparison, the expletive negative and the comparative particle introducing comparatives of inequality. The reasons for this 'double marking' will be considered on pages 184–6. The Italian constructions might justly be described as sharing some features of both of the other languages, while being identical to neither.

The following discussion of the means available for the expression of comparison in Italian should suffice to indicate that the evidence from Italian supports my thesis as to the role of expletive negative elements in comparison and the operation of a tensed verb constraint in comparatives of inequality. The discussion will consider the constructions of formal standard Italian and will focus

A consideration of other Romance languages

on constructions expressing full, rather than partial, comparison as the available data relate almost exclusively to these. While a more detailed consideration of the constructions available in non-standard, colloquial varieties would no doubt be of great interest, it is beyond the scope of the present study. Nevertheless, it is hoped that the relatively limited scope of this treatment can still furnish more than enough detail to exemplify the points at issue. The various construction types available for the expression of full comparison will be exemplified for both kinds of comparative and the role of expletive *non* in a subset of these constructions discussed. In particular, the interdependent relation holding between the occurrence of *non* and the subjunctive mood will be examined. It will be shown that, as for French, evidence supporting the traditional view of the expletive element as a marker of negation is weak and that there are stronger and more compelling reasons, both language-internal and language-external, for analysing the expletive negative of Italian as a marker of comparison parallel to the expletive *ne* of French. Once again, it is the availability of this marker of comparison which will be held to account for the fact that no tensed verb constraint appears to operate in Italian comparatives of inequality.

4.1.1 Expression of full comparison

The comparatives of inequality

There are three possible construction types:

1 a reduced sentential construction, e.g. (1):

(1) Siamo meno soddisfatti del tuo lavoro che[1] del suo
    We are less satisfied with your work than with his

2 a full sentential construction, e.g. (2):

(2) Maria è più intelligente[2] che tu non creda
    Maria is more intelligent than you think

3 four types of phrasal construction:

(a) an oblique phrasal construction:

(3) E più intelligente di[3] te[4]
    He is more intelligent than you

(b) a relativized phrasal construction involving *di quanto*:

(4) E arrivato più presto di quanto mi aspettavo
    He arrived earlier than I expected

(c) a relativized phrasal construction involving *di quello che*:

(5) Mi diede meno carta di quella che avevo chiesta
    He gave me less paper than I had asked for

(d) a relativized phrasal construction involving *di come*:

(6) E più piccolo di come lo immaginavo
    He is smaller than I imagined

The reduced sentential construction

The construction type exemplified in (1) is a reduced sentential construction, rather than an oblique comparative. Any category may surface after *che*, as a 'survivor' of the reduced clause, whereas in an oblique comparative involving *di*, which is not reduced, only a noun phrase may appear. Lepschy and Lepschy (1988: 113) state that '*che* is used [rather than *di*] when two terms are compared directly', and give the following as examples:

(7) Ho più stampe che quadri
    I have more prints than paintings
(8) Ugo è più furbo che intelligente
    Ugo is more crafty than intelligent
(9) Si comporta vilmente più che prudentemente
    He is behaving in a cowardly rather than in a cautious manner

In fact, these are all examples of partial comparison, with a (necessarily) reduced subordinate clause, hence the appearance of *che*.

Agard and Di Pietro (1965: 81) state that, while both *di* and *che* exist, we can 'take *di* as the norm'. Their 'normal' examples consist entirely of unreduced oblique phrasal comparatives, e.g.:

(10) Giovanni è più alto di Carlo
     Giovanni is taller than Carlo
(11) Io studio più di mio fratello
     I study more than my brother

(12) Paolo parla inglese molto meglio di me
    Paolo speaks English much better than me

They claim that *che* is used when 'the second item is balanced against the very word modified by *più* (or *meno*)', e.g.:

(13) Abbiamo più bicchieri che piatti
    We have more glasses than plates
(14) Giovanni è un ragazzo più stupido che mal educato
    Giovanni is a boy (who is) more stupid than badly educated

Such examples, like (7–9), are reduced sentential expressions of partial comparison. *Che* is also used when 'both items are functioning as attributive complements in a verb phrase' (p. 82), e.g.:

(15) Quell'espressione si usa più nel nord che altrove
    That expression is used more in the north than elsewhere
(16) Fa più freddo a Londra che a Roma
    It is colder in London than in Rome

Examples (15) and (16) are expressions of full comparison. That they are reduced sentential constructions rather than oblique phrasal constructions is evidenced by their reference to the 'verb phrase' – full in the matrix clause, but reduced in the subordinate clause.

Battaglia and Pernicone (1965: 168) also note that when a comparison involves two qualities and only one term of comparison, in other words, when it is a partial comparison, *che*, rather than *di*, is the 'comparative particle', e.g.:

(17) Tu sei più intelligente che studioso
    You are more intelligent than studious

They correctly state that the second clause must have been reduced:

> Questa presenza della congiunzione *che* è dovuta al fatto che in questo caso (quando, cioè, il confronto è fatto fra due qualità) si tratta, più che d'un complemento di comparazione, d'una proposizione comparativa ellittica . . . come se si dicesse: 'Tu sei *più* intelligente *che* (non sia) studioso'.

The use of *di* is ruled out: 'Questa construzione con *che* è l'unica quando la comparazione . . . è stabilita fra due aggettivi che si riferiscono allo stesso soggetto' (p. 501).

Battaglia and Pernicone also refer to the possibility of *non* occurring after *che* in reduced sentential comparatives: 'L'uso di *che non*, al posto del più semplice *che*, è affidato al particolare senso stilistico della frase' (501). As an example they give (18):

(18) Egli è più studioso che non intelligente
    He is more studious than intelligent

They claim that *non* here emphasizes the presumed lack of intelligence. Napoli and Nespor (1977: 86) feel that *non* may appear in reduced sentential contexts 'with marginal acceptability', giving (19a) (their (54)) as an example:

(19) a. ?Maria è più intelligente che non Carlo
    Maria is more intelligent than Carlo

Sentence (19a), unlike (18), is a reduced expression of full, rather than partial, comparison. Napoli and Nespor admit in a footnote that 'many speakers do not accept 54' (p. 94), and feel that partial comparison examples like (18) are more acceptable, though they disagree with Battaglia and Pernicone as to why this should be so. Notice that an alternative version of (19a), (19b), is more acceptable:

(19) b. E più intelligente Maria che non Carlo

In (19b) the postposed subject, *Maria*, and the second object of comparison, *Carlo*, directly precede and follow comparative *che*. As a result, the opposition expressed resembles (18) rather than (19a) in terms of superficial structure, making the contrast appear much more natural than it does in (19a). In (19b) two terms appear to be contrasted, *Maria* with *Carlo*, parallel to the contrast between *studioso* and *intelligente* in (18). Thus (19b) superficially resembles an expression of partial comparison. This is not the case in (19a). I shall return to this point on pages 186-8.

The full sentential construction

The full sentential construction, exemplified in (2), has no direct equivalent in Spanish, though it does in French:

(2) Maria è più intelligente che tu non creda
(20) Marie est plus intelligente que tu ne crois
(21) *María es más inteligente que tú crees

As in French, the Italian sentential construction contains an expletive negative. Unlike French, however, the verb of the subordinate clause is in the subjunctive, rather than the indicative, mood. This is necessarily so in the formal standard language; in colloquial usage, however, the subjunctive mood may be replaced by the indicative.

The expletive *non* Expletive *non* always occurs in full sentential constructions in Italian. Without this element the construction is ungrammatical:

(22) *Maria è più intelligente che tu creda

This would seen to indicate that in Italian expletive *non* plays the same role as the expletive *ne* of French in licensing the appearance of a tensed verb in the subordinate clause. Without *non*, the tensed verb may not appear. The fact that the verb is in the subjunctive mood appears to have no bearing on this; (22) would be equally unacceptable with the verb in the indicative. The tensed verb constraint, then, seems to apply to sentential comparatives of inequality in Italian, just as it does in French and Spanish; but Italian, like French, may escape the effects of this constraint because of the existence of the expletive element *non*, acting as an, in Italian, extra marker of comparison.

The obligatory nature of expletive *non* is not always recognized. Agard and Di Pietro (1965: 82) remark in a footnote, with reference to the following sentence, that 'when the core is finite, the pleonastic *non* is customary':

(23) L'inglese è meno difficile che io non credessi
English is less difficult than I thought

They make no comment on the mood of the finite verb, despite the fact that the subjunctive mood seems to be closely linked to the appearance of expletive *non*, nor do they make clear just what is meant by 'customary', though it is obviously a much weaker claim than that *non* is obligatory. Polizzi (1985: 447) gives the following as one of several examples of sentences expressing comparison:

(24) Ha capito più che non credessi
He has understood more than I thought

Although this full sentential construction is the only one of his examples to include expletive *non* + the subjunctive mood, the fact passes unremarked.

Mittwoch (1974: 40) refers to the use of a negative in 'certain types of comparative clauses in French, Italian and Spanish' as optional.[5] Battaglia and Pernicone (1965: 569) speak of

> l'uso mobile (cioè, a volontà) della congiunzione *non*, che si può esprimere o tacere senza che il senso si alteri . . . l'uso di *non* può considerarsi pleonastico, cioè superfluo; ma la sua presenza nella frase accentua spesso il distacco fra le due proposizioni comparative.

However, none of their examples, including 'optional' *non*, are actually sentential constructions; they are phrasal constructions involving *di quanto* or *di quello che*. Antinucci and Puglielli (1971: 54) also give a number of examples of phrasal comparatives including *non* and consider that 'il *non* in queste construzione è del tutto ridondante, vale a dire che queste frasi sono sinonime delle corrispondenti prive del *non*.'

There may well be reasons to consider the use of *non* in such relativized phrasal constructions as optional, a point to which I shall return on pages 158-64. It is interesting, however, that no example is given of the sentential construction, i.e. containing *più/meno . . . che non* + subjunctive verb, since this might not allow the assertion that the use of *non* is optional to be made.

As for French, the use of *non* is considered to signify some relation of negativity. Hence *non* may occur in a sentence like (2) because the assertion that Maria is intelligent is taken to contradict the listener's belief that she is not intelligent, whence the appearance of *non*. It is a simple matter to demonstrate that, just as in French, this cannot explain the occurrence of *non*. If this reasoning were correct, then (25), with *meno* replacing *più*, should be unacceptable:

(25) Maria è meno intelligente che tu non creda
Maria is less intelligent than you think

Example (25) is fully grammatical. The matrix clause assertion here cannot be said to contradict a belief that Maria is not intelligent; rather, it confirms such a belief. The occurrence of *non*, then, cannot be explained on this basis, any more than could the occurrence of French *ne*. Bergmans (1982: 205) quotes Leys as believing that '*non* in Italian *than*-clauses . . . has become part of the expression of irreality', a suggestion which echoes a common justification for the subjunctive mood in these clauses, and Napoli and Nespor (1976, 1977) present a detailed treatment of *non* in

A consideration of other Romance languages 153

Italian comparatives based on a similar, though more sophisticated, premise. As their data relate almost exclusively to the occurrence of *non* in phrasal, rather than sentential, comparatives, however, I shall consider their analysis in the section on phrasal comparatives.

The subjunctive mood It has been shown that the subjunctive mood usually cooccurs with expletive *non* in sentential comparative constructions. Some grammarians see this choice of mood as meaningful, giving an additional nuance to the comparative. Lepschy and Lepschy (1988: 235) see the choice of the subjunctive in the subordinate clause as stylistic and suggest that, more generally, the subjunctive 'suggests either a nuance of uncertainty or a more formal level'. Von Stechow (1984a: 189) suggests that the subjunctive + negation in Italian comparatives 'somehow marks the unexpected'. If, as I am claiming, the subjunctive mood is linked to the appearance of *non* in such constructions, then, whatever it 'marks', its actual appearance is anything but unexpected.

Napoli and Nespor (1976: 818; 1977: 90) believe that 'comparatives with the indicative ... are semantically distinct from comparatives with the subjunctive'. Battaglia and Pernicone (1965: 568) consider that the subjunctive mood emphasizes the hypothetical nature of the comparison:

> Le comparative di maggioranza e di minoranza hanno il verbo al modo indicativo o al modo congiuntivo, per quanto sia più frequente il secondo; ma il più delle volte l'uso dell'uno o dell'altro modo è affidato alla scelta di chi parla o scrive, il quale userà l'indicativo se l'azione della subordinata comparativa gli sembrerà reale e sicura, mentre ricorrerà al congiuntivo se vorrà sottolineare il carattere ipotetico di essa.

Interestingly, though Battaglia and Pernicone claim that both expletive *non* and the subjunctive mood are optional in comparatives, all the examples they give including expletive *non* also have the subordinate verb in the subjunctive mood. This clearly demonstrates the intimate connection between the two, which they do not explicitly make.

If the subjunctive mood were in any sense meaningful in constructions involving *più/meno che ... non* + subjunctive verb, it might be expected to be optional. This does not seem to be the case. While its use may be optional in phrasal comparatives, it appears to be obligatory in formal Italian in sentential comparatives, i.e. in clauses following the comparative clause introducer *che*, and, crucially, to be dependent upon the occurrence of expletive *non*. Regula and Jernej (1975: 316-17) state that the verb in a comparative construction may be in the indicative or subjunctive mood 'secondo il grado del modo di essere', but give examples in which the subjunctive mood occurs only in sentential comparatives with *non*, the indicative appearing in phrasal constructions. Napoli and Nespor (1977: 67) claim that 'there may be some speakers who use the indicative mood with . . . *non*', a claim repeated in their 1976 article (816), and that '*che* is not totally out with *non* in the indicative' (1977: 81), but they offer no evidence of this possibility, giving the following (their (40c)) as an example:

(26) ?*Maria è più intelligente che non è Carlo
Maria is more intelligent than Carlo is

This level of (un)acceptability scarcely supports the hypothesis that *non* may freely appear after *che* with a verb in the indicative. In fact, they are forced to accept explicitly that *che* must normally be followed by *non* + a subjunctive verb: 'For many Italians the complementizer *che* . . . can appear with the *non* comparatives but not with the comparatives without *non* in the indicative' (p. 83), giving (27a) and (27b) (their (44a,b)) as examples:

(27) a.*Maria è più intelligente che è Carlo
 b. Maria è più intelligente che non sia Carlo

It therefore appears that there is no evidence to suggest either that the subjunctive mood in sentential comparative constructions has any unique meaning of its own or that its occurrence is truly optional. The verb of the subordinate clause in comparatives of this type is obligatorily in the subjunctive mood, except in colloquial language. If the mood of the verb contributes nothing to the interpretation of the construction, why should the indicative be generally unacceptable? The answer to this question is linked to the appearance of the expletive *non*. I have claimed that, for Spanish, such an expletive element is unavailable to act as a marker of comparison since *no* would be indistinguishable from standard sentential negation, hence the unacceptability of full sentential constructions involving *más/menos* . . . *que* in this language; moreover, *que* itself is the marker of comparison, due to its distinctive use in comparatives of inequality only. In French, on the other hand, expletive *ne* is free to play this role since it is not the standard sentential negative, this being expressed by the disjoint negative *ne* . . . *pas*; in addition, *que* is not able to act as the marker of comparison as it is the universal comparative particle. *Non* in Italian, however, is unlike French *ne*, and like Spanish *no*, in that it is identical to the standard sentential negative. Why, then, is Italian *non* able to act unambiguously as an additional marker of comparison, licensing a tensed verb after *che*, while Spanish *no* could not? The answer is precisely because of the mood of the tensed verb; the subjunctive mood may distinguish this *non* clearly from the ordinary sentential negative, which does not trigger the subjunctive. A verb in the indicative mood following comparative *che* is therefore much less common, not because verbal mood contributes to the semantics of the construction, but simply because the clause is then less easily distinguishable from a negated noncomparative clause. By placing the verb of the *che* clause in the subjunctive mood, Italian can circumvent the problematic formal identity of expletive *non* and negative *non*. This is why expletive *non* and the subjunctive mood are so closely linked and mutually dependent in Italian sentential comparatives: *non* licenses the appearance of the tensed verb, while the mood of the verb allows *non* to act as a marker of comparison, clearly distinguishable from the negative. Obviously, *non* with true negative value may cooccur with the subjunctive mood in other constructions. I am not, therefore, suggesting that the subjunctive mood in Italian generally excludes a negative value for *non*, but rather that this value is excluded after comparative *che*; the expletive reading of *non* is compulsory here since the subjunctive verb may not appear without *non*. If it were a true negative, this would be inexplicable.

Some authors do recognize that neither *non* nor the subjunctive mood are truly optional after *più/meno . . . che*, though none seems to realize the significance of this. Stassen (1985: 217) states that 'use of *che* requires the presence of the negative item *non . . .* and the verb . . . in the subjunctive mood'. Seuren (1973: 535; 1984: 123) agrees: 'In formal standard Italian the negation *non* (together with the use of the subjunctive) is required in the *than*-clause whenever its complementizer is the comparative *che*.' Seuren's use of parentheses would seem to indicate, however, that the occurrence of the subjunctive is of little interest or importance.

The sentential construction with *che* is, in general, afforded less consideration in the literature than the relativized phrasal constructions *più/meno . . . di quanto/di quello che*. It is considered to be a highly formal means of expression, the phrasal constructions being preferred as more informal. Von Stechow (1984a: 189) discusses the following examples (his (21a,b) and (22c)):

(28) Luigi è più alto che non pensassi
(29) Luigi è più alto di quello che pensavo
(30) Luigi è più alto di quanto io pensavo
Luigi is taller than I thought

He feels that (29) and (30) are the more common variants, (28) being 'elevated style'. This perceived formality may well be linked to the status of the subjunctive mood in Modern Italian. Lepschy and Lepschy (1988: 81) note that there is, generally, 'a more and more limited use of the subjunctive, replaced in subordinate clauses by the indicative, in conformity with informal spoken style'. Migliorini (1984: 492) also remarks that

> Although Italian still makes use of the subjunctive for a wide variety of purposes, there has been some reduction in the last few decades . . . there is also a tendency in informal speech not to use the subjunctive in contexts where normative grammarians have usually prescribed it.

If the subjunctive mood is increasingly considered to be a marker of formal style, then it is unsurprising that the sentential comparative construction involving *non* + a subjunctive verb should appear formal. Conversely, since, as I have demonstrated, the subjunctive mood may be crucial to these constructions in that it serves to differentiate expletive *non* from the standard negative and hence cannot, at least in formal Italian, be displaced by the indicative mood, the sentential construction will necessarily be less commonly used than the phrasal construction, which does allow the verb to appear in the indicative mood. In this sense, Italian *più/meno . . . che* comparatives are unlike French *plus/moins . . . que* comparatives; the latter do not require a subjunctive verb (as *ne* is clearly distinct from true negation) and so are neither marked as formal nor require a phrasal alternative.

Notice that the fact that the subjunctive mood is less frequent in Modern Italian, and considered a marker of formal style, could have had either of two possible effects on the sentential comparative construction: either the construction might itself be considered formal and become less frequent or the subjunctive might be widely replaced by the indicative, making the construction less formal. That the first of these effects is in fact what has occurred reinforces my thesis that expletive *non* is crucial to the construction to avoid the effects of the tensed verb constraint and license the appearance of a tensed verb. As the sole purpose of the subjunctive mood in the sentential construction is to identify expletive *non* unambiguously as a non-negative marker of comparison, expletive *non* followed by the indicative mood is considerably less likely since *non* might appear to be the standard negative. However, completely impossible is a construction without *non* and with the verb in the indicative mood, as this would fall foul of the tensed verb constraint, due to the identity of comparative *che* and the tensed clause complementizer *che*. Unlike other constructions in Italian, where the subjunctive may be being replaced by the indicative, sentential comparatives must normally contain a verb in the subjunctive mood. As a result, the perceived formality of the subjunctive mood elsewhere in Italian has led to the sentential construction, which usually contains the subjunctive for the reasons I have outlined, being perceived as a formal means of expression.[6] The phrasal constructions, which I shall examine in the following section, will therefore generally be preferred; they do not require a subjunctive verb, as they need not contain an expletive element, this not being required to license the appearance of a tensed verb in what I shall show to be, as in French and Spanish, relative, rather than comparative, clauses.

The phrasal constructions

The oblique phrasal construction The oblique phrasal construction has been exemplified in (3) (repeated for convenience):

(3) E più intelligente di te

That this is a phrasal construction, with *te* the complement of *di*, is shown by the non-subject form of the second person pronoun and the use of *di* rather than *che*, the clause-introducing element. Examples (31) and (32), taken from Regula and Jernej (1975: 257), are further examples of the same construction:

(31) Erano giornate una più bella dell'altra
    They were days each more lovely than the next
(32) Nessuno fu più sapiente di Socrate
    No-one was more wise than Socrates

These contrast with constructions like (15) (repeated), where the category following *che* has 'survived' the reduction of the full tensed clause:

(15) Quell'espressione si usa più nel nord che altrove
    That expression is used more in the north than elsewhere

Notice that the tensed clause following *che* is not obligatorily reduced,[7] any more than the equivalent English gloss is. It is simply that the non-reduced tensed clause would add no further information, making the deleted categories semantically redundant.

Once again, it seems that the situation in Italian falls mid-way between the options available for French and Spanish. It has already been illustrated that French may be analysed as allowing only an oblique phrasal structure in constructions like (3), and Spanish as allowing only a reduced sentential structure. Italian, by contrast, allows both a reduced sentential structure and an oblique phrasal structure in such contexts, a possibility open to this language as a direct result of the availability of two 'comparative particles': *che* and *di*.

The relativized phrasal construction   Three further types of phrasal construction have been exemplified in (4-6) (repeated):

(4) E arrivato più presto di quanto mi aspettavo
(5) Mi diede meno carta di quella che avevo chiesta
(6) E più piccolo di come lo immaginavo

These constructions appear, superficially, equivalent to the Spanish construction with *de lo que*, and the French construction with *que ce que*. They display no gap in the second half of the comparison. In (5), the sequence *quella che* + tensed verb, following the comparative subordinator *di*, looks like the sequence pronoun – *che* + tensed verb found in relative constructions. Examples (4) and (6) are parallel, *quanto* and *come* acting as free or headless relatives.

These constructions of Italian, then, seem to pattern very much as the Spanish and French constructions, involving a restrictive relative clause in the second half of the comparison, headed by a relative pronoun (which is the complement of *di*).

It was pointed out in the previous chapter that the French phrasal construction, unlike its Spanish equivalent, is not required as a means of escaping the tensed verb constraint, since the full sentential construction, with expletive *ne*, is available. As a result, the acceptability of constructions involving *plus/moins . . . que ce que* is variable, the sentential construction normally being preferred. The Spanish *más/menos . . . de lo que* construction, on the other hand, is the only available option for the inclusion of a tensed verb in comparatives of inequality, due to the lack of a sentential construction (the result of the unavailability of an expletive element parallel to *ne/non*).

It might be expected, therefore, that in Italian, as in French, the existence of the sentential construction *più/meno . . . che non* + tensed verb would lead to the marginal acceptability of phrasal constructions, as they are not required to escape the tensed verb constraint. Examples (4) and (5), for example, could easily be expressed as sentential constructions:

(33) E arrivato più presto che non mi aspettassi
(34) Mi diede meno carta che non ne avessi chiesta

This is not, however, the case. In fact, quite the reverse appears to hold true: the phrasal constructions are usually preferred, due to the perceived formality of the sentential construction. This formality, as indicated above, appears to be linked to the use of the subjunctive in sentential constructions. So, although Italian has the same options as French, namely, both relativized phrasal constructions and a sentential construction with an expletive negative acting as a marker of comparison, the level of acceptability of these constructions is not the same. In French the sentential option is the norm, the phrasal construction having (usually) only marginal acceptability. In Italian, while both options are fully acceptable, a phrasal construction is often preferred. The lower frequency of the sentential construction in Italian might thus be directly ascribed to the fact that its expletive negative, *non*, is non-distinct from the standard negative, unlike French *ne*, since it is this formal identity which, I have argued, may necessitate the use of the subjunctive mood as a differentiating device; the perceived formality of the subjunctive mood, however, then reduces the frequency of use of the sentential construction.

Although the relativized phrasal constructions exemplified do not contain expletive *non*, it seems that they may. Equally, the verb of the relative clause appears to be optionally subjunctive. However, there seems to be little agreement in the literature on just what permutations are allowed and where.

Lepschy and Lepschy (1988: 113) state that 'comparative clauses can be constructed in a variety of ways', illustrating both *non* and the subjunctive mood used optionally in *più/meno . . . di quanto* constructions (though they do not indicate whether these options are linked) and optional use of the subjunctive mood in *più/meno . . . di quello che/di come* constructions, without *non*. They give no indication of any perceived differences between these various options, except to suggest (p. 236) that (35) is more 'informal' than (36):

(35) E più grande di quanto mi aspettavo
(36) E più grande di quanto mi aspettassi
   He is bigger than I expected

Agard and Di Pietro (1965), on the other hand, make no mention at all of the relativized phrasal constructions, while Polizzi (1985: 447) illustrates only the sentential construction and the *più/meno . . . di quanto* construction, e.g.:

(37) Era più onesto di quanto lo sono gli altri
   He was more honest than the others are
(38) Possedeva meno sicurezza di quanto ne dimostrava
   He had less sureness than he showed
(39) Ha capito più che non credessi
   He has understood more than I thought

In (37) and (38), unlike (39), there is no expletive *non* and the verbs are in the indicative mood. No mention is made of the significance of the expletive element and/or the subjunctive mood, nor are they mentioned as being optional in the phrasal examples. Constructions involving *più/meno . . . di quello che/di come* are not referred to.

Stassen (1985: 217) goes further and states that 'An alternative formation of Italian comparative clauses involves the use of the complex comparative particle *di quello che*. In this case the verb in the clause is in the Indicative Mood, and the negative item *non* is no longer present.'[8] His examples (86a–c) are as follows:

(40) Gianni è più grande che non pensassi
(41) *Gianni è più grande di quello che non pensassi[9]
(42) Gianni è più grande di quello che pensavo
   Gianni is bigger than I thought

He does not illustrate the variant which includes the subjunctive mood and excludes *non*, permitted by Lepschy and Lepschy, but does not seem prepared to allow it, as the quote indicates. Moreover, he does not refer at all to the *più/meno . . . di quanto* construction; this is exactly the reverse of the picture given in Polizzi (1985). Von Stechow (1984a: 189) gives the following as illustration of the range of options available (his (21a,b) and (22c)):

(43) Luigi è più alto che non pensassi
(44) Luigi è più alto di quello che pensavo
(45) Luigi è più alto di quanto io pensavo
   Luigi is taller than I thought

He considers the phrasal constructions illustrated in (44) and (45) to be 'the more common ones'. In (44) and (45) there is no expletive *non* and the verbs are in the indicative mood. Von Stechow gives no indication that either of these two elements is possible in such phrasal constructions.

Seuren (1984: 123) states categorically:

> In formal standard Italian the negation *non* (together with the use of the subjunctive) is required in the *than*-clause whenever its complementizer is the comparative *che*.[10] But when the clause is relativized by means of *di quello che* there is no negation and no subjunctive.

He does not mention the construction involving *più/meno . . . di quanto*.

Muller (1983: 313) gives an example of the *più/meno . . . di quanto* construction including both *non* and the subjunctive:

(46) Gianni è più alto di quanto non sia Mario
    Gianni is taller than Mario is

He states that in Italian 'le verbe est en principe au subjonctif.'

Apart from Lepschy and Lepschy (1988), only Battaglia and Pernicone (1965: 568–9) allow all four possibilities (one sentential, three relativized phrasal) for the expression of a comparison of inequality, listing *più . . . che*, *più . . . di come*, *più . . . di quanto* and *più . . . di quello che*. However, unlike Lepschy and Lepschy, who give no examples of expletive *non* in *più . . . di quello che* comparatives, they consider the use of expletive *non* and the subjunctive mood to be fully optional; for them, the use of *non* emphasizes the opposition between the two clauses, while the use of the subjunctive stresses the hypothetical nature of the comparison. Thus they allow all of the following:

(47) Abbiamo studiato più che tu non voglia ammettere
    We have studied more than you want to admit
(48) Ha parlato meno di quel che prevedevamo
    He spoke less than we expected
(49) S'è comportato peggio di come avevamo pensato
    He behaved worse than we had thought
(50) a. Il viaggio fu più lungo di quanto si pensasse
    b. Il viaggio fu più lungo di quanto si pensava
    The journey was longer than one thought
(51) a. La serata riuscì più divertente di quel che fosse stato previsto
    b. La serata riuscì più divertente di quel ch'era stato previsto

The soirée was more entertaining than had been expected
(52) a. Egli si è compromesso più di quanto si creda
b. Egli si è compromesso più di quanto non si creda
He has committed himself more than one thinks
(53) a. Abbiamo agito peggio di quel che tu possa immaginare
b. Abbiamo agito peggio di quel che tu non possa immaginare
We have acted worse than you can imagine

Sentence (47) illustrates the standard sentential construction with *non* + the subjunctive. Examples (48), (49), (50b) and (51b) exemplify the phrasal construction without expletive *non* and with the verb in the indicative. Examples (50a), (51a), (52a) and (53a) show phrasal constructions with the verb in the subjunctive mood but excluding expletive *non*, while (52b) and (53b) include both expletive *non* and the subjunctive mood. The only possibility which Battaglia and Pernicone implicitly do not allow is that of expletive *non* appearing in a phrasal comparative without the subjunctive mood. Hence, although they do not explicitly note this, the connection I have mooted between *non* and the subjunctive mood is supported by their examples.

Finally, Napoli and Nespor (1976; 1977) focus their analysis on the *più/meno . . . di quanto* construction, with optional *non* + subjunctive, completely ignoring the other phrasal constructions.

The picture with regard to the phrasal constructions, then, is very unclear. Authors differ widely as to which permutations of *non* and the subjunctive mood they will allow, if any. There seems, however, to be a general consensus (excluding those who totally disallow both *non* and the subjunctive in phrasal constructions) that

1 the sentential construction *più/meno . . . che* must normally include both *non* and the subjunctive
2 the *più/meno . . . di quanto* construction is the most common of the various phrasal possibilities and may (though it need not) include both *non* and the subjunctive mood.

Differences then arise as to the significance of these options, whether semantic or pragmatic. Napoli and Nespor present a detailed defence of a pragmatic analysis of expletive *non* in Italian comparatives, which will be discussed on pages 164–76.

This apparent confusion over what combinations of *non* and the subjunctive mood may be allowed in phrasal comparatives may seem to contrast sharply with the universal agreement that the sentential construction must normally include both *non* and a subjunctive verb. In fact, my thesis as to the role of *non* and the associated subjunctive mood in Italian comparatives makes this entirely predictable. I have claimed that the function of expletive *non* in sentential comparatives is to act as a marker of comparison, licensing the appearance of a tensed verb and saving the construction from the effects of the tensed verb constraint, exactly parallel to French *ne*. I have also claimed that the subjunctive mood of the verb has no semantic import, serving simply to differentiate this expletive *non* from true negation, with which it is isomorphic. This explains the obligatory nature of both elements in *più/meno . . . che* constructions in formal Italian. In phrasal constructions, however, there is no comparative subordinate clause, the clause headed by *quanto/quello/come* being a relative clause. As such, a constraint such as the tensed verb constraint, operating on comparative clauses, will not be applicable, just as it does not apply to French *plus/moins . . . que ce que* constructions or Spanish *más/menos . . . de lo que* constructions. Hence the phrasal constructions do not require the presence of *non* (+ associated subjunctive mood) to license the verb of the relative clause and make them acceptable. However, just as has been shown to be the case in French for expletive *ne*, Italian expletive *non*, as a result of its requirement as a marker of comparison in sentential constructions, has been imported by analogy, together with the subjunctive mood, into the phrasal constructions. This is so even though it is not actually required. The fact that the sentential construction is increasingly regarded as rather formal could only be expected to strengthen this tendency. It follows quite naturally, then, that expletive *non* in phrasal constructions should be so unstable and opinions as to its status so uncertain. *Non* + the subjunctive mood are optional in Italian phrasal comparatives because they are not required to license the appearance of a tensed verb; phrasal comparatives containing *non* + a subjunctive verb may therefore be perceived as being more formal than the straightforward construction excluding *non* and containing an indicative verb. *Non* + subjunctive mood are obligatory in the sentential construction to avoid the effects of the tensed verb constraint, *non* serving as an extra and essential marker of comparison. Their appearance in the phrasal constructions is due to this close association of expletive *non* with the concept of comparison. The fact that it is not actually required, however, necessarily leads to some confusion as to its level of acceptability. It does not in any way alter the meaning of the construction in which it appears, as is so often claimed. If it did, it would be difficult to explain why it should be obligatory in sentential constructions, but optional in phrasal constructions. Such a claim is tantamount to stating that alternatives like (54), (55) and (56) have different meanings, which they clearly do not:

(54) Il viaggio fu più lungo che non si pensasse
(55) Il viaggio fu più lungo di quanto si pensava
(56) Il viaggio fu più lungo di quanto non si pensasse
 The journey was longer than one thought

If *non* adds something to the meaning of (56), why is it that that 'something' cannot be removed from (54) without causing it to become relatively unacceptable?:

(57) ??Il viaggio fu più lungo che si pensasse

If *non* serves to negate some presumed presupposition, why is it possible to choose not to negate the presupposition in a phrasal construction (as in (55)), but difficult to do so in a sentential construction (as in (57))?

The function of *non* in Italian comparatives is exactly parallel to the function of *ne* in French comparatives. It is simply the added complication of the subjunctive mood, the function of which has been explained, and the associated perception of 'formality', which serves to confuse the picture by making the phrasal construction, in which these elements are purely optional, more common than the sentential construction, in which the role of *non* is perhaps easier to analyse. Nonetheless, I would claim that Italian expletive *non* is nothing other than a marker of comparison, licensing the appearance of a tensed verb in the sentential construction and appearing by analogy in the phrasal construction.

'Illogical' *non*

A presuppositional analysis In two virtually identical papers, Napoli and Nespor (1976; 1977) consider the function of expletive *non* in Italian comparatives, basing their analysis on the *più/meno . . . di quanto* and *più/meno . . . che* constructions. As their analysis is the most detailed in the literature, I will consider it in some detail, concentrating on their 1977 paper. Their hypothesis is that the inclusion of superficially 'illogical' *non* depends on the presence of certain pragmatic presuppositions: '*Non* appears when the speaker is assuming, but has not been told explicitly and therefore is not sure, that the assertion of the comparative is contradictory to some previously held belief – most often the belief of the listener, but not always' (1977: 62). This is reminiscent of Von Stechow's (1984a: 189) notion of 'unexpectedness' (see pages 153–7). The relevance, if any, of the subjunctive mood is not considered.

It is clear that this definition of the circumstances in which *non* may appear is somewhat vaguely formulated. Nonetheless, the assertion that the expletive element serves to negate some previously held assumption echoes similar explanations for the appearance of expletive *ne* in French comparatives. I do not believe that there is any more evidence for this assertion in the case of Italian than there is in French, as I hope to demonstrate.

Napoli and Nespor (1977: 63) set up the following context to illustrate the operation of their pragmatic principle (their context 2):

(58) Dario: Carlo è così intelligente che dubito che Maria possa vincerlo a scacchi
Carlo is so intelligent that I doubt that Mary can beat him at chess
Paolo: Ma ti sbagli! Maria è più intelligente di quanto non sia/è Carlo e potrebbe vincerlo senza molti sforzi
But you're wrong! Maria is more intelligent than Carlo is and she could beat him with little effort

They consider both versions of the comparative to be acceptable: if *non* is included, this signifies that Paolo assumes that Dario thinks that Maria is less intelligent than Carlo, thus *non* is used as he is contradicting Dario's belief; without *non*, Paolo is speaking more assertively and

> taking Dario's remark as equivalent to an explicit evaluation of Maria's intelligence . . . . Thus there are two possible responses here, with differing amounts of intensity on the part of the speaker's attitude towards his contradiction of the listener's evaluation of Maria and Carlo
>
> (1977: 63)

The definition of a suitable context for *non* has now become more complex: it is not just a question of whether the comparison negates some previously held assumption, but also of how the speaker views this contradiction. It is difficult to see how such an all-embracing description of a suitable context for *non* could ever fail to be applicable to any context, since presumably the 'intensity' of the speaker's attitude could be adjusted to fit the choice made as to whether or not to include *non*. This is, admittedly, a general problem faced by pragmatic explanations.

Notice, moreover, that if *più* is replaced by *meno* in a similar context, we would not expect *non* to be possible, as Paolo could not now be said to be contradicting Dario's previously held belief (that Maria is unintelligent); in other words, if Paolo's response to Dario were as follows:

(59) Paolo: Non ti sbagli! Maria è meno intelligente di quanto non sia/è Carlo e non potrebbe vincerlo senza molti sforzi
You're not wrong! Maria is less intelligent than Carlo is and she couldn't beat him without a lot of effort

The inclusion of *non* seems just as possible in this context, despite the fact that, far from contradicting Dario's belief about Maria's intelligence, Paolo is now agreeing with him.

Another, similar, context is illustrated (their context 4):

(60) Dario: Non ho capito per niente quest'ultima lezione, comunque non credo che valga la pena di chiedere aiuto a Maria
I didn't understand this last lesson at all, but I don't believe it's worth the trouble to ask Mary for help
Paolo: Secondo me fai male, dovresti chiederglielo. Maria è più intelligente di quanto tu non creda/(?)credi
As I see it you're making a mistake, you should ask her. Mary is more intelligent than you believe

They explain the acceptability judgements as follows:

> Here Dario is not explicit as to his evaluation of Maria's intellect. Thus Paolo assumes that she is more intelligent than Dario thinks, and uses *non* accordingly. However, if Paolo takes Dario's remark as a strong indication of his evaluation of her intellect, then he need not use *non*.
> (1977: 64)

Their claim, then, is that

> *non* appears when there is a bit of uncertainty or indefiniteness about the speaker's assumption. But it cannot appear if there is absolutely no justification for the speaker's assumption ... or if the speaker need not assume anything since explicit statements of the listener's opinion have been made.
> (1977: 64)

A consideration of other Romance languages 167

The impossibility of limiting such a wide definition (how much is 'a bit of uncertainty'?) has already been mentioned. Napoli and Nespor's explanation of the optionality of *non* rests heavily on the speaker's subjective evaluation of the context, but surely this is not predictable. Their analysis is 'after the fact'; it attempts to explain why *non* has been used in a specific context, but cannot predict when *non* will be selected. In fact, since *non* appears by analogy with the sentential construction, and is not required, its unpredictability is, so to speak, entirely predictable.

Non in questioned comparatives Napoli and Nespor go on (1977: 64–5) to point out that *non* may not appear in questioned comparatives, contrasting the following (their (7–9)):

(61) a. E più intelligente di quanto è Carlo?
b.*E più intelligente di quanto non sia Carlo?
Is she more intelligent than Carlo is?
(62) a. Non è più intelligente di quanto è Carlo?
b.*Non è più intelligente di quanto non sia Carlo?
Isn't she more intelligent than Carlo is?
(63) a.*E più intelligente di quanto tu credi?
b.*E più intelligente di quanto tu non creda?
Is she more intelligent than you think?
(64) a. E più intelligente di quanto tu credevi?
b. E più intelligente di quanto tu non credessi?
Is she more intelligent than you thought?
(65) a. E più intelligente di quanto lui crede?
b. E più intelligente di quanto lui non creda?
Is she more intelligent than he believes?

According to them, the explanation for the various acceptability judgements[11] is as follows. Example (61b) is unacceptable because the speaker would be both asking for information and appearing to contradict the speaker's belief at the same time; however, notice that if (61) were constructed as a sentential comparative, the opposite judgements would hold true:

(66) a.*E più intelligente che è Carlo?
b. E più intelligente che non sia Carlo?

The reason for the low acceptability of (61b) cannot, therefore, be semantic, as they claim, since the semantics of (66) must be identical.

Sentence (62b) they consider unacceptable because the speaker appears simultaneously to expect the listener to agree (matrix *non*) and to contradict him (embedded *non*). Once again, constructing (62) as a sentential comparative would lead to different judgements:

(67) a.*Non è più intelligente che è Carlo?
     b.?Non è più intelligente che non sia Carlo?

Sentence (67b) is fully grammatical. It is, however, an unlikely construction since expletive *non* following a negated matrix clause results in a sentence which is difficult to process – there appear to be too many negatives. This is also precisely what is wrong with (62b), and the reason why a phrasal construction like (62a), which need not contain expletive *non*, will be preferred.

The unacceptability of (63a) is explained on the grounds that 'one does not normally ask someone for a confirmation of something they do not believe' (p. 65). In fact, (63a) and (63b) are both out for this reason; it is simply an illogical question. Obviously, it is possible to imagine circumstances in which such questions might be appropriate and therefore logical in context. Nonetheless, it remains the case that, under normal circumstances, these questions appear strange. Whether or not *non* is present is irrelevant. The question would be just as unlikely constructed as a sentential comparative:

(68) ??E più intelligente che tu non creda?

Sentence (64a) is said to be acceptable because 'it is perfectly natural to ask the listener to confirm whether or not a past belief was correct', and (64b) because 'it is also natural to ask him now to confirm the opposite of what we expect he used to believe' (p. 65). In fact, (64a) and (64b) are simply alternatives, the version in (64b) being constructed by analogy with the sentential construction. Example (64) contrasts with (63), not in terms of the acceptability of expletive *non*, but simply because the past tense of the subordinate clause makes the question a logical one.

Exactly the same holds true of (65). They claim that the version in (65a) asks whether someone is more intelligent than a third person believes, while the version in (65b) asks whether someone is more intelligent than the questioner expects a third person to believe. This is not the case. The versions in (65a) and (65b) are simply alternatives, with identical meanings.

Napoli and Nespor sum up this examination of expletive *non* in questions thus:

> If the distribution of *non* were determined by factors other than semantic ones, it would be very difficult to explain the

acceptability [of (64b) and (65b) in contrast with (61b) and (62b)]. But with semantic criteria, one can explain the distribution . . . in a simple way.

(1977: 65)

As I have shown, however, it is not at all difficult to explain these acceptability judgements, without recourse to semantic criteria. Expletive *non* may or may not appear in phrasal comparatives, by analogy with the sentential construction, but it is less likely to appear in contexts where it will make the sentence difficult to process, i.e. in questions and/or after a negative matrix. As it is not required, it may be dispensed with. If semantic criteria lay behind these acceptability judgements, we would expect them to apply equally to the sentential construction. As I have illustrated, they do not. Therefore, either the semantics of the sentential construction and the relativized phrasal construction differ, which is highly unlikely, or the restrictions on the use of *non* in relativized phrasal comparatives are the direct result of its optional status, as the result of an analogical process, in these constructions.

***Non* after a negative matrix** Napoli and Nespor also consider the acceptability of expletive *non* in the subordinate clause of a comparative construction, the matrix of which is itself negated. They claim (p. 66) that in such a context 'special *non*', as they term it, is not acceptable, giving as examples the following (their (13a–c)):

(69) *Maria non è più intelligente di quanto non sia Carlo
    Maria is not more intelligent than Carlo is
(70) *Maria non è più intelligente di quanto tu non creda
    Maria is not more intelligent than you think
(71) *Maria non è più intelligente di quanto non creda Dario
    Maria is not more intelligent than Dario thinks

The reasons they adduce for this are complex. Example (70) is unacceptable because the speaker's assertion is in agreement with the listener's belief (that Maria is not intelligent), therefore *non* is excluded on semantic grounds. In (71), the same reasoning applies, as the speaker does not expect to contradict Dario's belief (that Maria is not intelligent). Example (69), on the other hand, is unacceptable because

if the presupposition were that someone expected Carlo to be more intelligent than Maria and that the assertion of the inequality would contradict this belief or expectation, then *non* [in the subordinate clause] could be used. But here the assertion is that Maria, in fact, is not more intelligent than Carlo. Thus, rather than contradicting the belief (presupposed to be held by someone) which *non* would reveal, the assertion agrees with it. So in (13a) [69] the semantic environment for *non* is not met, and it cannot (and does not) appear.

(1977: 66)

This complex semantic justification for the unacceptability of (69) ignores the fact that the unacceptability of (69–71) can be explained on the simple grounds that too many negatives in a comparative make it difficult to process, even if in reality only the first negative is a true negative. Napoli and Nespor claim, however, that 'regular *non*' may appear after a negative matrix clause, using the following (their (14) and (15)) as illustrations:

(72) Io non sono stata all'estero più giorni di quanti Maria non è andata a lavorare
I have not been abroad more days than Maria has not gone to work

(73) *Io non sono stata all'estero più giorni di quanti Maria non sia andata a lavorare
I have not been abroad more days than Maria has gone to work

They believe that (73) is unacceptable for the same reasons as (69) and that (72) is fully acceptable. It is far from obvious, however, that (72) is fully acceptable and, specifically, that it is very much more acceptable than (73). Both sentences are difficult to interpret. The only difference between them is that the expletive *non* of (73) need not appear, being optional, and so would tend to be excluded from the environment of a negative matrix clause. In (72), however, the *non* in the subordinate clause is a true negative and so cannot be excluded wihout changing the meaning of the sentence. It still suffers, nonetheless, from the level of unacceptability normally associated with having more than one negative in a comparison, whether expletive or not.

In fact, Napoli and Nespor do realize that semantic grounds are not required to explain this distribution of *non*, but reject the notion that there might be 'a constraint which says that our *non* cannot appear if the matrix verb is negated' (p. 67). According to them, this is not possible since the difference between expletive *non* and the true negative 'is not apparent'. The difference is, of course, clearly apparent here: expletive *non* appears with the verb in the subjunctive mood. They circumvent this by claiming that 'there may be some speakers who use the indicative mood with our *non*' (p. 67), a statement which turns out to amount to the less than convincing assertion that 'no-one has told us they would say [a phrasal comparative with expletive *non* and an indicative verb] . . . yet everyone thinks they might have heard someone else say it' (p. 80). As I have already indicated, there is evidence that expletive *non* may sometimes appear with a verb in the indicative mood, particularly in colloquial speech. Nonetheless, in standard formal Italian *non* and the subjunctive are strongly linked. This is what my analysis would predict. In addition, they offer the following sentences (their (13a–c)) as proof that the constraint in question does not involve the actual presence of *non* itself:

(74) a.*Maria non è più intelligente di quanto sia Carlo
b.*Maria non è più intelligente di quanto tu creda
c.*Maria non è più intelligente di quanto creda Dario
Maria is not more intelligent than Carlo is/you think/Dario thinks

Since expletive *non* is not present in (74a–c), they argue, it cannot explain the ungrammaticality. In fact, (74a–c) may appear unacceptable precisely because there is no justification for the subjunctive mood of the verb, the purpose of whose mood is to distinguish a preceding expletive *non* from the true negative. Without expletive *non*, the verb might be expected to appear in the indicative mood. It is Napoli and Nespor's failure to accept the clear link between expletive *non* and the subjunctive mood which leads them to reject the simple and obvious explanation for the distribution of expletive *non* in negated comparatives in favour of a highly complex and unsystematic semantic justification. It seems to me that the position is as follows, at least in the formal language. The Italian translation of, for example, *Maria is more intelligent than Dario thinks* must contain expletive *non* + a subjunctive verb if it is constructed as a sentential comparative:

(75) Maria è più intelligente che non creda Dario

It may optionally include *non* + a subjunctive verb, by analogy, when constructed as a phrasal comparative:

(76) a. Maria è più intelligente di quanto non creda Dario

b. Maria è più intelligente di quanto crede Dario

However, the possibilities are as follows for the negated statement *Maria is not more intelligent than Dario thinks*:

(77) ?Maria non è più intelligente che non creda Dario
(78) Maria non è più intelligente di quanto crede Dario
(79) ?*Maria non è più intelligente di quanto non creda Dario
(80) *Maria non è più intelligente di quanto creda Dario

Sentence (77) is grammatical, but the two negatives may make it difficult to interpret. Sentence (78) is fully acceptable. Example (79) is worse than (77) just because the cooccurrence of two negatives may be avoided in the phrasal construction, as shown by (78). Sentence (80) appears unacceptable because the verb is not actually required to be in the subjunctive mood, since expletive *non* is not present. Semantic criteria are not required to explain these judgements.[12]

Possible combinations of *non* + verbal mood Napoli and Nespor give the following (their (35a–d) and (36a–d)) to illustrate the preferences that hold for the expression of positive phrasal comparatives (1977: 80):

(81) a. Maria è più intelligente di quanto tu credi
b.*? Maria è più intelligente di quanto tu non credi
c. Maria è più intelligente di quanto tu non creda
d.(?)Maria è più intelligente di quanto tu creda
(82) a. Maria è più intelligente di quanto è Carlo
b.?* Maria è più intelligente di quanto non è Carlo
c. Maria è più intelligente di quanto non sia Carlo
d.(?)Maria è più intelligente di quanto sia Carlo

They consider (81b) and (82b) to be possible though, as already mentioned, they present no evidence for this. It is, however, essential for their analysis that this should be possible. In fact, these judgements fully support my thesis as to the possible occurrence of *non* in Italian phrasal comparatives. The (a) examples are fine, as they contain straightforward relative clauses, without expletive *non* or the subjunctive mood. Similarly, the (c) examples are fully acceptable, as, by analogy with the sentential construction, they contain expletive *non* and a subjunctive verb. The (b) examples are less generally acceptable as in Standard Italian expletive *non* requires a subjunctive verb to differentiate it from the true negative. The (d) examples, with the verb in the subjunctive mood, but without expletive *non*, are better than the (b) examples in that they do not contain a standard negative *non* where the expletive would be required (as appears to be the case in (81b) and (82b)), but not fully acceptable as there is no reason for the verb to appear in the subjunctive mood if expletive *non* is not present. In both examples the worst variant is the one containing expletive *non* followed by the indicative. This points up the importance of the subjunctive mood here, not as a semantically relevant option, but as a device for differentiating expletive *non*.

Relativized phrasal versus sentential comparatives

Napoli and Nespor (1977: 81) point out that 'subjunctive comparative clauses with *non* can be introduced by the complementizer *che* as well as by *di quanto*, while indicative comparatives without *non* can be introduced only by *di quanto*.' In this they fail to realize that it is the less common sentential, and not the phrasal, construction which is the source of the analogical extension of *non*. They also point out that in the sentential construction '*che* . . . is totally out without *non* in the indicative', describing this conclusion as 'unenlightening' (p. 81). In fact, it is extremely enlightening once it is accepted that *non* must appear in the sentential construction to license the appearance of a tensed verb and avoid the effects of the tensed verb constraint. The *di quanto* constructions are not subject to this constraint since they contain a relative clause, and hence are acceptable without *non* and with a verb in the indicative mood.

They claim that relativized phrasal comparatives may contain a subjunctive verb without expletive *non* and that, while this is marginal with present-tense verbs, 'in the past tense . . . the deletion of *non* is perfectly acceptable for many speakers we have questioned' (p. 82). They give the following (their (41a)) as an example:

(83) Maria è più intelligente di quanto (non) fosse suo fratello a quell'età
Maria is more intelligent than her brother was at that age

Napoli and Nespor quote Bolinger as suggesting that this is possible 'when the speaker allows for the possibility that he might be mistaken about his presumption of other people's opinions' and that 'the possibility of having mistaken a past opinion is stronger than the possibility of having mistaken a present one' (p. 82). I do not see how this can be considered explanatory. However, it is possible that a sentence like (83) might seem preferable to a present-tense version, like (84), simply because the past tense of the verb, disregarding its mood, together with the extra information *a quell'età*, justifies a full clause:

(84) Maria è più intelligente di quanto ?(non) sia suo fratello
Maria is more intelligent than her brother is

The present-tense version in (84) could be replaced by the oblique phrasal construction:

(85) Maria è più intelligente di suo fratello

Any perceived improvement, therefore, in (83) as compared with (84) is unrelated to the subjunctive mood of the verb.

In a parallel fashion, they claim that *non* with the indicative sounds better in the past tense than in the present, giving the following (their (42a) and (42b)) as examples:

(86) ?*Maria è più intelligente di quanto non è suo fratello
(87) ?(?)Maria è più intelligente di quanto non era suo fratello a quell'età

Both of these sentences are generally unacceptable. Once again, if (87) sounds slightly better, this is simply because it is more informative than (86), providing more contrasts with the matrix in the second half of the comparison. In fact, Napoli and Nespor admit that they have not found speakers who would produce these sentences (1977: 82).

Napoli's and Nespor's conclusions

Napoli and Nespor (1976: 833) attempt to relate the sentential and relativized phrasal constructions syntactically by positing a number of context-dependent deletion rules in deep structure, as well as the existence of an 'abstract S' to account for the insertion of expletive *non* and the subjunctive mood of the verb; the details of these claims, framed in terms of the syntactic model current at the time, need not concern us. However, even in terms of the syntactic theory current at the time of their analysis, their claims are untenable, as they come close to admitting (1977: 88), referring to the 'serious theoretical implications' of their proposals. Their analysis fails syntactically, as well as being semantically dubious. While they realize that there must be a connection between the sentential construction and the relativized phrasal construction, they fail to see what that connection is. They insist that *non* 'is not pleonastic, but rather a bona fide negative' (1977: 88), used 'when certain pragmatic presuppositions are present' (1976: 812). This is to disregard the fact that when the more formal sentential construction is used, *non* will always occur. They appear, therefore, to be claiming that the presuppositions present in the context of use of a comparative can vary according to the construction used; that a speaker using the *più/meno . . . che* construction automatically assumes that her assertion is contrary to the listener's beliefs, since expletive *non* will always be present, while the same speaker using the *più/meno . . . di quanto* construction may or may not make this assumption, depending on whether or not she chooses to include optional *non*. Surely the difference between the two construction types can only be one of style/register. Napoli and Nespor claim that expletive *non* appears when there is some uncertainty about the speaker's assumptions, but that 'the [phrasal] comparative without *non* can appear in all contexts' (1976: 813). If expletive *non* is triggered by certain presuppositions, how can it be possible for it to be absent when these presuppositions are present? The presupposition analysis does not work, any more than it did for French.

Napoli and Nespor also try to relate the expletive *non* of comparatives to *non* appearing in other contexts: 'If our analysis of *non* is correct, its appearance depends on the presuppositions of the speaker . . . . Therefore we would expect to find other syntactic environments in which it can appear. And in fact, we do' (1976: 835–6). The constructions they consider are as follows (their (88–91)):

(88) Chissà (a) che ti sposi/(b) che non ti sposi
 Who knows if he'll marry you/if he might not marry you
(89) Non sono sicura (a) se io debba/(b) se io non debba vederlo lunedì
 I'm not sure if I should/shouldn't see him on Monday
(90) Ci domandiamo (a) se dobbiamo/(b) se non dobbiamo riconsiderare la nostra analisi di *non*
 We wonder if we should/shouldn't reconsider our analysis of *non*
(91) Chissà (a) se vale/(b) se non valga la pena (di) comprarlo
 Who knows if it's worth/if it's not worth the trouble to buy it

In (88–90) the subjunctive is used with or without *non*. In other words, they are unrelated. This is quite unlike the case with the expletive *non* in comparatives, which must generally appear with a subjunctive verb. Only in (91) does *non* seem to cooccur obligatorily with the subjunctive, but the verb might just as easily be in the indicative mood, as shown by the acceptability of (92):

(92) Chissà se non vale la pena (di) comprarlo

These instances of *non*, therefore, interesting though they may be, cannot be related to the occurrence of expletive *non* in expressions of comparison of inequality.

Napoli and Nespor's discussion is rich in interesting data. However, their analysis entirely misses the point, possibly because they take the relativized phrasal construction as their starting point. *Non* appears optionally in the phrasal construction, together with an associated subjunctive verb, by analogy with its occurrence in the sentential construction. In the latter, however, its appearance is obligatory since it acts as a marker of comparison which serves to license the appearance of the tensed verb in a comparative subordinate clause. It is not obligatory in the phrasal construction as the tensed verb of the relative clause may appear with impunity. Its inclusion by analogy can be explained by the fact that, while the sentential construction is perceived as stylistically formal, expletive *non*, as the marker of comparison, may be 'imported' into the equivalent phrasal construction. This provides a simple and explanatory account of the structural possibilities available. Moreover, it is additionally motivated by language-external factors, specifically the parallels with French. The analysis of Napoli and Nespor, by contrast, is largely unmotivated and non-explanatory, and relies on *ad hoc* theoretical leaps of imagination.

The comparative of equality

According to Lepschy and Lepschy (1988: 114) a comparative of equality may be constructed using the following options: *tanto . . . quanto/così . . . come/altrettanto . . . quanto*. They give the following as examples of the first and third of these options:

(93) Riesce tanto nella pittura quanto nella scultura
    He is as good at painting as at sculpture
(94) Non ho tanti libri quanti mio fratello
    I haven't as many books as my brother
(95) E uno scrittore altrettanto noto all'estero quanto in Italia

He is a writer who is as well known abroad as in Italy
(96) C'erano tanti uomini quante donne
There were as many men as women

Sentence (93) involves the verb as the object of comparison and is a reduced sentential structure, expressing full comparison, as is (94), with the noun the object of comparison, and (95), with the adjective as the category of comparison. Sentence (96) is a reduced sentential construction expressing partial comparison. Lepschy and Lepschy point out that, in certain cases, '*che* may replace the adverbial *quanto*', though 'purists object to this use of *che* . . . the forms with *che* are more colloquial' (p. 114). *Che* may replace *quanto* in (93) and (95), in other words in those constructions where *quanto* is not being used adjectivally, but rather as an (invariable) clause introducer.

Agard and Di Pietro (1965: 82) do not mention the *altrettanto* . . . *quanto* construction, but give examples of the others as follows:

(97) Noi (non) abbiamo tanti soldi quanto voi
We (do not) have as many pennies as you
(98) Giovanna è una ragazza tanto brava quanto Carla
Giovanna is a girl (who is) as good as Carla
(99) Io (non) studio tanto quanto mio fratello
I (do not) study as much as my brother
(100) (Non) si mangia tanto bene qui quanto a Parigi
One (does not) eat(s) as well here as in Paris
(101) (Non) abbiamo tanti bicchieri quanti piatti
We (do not) have as many glasses as plates
(102) Giovanna è una ragazza così brava come Carla
(103) (Non) si mangia così bene qui come a Parigi

In (97) the category of comparison is a noun, in (98) an adjective and in (99) a verb. All are expressions of full comparison and, in theory, could be either oblique phrasal constructions, with *voi*, *Carla* and *mio fratello* the complements of *quanto*, or reduced sentential constructions. Sentence (100) is a reduced sentential construction, with an adverb as the category of comparison, while (101) is a reduced sentential construction expressing partial comparison. Examples (102) and (103) are alternative versions of (98) and (100), respectively, with *così . . . come* replacing *tanto . . . quanto*. This occurs in what Agard and Di Pietro describe as 'limited environments' (p. 82) and is possible only when the category of comparison is an adjective or adverb.

Polizzi (1985: 508) gives the following examples:

(104) Un libro è tanto utile quanto piacevole
   A book is as useful as (it is) pleasant
(105) Il freddo è (così) dannoso come il caldo
   Cold is (as) harmful as heat
(106) Quel ragazzo è (così) bello come il suo amico
   That boy is (as) handsome as his friend

Example (104) is a reduced sentential construction expressing partial comparison, with the adjectives as the categories of comparison. Sentences (105) and (106) are both expressions of full comparison, again with the adjective as the object of comparison. Like (97-9), (105) and (106) could theoretically be oblique phrasal constructions or reduced sentential constructions. The status of *così* is considered optional.

In Battaglia and Pernicone (1965: 168, 500, 567-8) the following examples are found:

(107) Tu sei (tanto) studioso quanto tuo fratello
(108) Tu sei (così) studioso come tuo fratello
   You are (as) studious as your brother
(109) Tu sei (tanto) bravo quanto audace
   You are (as) good as (you are) bold
(110) Egli è (tanto) generoso quanto te
   He is (as) generous as you
(111) Noi siamo (così) stanchi come voi
   We are (as) tired as you
(112) Tu sei tanto forte quanto delicato
   You are as strong as (you are) delicate
(113) La palla è tanto grossa quanto leggera
   The ball is as big as (it is) light
(114) Non è così bravo come dicevi
   He is not as good as you said
(115) E tanto schietto come appare
   He is as sincere as he seems
(116) Mi sentivo tanto triste quanto felice ero stato prima
   I felt as sad as I had been happy before
(117) Il bimbo mi fa tanta compagnia quanta me ne farebbe un amico
   The baby keeps me company as much as a friend would

Examples (107), (108), (110), (111), (114) and (115) are expressions of full comparison involving the adjective as the category of comparison. Examples (107), (108) and (111), as before, could, at least in theory, be either oblique phrasal constructions or reduced sentential constructions. Example (110), on the other hand, appears to be an oblique phrasal construction, since the pronoun te is not in the subject form (*tu*). Examples (114) and (115) are full sentential constructions, as shown by the appearance of the tensed verb.

Examples (109), (112), (113) and (116) all express partial comparison, again with the adjectives as the categories of comparison. Examples (109), (112) and (113) are reduced sentential constructions, while (116) is a full sentential construction. Interestingly, in (116) the second adjective, *felice*, appears to have been fronted in the subordinate clause, in a way reminiscent of the (obligatory) clause-fronting of the second compared category in the parallel Spanish construction involving the comparatives of inequality, via a process of topicalization. Example (117) is a full sentential construction expressing full comparison, with the noun as the category being compared.

Examples (93–117) serve to illustrate the full range of structures, expressing both full and partial comparison, and involving a range of syntactic categories as the objects of comparison.

For Battaglia and Pernicone, both *così* and *tanto* are optional, while the element introducing the second term of the comparison is not (1965: 567):

> si può dire, il periodo comparativo si vale d'una particella correlativa nella principale (*così, tanto* . . .), che assai spesso si suole tacere e sottintendere; mentre la subordinata è sempre legata alla principale mediante una particella comparativa: *come* (che è la più usata), *quanto* . . . . Quando si esprime la particella correlativa nella proposizione principale, vuol dire che s'intende sottolineare di più il valore comparativo, sicchè il suo impiego dipende da ragioni stilistiche, secondo l'intenzione e il gusto di chi parla o scrive.

Only Battaglia and Pernicone give examples of full sentential equative constructions – 'la comparazione . . . fra due proposizioni intere, di cui l'una è la principale (o reggente) e l'altra la subordinata comparativa' (pp. 566–7) – the others limiting themselves to examples of oblique phrasal or reduced sentential constructions. Battaglia and Pernicone, unlike Lepschy and Lepschy, make no mention of the possibility of *che* replacing *quanto* in any context. They do, however, appear to allow *come* to introduce a full clause after *tanto*[13] (see (115)) as an alternative to *quanto*, considering this to be the more usual of the two.

There appears, then, to be a certain degree of choice as to the construction used to express a comparison of equality in Italian. *Tanto* may modify any category, exhibiting gender and number agreement only with the noun, while *così* may modify only adjectives and adverbs; *quanto* may introduce the second term of the comparison only in equatives featuring *tanto* in the matrix clause and may also show gender and number agreement where the category of comparison is a noun. *Quanto* may be replaced by the more colloquial *che*, except when the object of comparison is a noun and it therefore exhibits gender and number marking (see (94), (96)); *come* always introduces the second term of the comparison when *così* appears in the matrix clause of the equative construction, in other words when the comparison involves an adjective or an adverb. Additionally, it seems *come* may act as an alternative to *quanto* and introduce the second term of the comparison after *tanto*, but only when this is a full clause.

Expletive *non*

Examples (93–117) illustrate a wide range of possibilities, both of construction types (oblique phrasal, reduced sentential, full sentential) and kinds of comparison (full or partial). It has been shown that the range of possibilities is fairly broad. However, in none of these examples does expletive *non* appear. Nor does the verb, in the subset of examples containing a tensed verb in the subordinate clause, appear in the subjunctive mood.

Napoli and Nespor (1976: 817–19; 1977: 67) note that expletive *non* cannot appear in comparatives of equality, giving the following as examples (their (16) and (17)):

(118) a. Maria è tanto intelligente quanto è Carlo
      b. *Maria è tanto intelligente quanto non sia Carlo
          Maria is as intelligent as Carlo is
(119) a. Maria è tanto intelligente quanto tu credi
      b. *Maria è tanto intelligente quanto tu non creda
          Maria is as intelligent as you think

They rightly reject the suggestion that *non* may not appear in such contexts as a result of the fact that in equative constructions two similar things are compared, while in a comparative of inequality

A consideration of other Romance languages

construction the objects of comparison are necessarily dissimilar, pointing out that a negated comparative of equality, which is semantically equivalent to a comparative of inferiority, also disallows *non*, as shown by the following (their (18)):

(120) a. Maria non è tanto intelligente quanto tu credi
 b. *Maria non è tanto intelligente quanto tu non creda
 Maria is not as intelligent as you think

However, they do consider the restriction to be semantic in origin and link it to their presupposition-based analysis of expletive *non* in comparatives of inequality. Recall that they claim that *non* occurs in such contexts when the speaker presupposes that a certain opinion is held by the listener, but not when an explicit evaluation has already been made by the listener. They further claim that 'since *tanto . . . quanto* requires explicit and precise knowledge while *non* requires inferred and imprecise knowledge, *non* is excluded from comparisons of equality on semantic grounds (i.e. *non* and *tanto . . . quanto* are semantically mutually exclusive)' (1977: 69).

It has already been demonstrated that the distribution of expletive *non* in comparatives of inequality cannot be explained by the above hypothesis. Rather, it is the result of a non-uniform analogical process between sentential and relativized phrasal comparatives. Hence the explanation for the non-appearance of expletive *non* in the equative construction cannot be based on such a hypothesis. Moreover, it is inexact to state that an equative construction may only be used when there is 'explicit and precise' knowledge of the objects of comparison. In fact, this is rarely the case, the relation of equality expressed by an equative construction more usually being rather imprecise. Expletive *non* does not appear in the equative constructions of Italian quite simply because, firstly, it is not required, the tensed verb constraint having been shown to apply only to comparatives of inequality, and secondly, no process of analogy has affected the structure of equative constructions. This second point may be explained by the fact that analogical 'crossing' of *non* into the equative construction might entail the subjunctive mood spreading into a new structure, against the prevalent trend in Modern Italian.

Napoli and Nespor also note that the verb of the subordinate clause in an equative construction may not appear in the subjunctive mood, as do Battaglia and Pernicone (1965: 567): 'La proposizione comparativa di uguaglianza ha il verbo al modo indicativo, perchè esprime un'azione reale e certa.' While Battaglia and Pernicone consider that this is because a comparison expressed by a comparative of equality is perceived as being less hypothetical than the corresponding comparatives of inequality, Napoli and Nespor (1977: 68) simply state: 'Since equalities cannot have the subjunctive, *non* cannot appear.' They offer no explanation of why the subjunctive mood cannot appear in an equative construction. In fact, their statement would be correct if reversed: the situation is rather that since equatives cannot have *non*, the subjunctive is quite unnecessary.

Saltarelli (1974: 217) also considers the question of why the subjunctive may appear in the second half of a comparative of inequality, but never in an equative construction. He does offer an explanation for this and one which is semantically based. His claim is that in a comparative of equality 'the second term of comparison is referentially identified, and therefore the indicative is used'. One of the examples he gives (his (35b)) is reproduced below:

(121) E alta quanto tu credi
She is (as) tall as you think

(In (121) *tanto* has been omitted.) For Saltarelli, since 'the utterer is now asserting a degree of height equal to the degree of height believed by the subject of the second term, he knows then that this proposition refers to a fact of the real world'. However, simply negating (121) would alter this state of affairs:

(122) Non è tanto alta quanto tu credi
She is not as tall as you think

In (122) the proposition does not refer to a fact of the real world as what the subject of the second term believes is stated to be false. Nonetheless, the subjunctive may not appear. The use of the subjunctive in Italian comparatives clearly cannot be explained on these semantic grounds. As has already been argued, the subjunctive mood appears as a direct result of the presence of expletive *non* in comparatives of inequality, serving to distinguish it from the true negative.

It might be objected that my earlier assertion, that expletive *non* does not appear in the equative constructions of Italian because these are unaffected by the tensed verb constraint, does not appear to hold true in French, where expletive *ne* may appear in the equative construction. However, the situation in Italian is distinct from that of French in several respects. I have argued that expletive *ne* may appear in the French equative construction via a process of analogy. This is possible because of the close formal parallelism of the constructions *plus/moins* . . . *que* and *aussi/autant* . . . *que*, both types sharing the same 'comparative particle', *que*. This is not the case in Italian, where the comparatives of inequality and equality do not share the same particle, *che* appearing to be only rarely acceptable after *tanto* and never after *così*. Moreover, in French a comparative of inequality sentential construction strongly requires the presence of expletive *ne*. There is no fully viable phrasal alternative without *ne*, as there is in Italian. As a result, expletive *ne* is intimately associated with the concept of comparison and its being 'imported' into the equative construction, as a marker of comparison, is unsurprising, even though it is not required. In Italian the sentential construction *più/meno* . . . *che*, which also strongly requires the presence of expletive *non*, does have a phrasal alternative, which is actually the more common construction and, crucially, does not require expletive *non* (though it may optionally include this element). Hence the frequency of occurrence of expletive *non* is lower and it becomes correspondingly less likely that this element would spread beyond the comparatives of inequality. Finally, it has been noted that the subjunctive mood is increasingly being replaced by the indicative in Modern Italian. The fact that expletive *non* must normally be accompanied by a subjunctive verb, unlike French expletive *ne*, to signal clearly that it is the expletive rather than the isomorphic negative particle, must also make it less likely that *non* would be 'imported' into the equative constructions, causing the subjunctive mood actually to replace the indicative in this context; this would run counter to the obvious trend in the opposite direction.

All of these factors combined serve to differentiate the position of equative constructions relative to the comparatives of inequality in Italian quite clearly from that of the corresponding structures in French. No tensed verb constraint applies to equative constructions, hence they do not require the presence of an element capable of licensing the appearance of a tensed verb, which is at least partly the function of the expletive negative in comparatives of inequality. For the reasons outlined above, it is unsurprising that expletive *non* has not spread to the equative constructions of Italian, as expletive *ne* has (partially) in French. Of all these reasons, however, the most interesting, perhaps, is the fact that Italian *che*, unlike French *que*, does not act as a universal comparative clause introducer and may therefore be regarded as a marker of comparison itself.

The clause introducer

It seems that the range of constructions available for the expression of comparison is the same for both the comparatives of inequality and the comparatives of equality. This resembles the situation in French, but is unlike the situation in Spanish, where the range of structural possibilities for the equative construction is greater than for the comparatives of inequality, which do not normally allow a full clause to follow *que* in expressions of full comparison. In Chapter 3 I argued that this was related to the fact that the two types of comparatives in Spanish do not share the same clause introducer or 'comparative particle', having both *que* and *como*, while in French there is only one 'comparative particle': *que*. Since Italian is like Spanish in that it has more than one 'comparative particle',[14] *che*, like *que*, being a marker of comparison, it might seem surprising that its range of structural possibilities resembles the range found in French, rather than Spanish. This is a direct consequence of the availability of expletive *non* as an additional marker of comparison which can license the appearance of a tensed verb after *che* in sentential comparatives of inequality. Recall that *no* may not serve this purpose in Spanish. I have argued that this may be because it would be indistinguishable, after comparative *que*, from the true negative, after the tensed clause subordinator *que*. The same situation exists in Italian, where expletive *non* is identical to the standard negative and comparative *che* is also non-distinct from the tensed clause subordinator *che*.[15] However, expletive *non* is, in formal Italian, clearly differentiated by the subjunctive mood of the verb in a comparative clause, thus enabling it to act, like *ne*, as a marker of comparison and allow full clauses to follow comparative *che*. Had Spanish developed along similar lines, then the subjunctive mood might have been expected, in this language also, to be used to facilitate the use of *no* as a comparison marker, rather than simply a negative. Why this did not occur must be an open question, which cannot be answered from a synchronic perspective.

Italian, then, appears to possess two 'markers of comparison', both *che* and *non*; comparatives of inequality are doubly marked as such. This might seem surprising, but it is clearly advantageous. While *che*, as it is not the universal comparative particle of Italian, is distinctive in introducing comparatives of inequality rather than equality, it is nonetheless subject to the disadvantage of being formally identical to the tensed clause complementizer. I have argued that this formal identity has as a consequence a tensed verb constraint, disallowing a tensed verb after such comparative particles due to the risk of the clause being misinterpreted as a non-comparative clause. The availability in Italian of an additional marker of comparison, expletive *non*, however, means that the tensed verb constraint can be overridden; *non* marks the clause, in a less ambiguous fashion, as a comparative of inequality. Thus the use of two markers of comparison in Italian is explicable on these functional grounds: it extends the structural possibilities available. Notice also that it might be argued that *che* is not itself a true marker of comparison since it seems that, while it does not normally introduce equative constructions, it may (see pages 176–83). It is not therefore entirely distinctive in comparatives of inequality, unlike Spanish *que*, and this fact about the distribution of comparative *che* provides a further reason for the requirement of an additional marker of comparison.

Stassen (1985: 219) considers Italian *che* to be 'historically an adverbial case form of the relative/interrogative pronoun', and states that it is in complementary distribution with *di* (p. 337), as does Seuren (1984: 123): 'Italian . . . has two comparative particles, *di*[16] (from Latin *de* meaning "from") and *che* (from Latin *quo*), the Italian counterpart of French *que*. These two particles are in complementary distribution.' Small (1924: 53), on the other hand, while noting that Latin *de* 'still survives in Rumanian and Italian after the comparative without restriction', considers that Italian *che*, along with French and Spanish *que*, developed from the Latin comparative construction with *quam*, rather than from *quo*.

Battaglia and Pernicone (1965: 167) appear to see *che* as a conjunction, stating that the second term of a comparison in Italian is 'introdotto dalle preposizioni *di* o dalla congiunzione *che*'. Elsewhere they remark that *di* 'è in concorrenza con la particella *che*' (p. 414) and also that *che* is a subordinator which 'introduce . . . la proposizione comparativa' (pp. 441–2).

The position with regard to the distribution of *di* and *che*, however, is not quite as clear-cut as Seuren suggests. Napoli and Nespor (1976: 834; 1977: 86) point out that *che* may alternate with *di*, exemplified as follows (their (52) and (53)):

(123) Maria è più intelligente di Carlo
(124) Maria è più intelligente che Carlo
Maria is more intelligent than Carlo

They do, however, state that not many speakers would use (124). It seems likely that for those who do, (124) is constructed as a reduced sentential structure, unlike (123), which is an oblique phrasal construction. Battaglia and Pernicone (1965: 168) also claim that 'A volte s'incontra il costrutto con la congiunzione *che* al posto della preposizione *di* per il secondo termine di paragone: *Roma è più antica che Firenze; Io sono molto più stanco che te*' ('Rome is older than Florence', 'I am much more tired than you').

Expletive non *in a reduced clause*

As I have argued that the function of expletive *non* in a comparative subordinate clause is to act as an additional marker of comparison and enable a tensed verb to appear, it might be expected that it need not occur in a reduced comparative, i.e. where the tensed verb has been deleted. However, Regula and Jernej (1975: 244) give the following as acceptable:

(125) Costa più il condimento che non la carne
    The condiment costs more than the meat

For them, this is semantically equivalent to (126):

(126) La carne non costa tanto quanto il condimento
    The meat does not cost as much as the condiment

They state that 'La negazione si spiega per influsso del pensiero'.
  Napoli and Nespor (1977: 86) also claim that the following sentence (their (54)) has 'marginal acceptability':

(127) ?Maria è più intelligente che non Carlo
    Maria is more intelligent than Carlo

They note (p. 93) that the equivalent sentence with *di* is completely unacceptable:

(128) *Maria è più intelligente di non Carlo

In contrast to (127), which they admit (p. 94) that many speakers do not accept, they point out that (129) is accepted by most:

(129) E più studioso che non intelligente
    He is more studious than intelligent

Napoli and Nespor claim that *non* in (129) and (127) is their '*non* of presupposition' (p. 94) and that it does not, therefore, serve to emphasize any presumed lack of intelligence, which is the more usual explanation.

A consideration of other Romance languages 187

Example (127) seems to be somewhat unacceptable, but better than (128). Recall that postposing the matrix subject *Maria* improves (127) dramatically (see example (19b)); it contrasts strongly with the much more acceptable (125) and (129). In fact, (127) and (128) are very different from (129). The former both express full comparison, while the latter expresses partial comparison. Example (125), on the other hand, while it also expresses full comparison (with the verb as the object of comparison) superficially resembles an expression of partial comparison, *il condimento* seeming to be balanced against *la carne* in much the same way as *studioso* is balanced against *intelligente* in (129). As proof of this, notice that changing the word order, i.e. removing *il condimento* from the immediate vicinity of *la carne*, makes the sentence less acceptable with *non*:

(130) ?Il condimento costa più che non la carne

It seems, then, that expletive *non* may be acceptable for some speakers in an expression of partial comparison, but less acceptable in an expression of full comparison, like (127) (or (130)). Napoli and Nespor claim that expletive *non* may appear in reduced comparatives because the same set of presuppositions hold in such contexts as hold in non-reduced structures. This will not, however, explain why (127) is much less acceptable than (129). Presuppositions cannot vary according to the type of comparison (full or partial); in other words, it cannot be that in expressions of full comparison presuppositions become irrelevant if the structure is reduced, but remain relevant if the reduced construction in question expresses partial comparison.

I would suggest that what is relevant in these constructions is not semantic or pragmatic, but syntactic. It has already been noted that *che* may sometimes alternate with *di* in the oblique phrasal structure (see pages 157–8), i.e. (131) may alternate with (132):

(131) Io sono molto più stanco che te
(132) Io sono molto più stanco di te
    I am much more tired than you

As the form of the pronoun *te*[17] shows, it may be analysed as the complement of *che/di* and not the 'survivor' of a reduced clause. Therefore, a sentence like (127) could also be analysed as an oblique phrasal construction, with *Carlo* the complement of *che*, rather than a reduced sentential construction. Oblique phrasal constructions cannot contain the expletive negative, whose presence is required only when a tensed verb follows *che*, that is when there is a full comparative clause. Since a tensed verb need not be posited as having featured in the derivation of (127), and cannot possibly have been present in (128), the appearance of *non* is unacceptable.

Example (129), on the other hand, is an expression of partial comparison. As such, it is obligatorily reduced, the copula of the subordinate clause having been deleted. *Non* would, therefore, have been present in the unreduced version of (129), licensing, as usual, the tensed verb. Hence there is a source for *non* here, unlike (127) and (128), which explains the greater degree of acceptability. *Non* should not, of course, be expected to 'survive' deletion of the tensed verb, as it no longer has a role to play. However, its status as a marker of comparison might make it acceptable for some. Nonetheless, it is important to notice that the fully acceptable versions of (125–30) are those in which *non* is omitted.

For some speakers, then, it seems that expletive *non* may occur in a reduced comparative, i.e. when there is no tensed verb present. Yet, even for these speakers, the acceptability of such constructions depends on the history of the construction: *non* may only appear if a tensed verb has been deleted, that is, if a tensed verb could have appeared. *Non* survives in such structures as a simple marker of comparison with no real function. The (marginal) acceptability of such constructions, then, does not vitiate my contention that the function of expletive *non* in comparatives is to act as a marker of comparison capable of licensing the appearance of a tensed verb. Rather, as has been shown, they support this thesis. Such sentences cannot be explained by a presupposition-based analysis of the type proposed by Napoli and Nespor.

4.1.2 Summary of the situation in Italian

The preceding discussion of the comparative constructions of Italian has been necessarily limited. In particular, little has been said about the expression of partial comparison, the discussion having focussed on constructions expressing full comparison. Nevertheless, I hope that even this limited examination of the comparative constructions of Italian has served to demonstrate that the general constraint on comparatives of inequality which I am proposing – that they must contain a marker of comparison – applies as much to Italian as it does to Spanish and French.

Italian, like French, is able to escape the effects of the tensed verb constraint because of the existence of an extra element, expletive *non*, which is able to act as an additional marker of comparison and license the appearance of a tensed verb. I have argued that expletive *non* does not have negative import, any more than does French expletive *ne*, and that the subjunctive mood of the verb of the comparative subordinate clause supports this thesis, serving as it does to differentiate expletive *non* from the standard negative of Italian, which is also *non*. It has been demonstrated that a presupposition type of analysis, such as that proposed in Napoli and Nespor (1976, 1977), cannot adequately explain the distribution of *non* in Italian comparatives of inequality. In particular, the presupposition analysis fails to account for the interdependence of expletive *non* and the subjunctive mood.

Nor can the presence of expletive *non* be explained on the basis of some presumed negativity. Stassen (1985: 221) claims that Italian belongs to the group of languages which 'seem to have a negative sentence in their input-sentence', and Seuren (1984) also concludes that the expletive *non* of Italian has negative import. Yet there is no evidence for this other than the occurrence of the expletive negative element and, as von Stechow (1984a: 189) states, 'It is not even clear . . . that a language with an occasionally overt negation like Italian *has* to be analyzed along Seuren's lines.' While I would not agree with von Stechow that the negative element is to be interpreted as being linked to the hypothetical nature of comparison, he is correct in pointing out that the concept of negation does not necessarily have much to do with comparison.

Expletive *non* appears in the sentential *più/meno . . . che* construction in order to license the appearance of the tensed verb in a comparative of inequality. By a process of analogy it may also occur in the relativized phrasal constructions, for example, the *più/meno . . . di quanto* construction. When it does, the verb is normally in the subjunctive mood, which serves, as in the sentential construction, to differentiate this expletive *non* from negative *non*. Expletive *non* need not appear in the phrasal construction, however, as it is not required. The tensed verb in such constructions is in a relative clause, not a comparative subordinate clause, and so is unaffected by the tensed verb constraint. Hence the phrasal construction is equally acceptable without expletive *non*, in which case the verb will generally be in the indicative mood. That the phrasal construction is more common than the more formal sentential construction has been linked to the fact that the verb in the latter must normally be in the subjunctive mood, for the reasons stated, and the subjunctive mood is tending to be replaced by the indicative in Modern Italian. The phrasal constructions, which do not require either expletive *non* or, consequently, the subjunctive mood, will therefore be preferred.

It has previously been demonstrated that the tensed verb constraint does not apply to the comparative of equality construction. The situation in Italian confirms this: expletive *non* does not appear in the equative constructions. No process of analogy appears to have affected these structures, unlike the situation in French. This is unsurprising since it would be unlikely that the subjunctive mood, which accompanies expletive *non*, should spread to structures in which it is not required if the trend elsewhere in Italian is for it to disappear. Moreover, whereas in French the equative construction shares the same clause introducer, *que*, as the comparatives of inequality, in Italian this is not the case, *quanto* or *come* being used rather than *che*, hence the formal parallelism is much reduced.

It is clear that Italian shares some of the features of French and some of the features of Spanish. It is like French in two ways: firstly, there is an expletive negative element acting as a marker of comparison in the sentential comparative of inequality construction; and secondly, the range of construction types available for the expression of comparison is, in Italian just as in French, identical for both the comparatives of inequality and the comparatives of equality. Equally, it is unlike French in two ways: firstly, the expletive element also appears, by analogy, in the phrasal constructions, which does not occur in French;[18] secondly, Italian expletive *non* does not appear in the equative constructions, whereas French expletive *ne* may, by analogy. This is linked to both the formal status of the subjunctive and, more importantly, the fact that there is not a universal comparative particle in Italian as there is in French, whence the lowered formal parallelism between the two types of comparative.

The features which Italian shares with Spanish are as follows: there is a phrasal construction, resembling the *más/menos . . . de lo que* construction of Spanish, in which a tensed verb may appear, as the tensed verb constraint does not apply to a non-comparative (here, a relative) subordinate clause; like Spanish, Italian does not have a single 'comparative particle', *che* and *quanto/come* being parallel to *que* and *como* in Spanish, hence *che*, like *que*, may be considered a marker of comparison; Italian also does not have a distinctive expletive negative element, *non*, like Spanish *no*, being isomorphic with the standard negative. However, unlike Spanish,

A consideration of other Romance languages

Italian is able to make use of this expletive element as an additional marker of comparison, since the subjunctive mood of the verb helps to differentiate it from the true negative. As a result, a tensed verb may appear after *che* in the *più/meno . . . che* construction, which, for expressions of full comparison, it may not in the Spanish *más/menos . . . que* construction.

Italian, then, shares features of both French and Spanish, but is identical to neither. Despite this fact, my analysis of the data of Italian has shown that they support the same thesis as do the data of French and Spanish: a tensed verb constraint arises when the comparative particle, whether or not it is itself a marker of comparison (i.e. unique to comparatives of inequality), is formally identical to the tensed clause complementizer. The existence of such a tensed verb constraint is supported by the data of Italian.

Bergmans (1982: 196) quotes Leys (1980: 103) as stating that 'It becomes a pure matter of specific language organization and standardization whether pleonastic negation is retained in comparative clauses or not.' This is not the case. Whether an expletive negative occurs in a comparative clause depends on whether or not it is required as a marker of comparison. This will itself depend, firstly, on the type of comparison being expressed (whether it is a comparison of inequality or equality); secondly, on whether or not the comparative particle itself is able to act as a marker of comparison; and thirdly, on the availability of a distinctive negative particle (like French *ne*) or of some means of distinguishing the expletive from the real negative (as in Italian's use of verbal mood). With regard to the second point, if the marker of comparison and the tensed clause complementizer are isomorphic, this may lead, as in Italian, to the requirement for a less ambiguous marker of comparison if the structural possibilities are not to be limited.

I would agree with Seuren (1984: 124) that 'in Italian . . . the evidence is relatively messy, and a great deal of mixing of construction types seems to have been going on.' Nonetheless, as I hope the preceding analysis has shown, the evidence, however messy, supports my contention that a tensed verb constraint is operative in constructions expressing comparison.

4.2 COMPARATIVE CONSTRUCTIONS IN PORTUGUESE

The comparative constructions of Portuguese appear to resemble closely the corresponding constructions of Spanish, while having little in common with those of French. They display marked differences of structure in that there is no universal 'comparative particle', the comparative clause introducers being different for the comparatives of inequality and the comparative of equality. Consequently, the syntactic structures available for the expression of comparison are not the same: the comparatives of inequality allow both phrasal and sentential constructions, as in Spanish. Most importantly, the comparative particle *que* may be regarded as the marker of comparison, and there is no expletive negative element available to act as an additional marker of comparison, as there is in Italian and French (where *ne* is the sole marker of comparison). As a direct result, the tensed verb constraint applies to the comparatives of inequality and disallows the appearance of a tensed verb in the sentential construction.

The following, brief, examination of the means available for the expression of comparison in Portuguese will concentrate on constructions expressing full comparison, for both the comparatives of inequality and the equative construction. It will be shown that the lack of an expletive negative element in Portuguese means that a tensed verb may not appear in the subordinate clause of the sentential comparative of inequality construction, while it may appear freely in the equative construction.

4.2.1 The comparatives of inequality

There are two possible construction types:

1 a reduced sentential construction, e.g. (133):

(133) Ama o seu pai menos que a sua mãe
He loves his father less than his mother

2 a relativized phrasal construction involving *do que*:

(134) Bebe mais do que come[19]
He drinks more than he eats

The reduced sentential construction

The construction type exemplified in (133) is a reduced sentential construction rather than an oblique phrasal construction. The category that has 'survived' after *que* is the object noun phrase *a sua mãe*. It is not possible for the comparative clause to be non-reduced:

(135) *Ama o seu pai menos que ama a sua mãe
He loves his father less than he loves his mother

It is possible, however, for *do que* to alternate with *que*.[20] Example (136) is an acceptable alternative to (133):

(136) Ama o seu pai menos do que a sua mãe

Willis (1980: 328) points out that '*Than* is usually rendered by *que* or *do que*, but chiefly the latter.' Teyssier (1976: 260) states that 'on a le choix entre *do que* ou *que* seul.' For Mattoso Camara (1972: 214) '*que* and *do que* . . . alternate in Modern Portuguese . . . the second noun of a comparative sentence may be governed by either *que* or *do que*'. In fact, the category which survives the clause following (*do*) *que* need not be a noun phrase:

(137) Há menos gente em Roma que em Londres
There are fewer people in Rome than in London

In (137) a prepositional phrase follows *que*.
The following is also a reduced sentential construction:

(138) O João é mais forte[21] que[22] eu
João is stronger than I

Example (138) cannot be an oblique phrasal construction with *eu* the complement of *que*, as the subject form of the pronoun *eu* shows. The pronoun is obligatorily in subject form, as Teyssier (1976: 86) points out: 'ce sont les formes sujets que l'on emploie obligatoirement après *mais que* . . . *menos que*.' If an oblique phrasal construction were possible, (139) should be acceptable, but it is not:

(139) *O João é mais forte que mim
João is stronger than me

It follows that when the category following *que* in such constructions is a full lexical noun a reduced clause structure will also be the most likely source:

(140) O João é mais forte que o Pedro[23]
João is stronger than Pedro

Although in the case of a lexical noun there is no overt indication of its status, nothing is gained by positing a second structure here, that is, an analysis of *o Pedro* as the complement of *que*. Such an additional option would be superfluous. The situation in Portuguese, in this instance, exactly parallels that of Spanish.

Examples (133), (136–8), (140) are expressions of full comparison. In (133) and (136) the category of comparison is the verb, in (137) it is the noun, while in (138) and (140) it is the adjective. Example (141) is an expression of partial comparison, involving the nouns as the objects of comparison:

(141) Quero mais vinho (do) que água[24]
    I want more wine than water

I shall return to the use of *do que* as an alternant of *que* in reduced sentential comparatives on pages 195–6.

The relativized phrasal construction

The relativized phrasal construction has been exemplified in (134). (142–5) are further examples of this construction:

(142) Compra mais livros do que vende[25]
    He buys more books than he sells
(143) Trabalha mais do que eu pensava[26]
    He works more than I thought
(144) E mais fácil do que parece
    It is easier than it seems
(145) E menos estudioso do que eu imaginava[27]
    He is less studious than I imagined

Examples (134), (142–5) are constructions expressing full comparison. In (134), either the verb or a lexically unfilled noun object is the category of comparison (depending on whether the verbs are interpreted as intransitive or transitive: if they are intransitive, then (134) expresses partial comparison); in (142) the noun is the category of comparison, in (143) it is the verb which is being compared and in (144) and (145) the adjective is the object of comparison.

This *mais/menos . . . do que* construction appears to be almost identical to the Spanish phrasal construction with *de lo que*. There is no gap in the second half of the comparison; the sequence *o – que* + tensed verb following the preposition *de* (combining with *o* to give *do*) is the sequence pronoun – relative + tensed verb found in relative constructions. The Portuguese relativized phrasal construction, however, does differ from its Spanish equivalent in that the pronoun heading the relative clause is invariable. It cannot show gender and/or number marking, unlike the *lo* of *de lo que*, hence the unacceptability of (146a):

(146) a. *Compra mais livros dos que vende
      b. *Compra mais livros que vende

In (146a) the pronoun *os*, showing gender and number agreement with the matrix noun *livros*, is not acceptable. *Do que* may not be replaced by *que*, hence the ungrammaticality of (146b), although, as has been demonstrated, *que* may be replaced by *do que* in any context. In fact, a tensed verb may never follow *que*. According to Willis (1980: 328) '*Do que* is obligatory if the second element of comparison contains its own verb.'[28] The situation is, then, that *do que* is acceptable in all contexts after *mais/menos*, but *que* is not; as Mattoso Camara (1972: 214) notes, '*do que* [has] extended to all contexts.'

That a tensed verb may only surface in the *mais/menos . . . do que* construction is exactly as predicted by the thesis being defended here. The clause introduced by *do que* is a relative clause, not a comparative subordinate clause. As a result, the tensed verb may appear with impunity as the tensed verb constraint will not apply in such contexts. In the *mais/menos . . . que* sentential construction, however, the clause following *que* is a comparative subordinate clause. As the comparative particle *que* is non-distinct from the tensed clause complementizer *que*, a tensed verb is disallowed in such contexts, unless an expletive element is available to act as an additional marker of comparison, disambiguating the status of the clause and thus licensing the appearance of a tensed verb. As has been shown to be the case in Spanish, there is no such element in Portuguese, as Teyssier (1976: 264) notes: 'Les emplois dits "explétifs" de *ne* en français n'ont aucun correspondant en portugais.' Hence a tensed verb may not follow *mais/menos . . . que* and such sentential constructions always contain an obligatorily reduced clause.

However, this does not explain why *do que* may replace *que* in such reduced sentential constructions, as well as appearing in the relativized phrasal construction. The answer to this may lie in the form of *do que*. As the pronoun *o* is invariable, never displaying either gender or number marking, it seems likely that the sequence *do que* has become opaque: that is, it is no longer consciously analysed as introducing a relative construction, but is reanalysed as a complex 'comparative particle', parallel to *que*. The morphological adjustments to the pronoun necessary for the use of *de lo que* in

Spanish, on the other hand, would make it unlikely that this sequence could replace the simpler *que* in reduced comparatives. Given that the construction involving *do que* is the only one possible for the expression of non-reduced comparatives, therefore, this fact, together with its invariable morphological form, makes it unsurprising that its use should spread to reduced constructions, making *do que* the universal analytical 'comparative particle' in comparatives of inequality. From this perspective, what is surprising is that *que* should continue to be used at all, and it is, in fact, much less common than *do que*.

4.2.2 The comparative of equality

As for the comparatives of inequality, there are two possible construction types:

1 a reduced sentential construction, e.g. (147):

(147) Gosto tanto[29] de cinema como de teatro[30]
I enjoy the cinema as much as the theatre

2 a full sentential construction, e.g. (148):

(148) Não é tão fácil quanto parece[31]
It is not as easy as it looks

While there is the same number of construction types, i.e. two, for both the equative and the comparative of inequality constructions, they do not share the same structural possibilities. The comparative of equality has no relativized phrasal construction, while the comparatives of inequality have no non-reduced sentential construction.

The reduced sentential construction

In (147) the prepositional phrase *de teatro* has survived the reduced clause. Sentences (149–52) are further examples of this construction:

(149) Ela não tem tanto dinheiro como tu[32] ·
She does not have as much money as you
(150) Ela não trabalhou tanto como eu
She did not work as much as I
(151) Bebemos tanta água como vinho[33]

A consideration of other Romance languages

We drink as much water as wine
(152) Ele é tão rico como o irmão
He is as rich as his brother

As for the comparatives of inequality, these constructions must be reduced sentential constructions rather than oblique phrasal constructions. This is shown by the (obligatory) subject form of the pronouns *tu* and *eu*, in (149) and (150) respectively. Examples (147), (149), (150) and (152) are expressions of full comparison. In (147) and (150) the verb is the category of comparison; in (149) it is the noun and in (152) the adjective. Example (151) is an expression of partial comparison, with the nouns *água* and *vinho* the objects of comparison.

The full sentential construction

The full sentential construction, exemplified in (148), has a different comparative clause introducer, *quanto*. Sentence (153) is a further example of this construction type:

(153) João é tão aplicado quanto Maria é preguiçosa[34]
João is as industrious as Maria is lazy

According to Willis (1980: 329) '*tão* . . . *quanto* . . . replaces *tão* . . . *como* when a second finite verb is introduced.' Hundertmark-Santos Martins (1982: 513), however, although she lists the *tanto* . . . *quanto* construction, does not exemplify it or explain the difference between it and the *tanto* . . . *como* construction. Similarly, Mattoso Camara (1972: 215) notes the existence of '*tão* . . . *como* (or *quanto*)', while giving no indication of when *quanto* is to be preferred to *como*.

Teyssier (1976: 261) is more forthcoming, but disagrees with Willis in describing the use of *quanto* as an archaic form: '*Tanto (tão)* . . . *quanto (quão)* est un tour latinisant senti en général comme littéraire et classique.' The following example is given:

(154) Trabalha tanto quanto pode
He works as much as he can

He goes on to state that 'La construction vivante dans la langue d'aujourd'hui est *tanto (tão)* . . . *como*.' However, none of the examples which follow contain a tensed verb. They are all reduced sentential constructions and so would not require *quanto* as the 'comparative particle'.

It seems, then, that *como* and *quanto* alternate as the particles introducing the subordinate clause of an equative construction; they are in complementary distribution (unlike *do que/que*), *como* introducing a reduced clause and *quanto* a full sentential clause; this is unlike the case in Spanish, where *como* may introduce both reduced and non-reduced clauses.

Of the examples of full sentential constructions given, (148) and (154) are expressions of full comparison, with the adjective and verb, respectively, as the categories of comparison. Example (153), on the other hand, is an expression of partial comparison, the adjectives *aplicado* and *preguiçosa* being compared.

4.2.3 The clause introducer

While the number of construction types available for the expression of comparison is the same for the comparatives of inequality and the comparative of equality, being two in each case, the only construction they have in common is the reduced sentential construction. A relativized phrasal construction is available only for the expression of a comparison of inequality, while a full sentential construction may only be used to express a comparison of equality. This is unlike the situation in French, Italian or Spanish. Unlike French, Portuguese does not have a universal 'comparative particle' equivalent to *que*; Portuguese *que*, therefore, is itself a marker of comparison. While the range of clause introducers is superficially similar to the range available in Italian, the lack in Portuguese of an expletive element which may act as an additional marker of comparison limits the range of structures allowed. Unlike Spanish, Portuguese has two alternative 'comparative particles' to introduce the subordinate clause of the equative construction, and does not appear to allow a relativized phrasal structure (parallel to Spanish *tanto . . . como lo que*) for the expression of a comparison of equality.

Mattoso Camara (1972: 73, 214) believes that the comparative particle *que* of Portuguese derives from Latin *quam*, rather than from an adverbial case form of the relative/interrogative pronoun of Latin, as Stassen (1985: 219) states. Portuguese *que*, however, unlike *que* in French and Spanish and *che* in Italian, is increasingly being replaced by *do que* in all instances of a comparative of inequality.

There appear, then, to be four clause introducers available to act as 'comparative particles' in Portuguese. For the comparatives of

A consideration of other Romance languages 199

inequality, these are, in principle, *que* and *de*. For the equative construction they are *como* and *quanto*. *Que*, as in Spanish, may not be followed by a tensed verb. *De*, again as in Spanish, is followed by a pronoun heading an ensuing relative clause, giving the sequence *do que*. However, unlike Spanish, and for reasons already mentioned, this sequence *do que* seems to have been reanalysed synchronically as a complex 'comparative particle'. As a result, it alternates with *que* when introducing a reduced comparative clause, as well as being obligatory when a tensed verb is present in the second half of the comparison. *Que* and *do que*, then, are not in fully complementary distribution.

Como and *quanto*, on the other hand, are in complementary distribution, *como* introducing a reduced comparative clause and *quanto* introducing a full clause, i.e. a comparative clause in which a tensed verb occurs. Despite the fact that the construction with *quanto* is somewhat literary in style, it does not seem to be possible for a non-reduced clause to be introduced by *como*.

4.2.4 Summary of the situation in Portuguese

The preceding examination of the options available in Portuguese for the expression of comparison has been relatively limited and, in particular, little has been said about the expression of partial comparison. Nonetheless, even a brief discussion of the structural possibilities which exist in Portuguese demonstrates that, for this language also, the general constraint on comparatives of inequality which I am proposing, namely, that they must contain a marker of comparison, holds true. As in Spanish, this marker is the comparative particle itself. Once again, its formal identity with the standard tensed clause complementizer means that a tensed verb may not occur in the subordinate clause of the *mais/menos . . . que* construction. Unlike Italian, Portuguese does not make use of an expletive negative to act as an extra marker of comparison, thus licensing the appearance of a tensed verb and escaping the effects of the tensed verb constraint. Instead, to express a comparison of inequality involving a tensed verb in the second half of the comparison, Portuguese uses a relativized phrasal construction, *mais/menos . . . do que*. In this it is exactly parallel to Spanish. As the tensed verb constraint does not apply to equative constructions, a tensed verb may surface freely after *tanto . . . quanto*, and a relativized phrasal option is not required.

Of the three languages examined so far, then, Portuguese is most like Spanish in displaying the effects of the tensed verb constraint so strikingly due to the lack of an expletive negative. More importantly, it provides further evidence for one of the theses being defended here, that there exists a general constraint against the appearance of a tensed verb in the second half of a comparative of inequality whenever the comparative particle and the tensed clause complementizer are non-distinct.

4.3 COMPARATIVE CONSTRUCTIONS IN RUMANIAN

The comparative constructions of Rumanian, like their Portuguese equivalents, seem to resemble the constructions of Spanish, rather than those of French. There is no single 'comparative particle', the equative construction and the comparatives of inequality having different comparative clause introducers: for the comparatives of inequality these are *ca* (related to *que*) and *decît* (a fusion of preposition + quantifier); for the comparative of equality they are *ca şi* and *cum*. As a result, the comparative particle *ca* may be considered the marker of comparison and the two types of comparative display marked differences in structure. There is no expletive negative element available to act as an additional marker of comparison, as there is in Italian and French (where it is not, of course, additional). Consequently, the tensed verb constraint applies to the comparatives of inequality and disallows a tensed verb in the subordinate clause of the sentential construction.[35] However, as will be shown, the sentential construction is itself rare.

As for Portuguese, the following examination of the means available for the expression of comparison in Rumanian will deal mostly with constructions expressing full comparison, for both types of comparative (of equality and inequality). It will be shown that, as Rumanian does not possess an expletive negative element, a tensed verb may not appear in the subordinate clause of a sentential comparative of inequality, though this fact is obscured by the rarity of the sentential construction.

4.3.1 The comparatives of inequality

There are two possible construction types:

1 a reduced sentential construction, e.g. (155):

(155) Ion e mai mic ca Radu[36]

Ion is smaller than Radu

2 two types of phrasal construction:

(a) an oblique phrasal construction:

(156) E mai puţin fericit decît mine[37]
He is less happy than me

(b) a (non-oblique) phrasal construction involving *decît*:

(157) Ion scrie mai repede decît citeşte Radu
Ion writes more quickly than Radu reads

The reduced sentential construction

The construction type exemplified in (155) appears to be a reduced sentential construction, the category which has 'survived' after *ca* being the subject of the subordinate clause, *Radu*. However, the lack of subject case marking on lexical nouns in Rumanian means that *Radu* could possibly be the complement of *ca*, rather than acting as the subject of the reduced clause. In (158), however, the lexical noun following *ca* is an object:

(158) ?Te iubesc mai mult ca pe Ana[38]
I love you more than Ana

The marker *pe*, used with personal names, marks *Ana* unambiguously as an object. Example (158), therefore, must be a reduced sentential construction.

Example (158) is not fully acceptable. However, this need not be due to its being a reduced sentential construction. As Mallinson (1986: 166–7) points out, *ca* is 'An alternative marker introducing the standard of comparison . . . . Although it is claimed by some Rumanian grammarians that *ca* is increasing as a comparative element, it seems to be restricted to introducing nominal standards of comparison.' *Decît* is therefore preferred to *ca* in all contexts, which may account for the relative oddness of (158). Example (159), by contrast, appears to be totally unacceptable:

(159) *Ion e mai mic ca este Radu[39]
Ion is smaller than Radu is

Example (159) is a non-reduced sentential construction, with a tensed verb following *ca*. It is the appearance of this tensed verb which accounts for the sentence's ungrammaticality. As there is no expletive negative element in the clause *este Radu* to act as an additional marker of comparison and license the appearance of a tensed verb, the tensed verb constraint applies. Replacing *ca* with *decît* restores the sentence's grammaticality:

(160) Ion e mai mic decît este Radu

This is because (160), as will be demonstrated, is not a sentential construction, hence the tensed verb constraint does not apply, *este Radu* no longer being a comparative subordinate clause.

The phrasal constructions

The oblique phrasal construction

The oblique phrasal construction has been exemplified in (156). *Decît* may be replaced by *ca* in such structures:

(161) Ion e mai mic ca mine
      Ion is smaller than me

However, *decît* is more usual. That these constructions are oblique phrasal constructions, with the pronoun *mine* the complement of *decît/ca*, is shown by the form of the pronoun. According to Mallinson (1986: 166) 'any personal pronoun forming the standard of comparison cannot be in the subject form.' Hence (162) is ungrammatical:

(162) *Ion e mai mare decît eu
       Ion is bigger than I

An oblique phrasal structure is therefore available after *decît*, with the following noun the complement of the 'comparative particle'.

The non-oblique phrasal construction involving *decît*

The non-oblique phrasal construction involving *decît* has been exemplified in (157) and (160). The following are further examples of this construction:

(163) Maşina costă mai mult astăzi decît a costat ieri
      The car costs more today than it cost yesterday

(164) Noi sîntem mai fericiţi decît sînt prietenii lui
We are happier than his friends are
(165) El va cumpăra mai multe cărţi decît vom cumpăra noi
He will buy more books than we will buy
(166) Ion scrie o carte mai repede decît Radu scrie o scrisoare
Ion writes a book more quickly than Radu writes a letter

Examples (157), (160), (164–6) are expressions of full comparison. In (157) and (166) the category of comparison is the adverb. In (160) and (164) the adjective is being compared, while in (165) it is the noun which is the object of comparison. Example (163) is an expression of partial comparison, with the verbs as the objects of comparison.

As has been stated, *decît* is the standard 'comparative particle' of Rumanian in comparatives of inequality. As the previous examples show, a tensed verb may appear with impunity after *decît* (unlike after *ca*). Yet none of these examples contains an expletive negative element to license the appearance of the tensed verb. Clearly, the tensed verb constraint does not apply to *mai/mai puţin . . . decît* comparatives. This might appear to vitiate the argument that such a constraint exists. However, these constructions involving *decît* as the subordinate clause introducer are not sentential but relativized phrasal comparatives.

Superficially, synthetic *decît* does not seem to resemble Spanish *de lo que* or Portuguese *do que*. However, *decît* may be analysed as a combination of the preposition *de* + *cît*, an expression of quantity expressible in English as 'how much'. This shows it to be exactly parallel to the *di quanto* of the Italian phrasal comparative construction *più/meno . . . di quanto*.[40] The preposition *de*, then, introduces a relative clause headed by *cît*, acting as a free relative exactly like *quanto* in the Italian construction. However, as *decît* has been reanalysed as a synthetic 'comparative particle', this structure has become opaque. Nevertheless, my analysis explains why a tensed verb may follow *decît* but not *ca*: the tensed verb following *decît* appears in a relative clause, not a comparative subordinate clause, so the tensed verb constraint does not apply. By contrast, this constraint does apply, as expected, when the tensed verb follows *ca*, due to the near identity of *ca* and *că*, the tensed clause complementizer; in such cases it appears in a comparative subordinate clause, not a relative clause. The lack of an expletive negative element makes this latter option ungrammatical. This analysis might also explain why *ca* should be so rare in comparison with *decît* as the 'comparative particle': only *decît* allows a full clause in the second half of the comparison, since only the relativized *decît* structure is immune to the tensed verb constraint.

Decît may also introduce a reduced clause, e.g.:

(167) Moartea e mai permanentă decît viaţa[41]
   Death is more permanent than life
(168) Ieri a fost mai frig decît astăzi
   Yesterday it was colder than today
(169) Noi sîntem mai fericiţi decît prietenii lui
   We are happier than his friends
(170) El va cumpăra mai multe carţi decît noi
   He will buy more books than us
(171) Cartea mea e mai scumpă decît cartea ta
   My book is dearer than your book
(172) Mi-a dat mai mulţi bani decît Anei
   He gave more money to me than (to) Ana
(173) El e mai fericit decît ieri
   He is happier than yesterday
(174) E mai mult galben decît alb
   It is more yellow than white
(175) Ion de obicei vine mai mult devreme decît tîrziu
   Ion usually comes more early than late
(176) Locuiesc mai mult în Anglia decît în Australia
   I live more in England than in Australia

Sentences (167–76) show clearly that adjectives, adverbs, nouns and prepositional phrases may all follow *decît*. Sentences (167–73) are expressions of full comparison involving the adjective (167, 169, 171, 173) and the noun (168, 170, 172) as the categories of comparison; (174–6) are expressions of partial comparison involving the adjectives, adverbs and prepositional phrases, respectively, as the categories of comparison.

In none of (167–76) does a tensed verb appear, as these are all examples of reduced comparatives. It might seem surprising that the clause following *decît* may be reduced. This is certainly not the case where the Spanish *de lo que* construction is concerned. In fact, the situation in Rumanian is similar to that of Portuguese, where, I have argued, *do que* has been reanalysed as a general 'comparative particle', thus allowing it to alternate with *que* and allow a reduced clause to follow. I have claimed that this is facilitated by the invariable form of *do*, with no gender or number marking on the (fused) pronoun *o*. Where *decît* is concerned, this tendency is much more pronounced. Though I have argued that this form represents a fusion of the preposition *de* + the quantifier *cît*, parallel to Italian *di quanto*, and that structures in which it occurs may therefore justifiably be analysed as relativized phrasal constructions, it is evidently not interpreted as such by native speakers. Rather, it has been reanalysed as a synthetic 'comparative particle'. As such, it may introduce a reduced clause, as may Portuguese *do que*. Portuguese *do que* and Rumanian *decît* appear to be taking over in their respective languages as unique 'comparative particles' in comparatives of inequality, making *que/ca* virtually redundant; this process is predictable given the limited structural possibilities for clauses following *que/ca*, due to the lack of an expletive element. In addition, it is facilitated by the morphology of *do que/decît*, exhibiting no number or gender agreement (unlike Spanish *de lo que*). Nevertheless, only an analysis of *decît* as being composed of the sequence preposition – free relative is capable of explaining why a tensed verb may surface in the second half of such a comparison without ensuing ungrammaticality.

This analysis, therefore, is not only formally motivated, but also has explanatory power.

4.3.2 The comparative of equality

For the comparative of equality there are three possible construction types:

1 a reduced sentential construction, e.g. (177):

(177) M-a tratat la fel de rău ca (şi) pe tine
He treated me as badly as (he did) you

2 an oblique phrasal construction, e.g. (178):

(178) E la fel de înalt ca mine
He is as tall as me

3 a full sentential construction, e.g. (179):

(179) Scriu tot aşa de corect cum citeşti tu[42]
I write as correctly as you read

The first term of a comparison of equality is introduced by *la fel de* (literally, 'at manner of'), *tot aşa de* ('yet thus of') or *tot atît de* ('still so much of'). These may also be optionally omitted, e.g.:

(180) E rău ca odinioară
  He is (as) bad as formerly

The comparative clause introducer is either *ca* alone or *ca şi*. According to Mallinson (1986: 175) '*ca* can also be followed by ... *şi* ... with no discernible change in the meaning.'

The comparative of equality has no non-oblique phrasal construction parallel to the *mai/mai puţin* ... *decît* construction. On the other hand, there is a full sentential construction available, an option which does not exist for the comparatives of inequality.

The reduced sentential construction

In (177) the object noun phrase *pe tine* has survived the reduced clause. Sentences (181) and (182) are further examples of this construction:

(181) Viaţa mea nu e tot atît de bună ca a ta
  My life is not as good as yours
(182) Munca noastră nu e tot atît de productivă ca a voastră
  Our work is not as productive as yours

All three sentences express full comparison, with the adverb in (177) and the adjective in (181) and (182) as the objects of comparison.

Mallinson (1986: 177) states that 'with equative structures reduction is much more drastic than in comparative structures and often ... it will be a single constituent that is left behind.' In fact, Mallinson gives no examples in which a tensed verb follows *ca (şi)* in an equative construction, though he does not actually say that this restriction holds.

The oblique phrasal construction

This is exemplified in (178). As for the comparatives of inequality, proof that this is indeed a phrasal, rather than a reduced sentential, construction rests on the form of the pronoun, *mine*, following *ca*. This may not be replaced by the subject form:

(183) *E la fel de înalt ca eu
He is as tall as I

Thus *mine* in (178) must be the complement of *ca*, rather than the 'survivor' of a reduced clause.

The full sentential construction

Sentence (179) exemplifies a non-reduced sentential construction. It is an expression of full comparison, with the adverb as the object of comparison. As already stated, Mallinson (1986) gives no example of a clause containing a tensed verb in the second half of a comparison of equality, describing the process of reduction as 'rather drastic'. Sentence (179), taken from Baciu (1978: 94), illustrates that a tensed verb may appear, but the 'comparative particle' is *cum*, rather than *ca*. It seems, then, that there are two comparative clause introducers for the equative construction in Rumanian, *ca* (*şi*) and *cum*, parallel to *como* and *quanto* in Portuguese, but only *cum* allows a full clause to follow. The construction with *cum* is parallel to the Spanish *tan(to)* . . . *como* equative construction. It is clear that the comparative of equality constructions are not subject to the effects of the tensed verb constraint, as expected, unlike the comparatives of inequality, which must resort to a relativized phrasal construction to avoid the effects of this constraint.

4.3.3 The clause introducer

There are two structural possibilities shared by the comparatives of equality and the comparatives of inequality: the reduced sentential construction and the oblique phrasal construction. Where they differ is in the availability of a (non-oblique) relativized phrasal construction (allowed for the comparatives of inequality: see, for example, (157)) and a full sentential construction (allowed for the comparatives of equality: see (179)). This is unlike the situation in French, Italian or Spanish. Unlike French, Rumanian does not have a universal 'comparative particle' equivalent to *que* (though *ca* may be used in both types of comparative, with the restrictions mentioned). While the range of comparative particles is at least partially similar to the range found in Italian, the lack in Rumanian of an expletive negative element which may act as an additional marker of comparison limits the range of possible structures. Unlike Spanish, Rumanian has two alternative comparative particles to introduce the subordinate clause of the equative constructions. In fact, Rumanian most closely resembles Portuguese. For the expression of comparatives of inequality, Rumanian has the clause introducers *ca* and *decît*, while Portuguese has *que* and *do que*. Where the equative construction is concerned, Rumanian has *ca (şi)* and *cum*, while Portuguese has *como* and *quanto*. Also, in both Rumanian and Portuguese these latter are in complementary distribution, while the former are only partially so (where the ensuing clause is reduced).

There seem, then, to be four clause introducers available to act as 'comparative particles' in Rumanian. For the comparatives of inequality these are, in principle, *ca* and *decît*. *Ca*, the less usual alternant, may not be followed by a tensed verb, just like Spanish and Portuguese *que*. *Decît*, analysed as a fusion of *de* + *cît*, parallels Italian *di quanto* most closely at the formal level, and functions like Spanish *de lo que* and Portuguese *do que*; *de* is followed by a free relative heading an ensuing relative clause. However, the structure of *decît* is opaque and it is therefore interpreted synchronically as a simple 'comparative particle'. As a result, it may, like *ca*, introduce a reduced clause as well as being obligatory when a tensed verb occurs in the second half of the comparison.

Ca (şi) and *cum*, on the other hand, are in complementary distribution, *ca (şi)* introducing a reduced comparative clause and *cum* introducing a full clause containing a tensed verb.

4.3.4 Summary of the situation in Rumanian

The preceding discussion of the means available in Rumanian for the expression of comparison has necessarily been limited. Nevertheless, even a limited examination of the data has demonstrated that the general constraint on comparatives of inequality being proposed here, that they must contain a marker of comparison, applies equally to Rumanian and has as a predictable consequence a tensed verb constraint due to the near identity of the comparative particle *ca* and the tensed clause complementizer *că*. A tensed verb may not appear in the subordinate clause of a comparative of inequality unless the clause introducer is *decît*; it is disallowed in the (less common) *mai/mai puţin . . . ca* construction. Rumanian is like Portuguese and Spanish in that it does not have available an expletive negative particle to act as an extra marker of comparison and license the appearance of a tensed verb, thus escaping the effects of the tensed verb constraint. Instead, Rumanian employs a relativized phrasal construction, *mai/mai puţin . . . decît*, to express a comparison of inequality involving a tensed verb in the second half of the comparison. The synthetic form of *decît* makes this analysis less immediately obvious than in the case of Spanish *de lo que* or Portuguese *do que*. Nonetheless, it has been shown that, despite its opacity, *decît* is formally parallel to Italian *di quanto* (and may occasionally be replaced by the less opaque *de cum*, parallel to Italian *di come*). The analysis of *mai/mai puţin . . . decît* comparatives as relativized phrasal constructions, then, is formally motivated and, more importantly, explains why a tensed verb may follow *decît* but not *ca*: the tensed verb constraint applies only to comparative subordinate clauses, not to relative clauses.

As the tensed verb constraint does not apply to equative constructions, a tensed verb may surface after *la fel de/tot aşa de/tot atît de . . . cum* and a relativized phrasal option is not required. Nevertheless, the data indicate that such structures are unusual and that equative constuctions are almost always reduced, in which case *cum* is replaced by the clause introducer *ca (şi)*.

Of the languages surveyed so far, Rumanian is most like Spanish and Portuguese in lacking an expletive negative element. As a result, it displays the effects of the tensed verb constraint quite clearly, though the opaque form of the clause introducer *decît*, combining the preposition *de* and *cît*, the head of the ensuing relative clause, makes this fact about Rumanian rather more difficult to perceive than it is in Spanish and Portuguese. Most significantly, however, the situation in Rumanian, though superficially dissimilar to the other languages under consideration, has been shown to provide yet more evidence for the thesis that there exists a general constraint against the appearance of a tensed verb in the second half of a comparative of inequality whenever the marker of comparison (the comparative particle) and the tensed clause complementizer are not fully distinct items.

4.4 COMPARATIVE CONSTRUCTIONS IN CATALAN

Catalan comparative constructions appear to share some of the features of both their Spanish and French equivalents. As in Spanish, there is no single comparative clause introducer, the equative construction and the comparatives of inequality having different 'comparative particles'. Consequently, the structures available for the expression of the two types of comparison differ and the comparative particle *que* may itself be considered to be a marker of comparison. Unlike Spanish, however, Catalan does make use of an expletive negative as an additional marker of comparison. As a result, the tensed verb constraint does not apply to the comparatives of inequality, just as in French and Italian.

The following brief discussion of the construction types used in Catalan to express comparison should suffice to demonstrate these facts. As before, most of the example sentences will express full comparison.

4.4.1 The comparatives of inequality

There are three possible construction types:

1 a full sentential construction, e.g. (184):

(184) Aparenta més anys que no té[43]
He looks older than he is

2 a reduced sentential construction, e.g. (185):

(185) En Pau era menys esportiu que el seu germà[44]
Paul was less interested in sport than his brother

3 a relativized phrasal construction involving *del que*, e.g. (186):

(186) Dóna més del que promet
He gives more than he promises

The full sentential construction

The construction type exemplified in (184) is a full sentential construction, the clause following *que* being non-reduced. The following are further examples of this structure:

(187) Va resultar més fácil que no semblava
It proved to be easier than it looked
(188) Vàreu tardar menys a fer-ho que no ens havíem imaginat[45]
You took less time to do it than we had imagined
(189) El projecte tindria així menys possibilitats que no té en la seva solució actual
The project would thus have fewer possibilities than it has in its present form
(190) Parla menys que no creuries pel seu posat festiu

He speaks less than you would think by his cheerful manner
(191) Tu has caçat més ànecs que no he pescat jo truites[46]
You have shot more ducks than I have caught trout

Sentences (184) and (187-90) are expressions of full comparison, with the noun, adjective, verb, noun and verb, respectively, as the categories of comparison. Sentence (191) is an expression of partial comparison, the nouns *ànecs* and *truites* being the categories of comparison. Such constructions are ungrammatical without *no*:

(192) *Va resultar més fàcil que semblava

According to Badia Margarit (1980: 36-7), 'cuando se expresa el verbo subordinado . . . es indispensable el uso del adverbio [*no*] . . . en estas oraciones es preceptivo el uso de *no*.' This is exactly as my analysis would predict. Expletive *no* in Catalan acts as an extra marker of comparison, exactly parallel to Italian *non* and French *ne* (though *ne* is the sole comparison marker of French), serving to license the appearance of a tensed verb in the comparative subordinate clause. Without the presence of *no*, the tensed verb constraint applies, rendering the sentence ungrammatical.[47]

As I have demonstrated for French and Italian, this expletive negative is without negative force. It is described by Badia Margarit (1980: 272) as 'un adverbio . . . sin valor negativo'. Its role is simply to act as a comparison marker. What is somewhat surprising, however, is that, unlike French expletive *ne*, which is not the standard negative, and Italian expletive *non*, which is differentiated from the standard negative by the use of the subjunctive mood in comparative clauses, Catalan expletive *no* is identical to the standard sentential negative and is not differentiated from this syntactically. Perhaps because of this, it only occurs after non-negated matrix clauses:

(193) ??*No va resultar més fàcil que no semblava
It did not prove to be easier than it looked

Example (193) is highly unacceptable, since the true negative in the matrix tends to force an interpretation in which expletive *no* is actually negating *semblava*, i.e. 'It did not prove to be easier than it did not look.' Example (193), therefore, is unacceptable for two reasons: firstly, this interpretation is difficult to process; and secondly, under this interpretation there is no expletive element (*no* cannot play two roles at once), hence the presence of the (unlicensed) tensed verb renders the sentence ungrammatical.

As the presence of expletive *no* enables a full clause to follow *que*, it is also possible for the second compared element to be embedded more than one clause down, e.g. (194):

(194) Ven més que no diuen que compra[48]
He sells more than they say that he buys

This process of embedding is only possible in languages which have an expletive negative element; it is not, therefore, possible in Spanish, as has been shown in Chapter 2.

The reduced sentential construction

The construction type exemplified in (185) is a reduced sentential construction, the category which has 'survived' after *que* being the subject of the subordinate clause, *el seu germà*. The following are further examples of this construction:

(195) La nit era més humida que freda
The night was more humid than cold
(196) La literatura llatina resulta menys interessant que la grega
Latin literature is less interesting than Greek
(197) Aquest propietari és més ric que tots els altres del poble plegats
This land-owner is richer than all the others in the town together
(198) La pel·lícula és menys interessant que la novel·la corresponent
The film is less interesting than the corresponding novel
(199) Estarem més bé a fora que a dintre[49]
We shall be better off outside than inside
(200) Pitjor serà la cura que la malaltia
The cure will be worse than the illness
(201) Tu tens més pràctica que jo en qüestions de comerç
You have more experience than I in business matters

Sentences (185) and (196–201) are expressions of full comparison. The adjective is the category of comparison in (185), (196–8) and (200). In (199) the adverb is compared and in (201) the noun. Example (195) is an expression of partial comparison, the adjectives *humida* and *freda* being contrasted.

It seems, however, that a negative may optionally be inserted in such structures,[50] e.g. (202):

(202) Pitjor serà la cura que no la malaltia

This expletive *no* may even be accompanied by *pas*, e.g. (203):

(203) Pitjor serà la cura que no pas la malaltia

According to Yates (1975: 164), 'when a verb is suppressed in the second part of the comparison . . . the *no* . . . can be reinforced with *pas* or omitted altogether.' For Badia Margarit also (1980: 37), 'cuando se omite el verbo subordinado . . . se puede posponer siempre el refuerzo *pas* al adverbio *no* . . . es correcto tanto reforzar el adverbio *no* con *pas*, como prescindir del propio adverbio.'

The position appears to be that in reduced sentential constructions either *no* or *no pas* may optionally occur after *que*. On the other hand, *pas* may never cooccur with *no* in full sentential constructions. This raises two questions; first, why does the expletive negative appear when there is no tensed verb; and second, why may it be accompanied by *pas* in such contexts only?

To answer these questions, it is first worth pointing out that it is not the case, as grammars suggest, that the negative is always entirely optional in reduced sentential comparatives. Taking (199) as an example, alternative versions including *no/no pas*, e.g. (204), are not entirely equivalent:

(204) a. Estarem més bé a fora que no a dintre
b. Estarem més bé a fora que no pas a dintre

These versions are perceived as being marked stylistically as highly formal and may thus be considered somewhat stilted, the version excluding the negative(s) being much preferred.

While this preference may be linked to perceived formality, there are contexts in which *no/no pas* may be virtually excluded. For example, while (201) is fully acceptable, the versions below are much less so:

(205) a. ?Tu tens més pràctica que no jo en qüestions de comerç
b. ?Tu tens més pràctica que no pas jo en qüestions de comerç

The same is true of (185):

(206) a. ?En Pau era menys esportiu que no el seu germà
b. ?En Pau era menys esportiu que no pas el seu germà

These judgements contrast sharply with the perceived correctness of, for example, (199) and (204), or of the following versions of (195):

(207) a. La nit era més humida que no freda
b. La nit era més humida que no pas freda

The difference between the sentences appears to be related to the perceived strength of contrast in the comparison. In (204), *a dintre* contrasts strongly, both formally and semantically, with *a fora*. In (207), the same is true of the adjectives *freda* and *humida*. It seems the weaker the perceived contrast, the less acceptable the inclusion of *no/no pas* will be: hence (201) is preferred to (205), since *jo* is not perceived to be strongly contrasted with *tu*. Notice that if a noun contrasting with *pràctica* is involved, the 'negated' version becomes much more acceptable:

(208) a. Tu tens més pràctica que no coneixements en qüestions de comerç
b. Tu tens més pràctica que no pas coneixements en qüestions de comerç
You have more experience than knowledge in business matters

Similarly, (185) is preferred to (206) because the contrast between *el seu germà* and *en Pau* is weak. Rather, a contrast with the adjective *esportiu* is expected and this will allow the inclusion of *no/no pas*:

(209) a. En Pau era menys esportiu que no artistic
b. En Pau era menys esportiu que no pas artistic
Paul was less interested in sport than (he was) artistic

This indicates that the function of *no* in such comparisons is simply to underline a perceived contrast. If either the syntactic structure or the interpretation of the comparative does not point to such a contrast, the acceptability of *no/no pas* in the reduced clause may be markedly reduced.[51] Thus the function of *no* in such structures is not that of licensing a tensed verb, though it clearly could not have been incorporated had it not occurred elsewhere in expressions of comparison.

Pas is not allowed in non-reduced sentential constructions: 'La locución *no pas* puede aparecer también en vez del simple *no*, en las oraciones comparativas, cuando se omite el verbo subordinado' (Badia Margarit, 1980: 47). The preceding examples indicate why *pas* may cooccur with *no* in reduced clauses only: it serves to differentiate this use of *no* from the expletive negative of the full sentential construction. Catalan *pas* is not equivalent to the French negative *pas*. According to Badia Margarit (p. 43), *pas* has various interpretations, 'el más importante de los cuales tiene valor adversativo'. There is no difference in meaning between *no* and *no pas*: 'cuando cualquier parte de una oración no negativa va precedida del adverbio *no*, éste admite por lo común el adverbio *pas* pospuesto, sin que el cambio de *no* en *no pas* altere esencialmente el sentido de la oración' (Badia Margarit, 1980: 46). *Pas*, therefore, serves to underline the perceived contrast in the comparison, reinforcing *no*. As has been demonstrated, where this contrast is weaker neither *no* nor *no pas* will normally be included.

The answers to the two questions posed earlier are, therefore, that expletive *no* may appear (optionally) in reduced clauses, where there is no tensed verb, as its function is not to license a verb, but rather to emphasize a perceived contrast. Hence *pas* may accompany it as a typical marker of contrast, but may not occur in full clauses, where the role of *no* is very different. *No*, with or without *pas*, is generally omitted in such reduced comparatives if the perceived contrast is not strong. Moreover, the inclusion of *no/no pas*, when the context allows, may mark the sentence as formal. While this use of *no* must be distinguished from expletive *no* in the full sentential construction, for all the above reasons and, particularly, because it is never optional in the latter construction, it is clear that its apparently general availability as a marker of comparison must be linked to its basic function as an additional marker of comparison in tensed comparative clauses.

Nonetheless, *no (pas)* in reduced clauses, just as in full clauses, cannot be considered to have negative import. In fact, when there is a risk of it, i.e. *no* without *pas*, being interpreted as true negation in the second half of the comparison, for example when it precedes an infinitive, it is usually avoided: 'en este caso es de aconsejar ... suprimir simplemente el adverbio *no*' (Badia Margarit, 1980: 37). As it is not a negative itself, *no* may even cooccur with a true negative, though it must be reinforced by *pas*, e.g. (210):

(210) Més s'estima restar a casa avui que no pas no veure les festes
He prefers to stay at home rather than not to see the celebrations

The sequence *no pas no* is possible only because *pas* serves to differentiate the first *no* (the marker of comparison) from the second *no* (the true negative). As *pas* cannot occur in full clauses, a sequence *no . . . no* is not possible in such clauses (see (193)).

The phrasal construction involving del que

The phrasal construction is exemplified in (186) (repeated):

(186) Dóna més del que promet

This is an alternative to the *més/menys . . . que* construction. Example (211) is the sentential version of (186):

(211) Dóna més que no promet

Similarly, the sentential examples given, e.g. (184), (187), (188) and (190), may be constructed as phrasal comparatives:

(212) Aparenta més anys dels que té
(213) Va resultar més fàcil del que semblava
(214) Vàreu tardar menys a fer-ho del que ens havíem imaginat
(215) Parla menys del que creuries pel seu posat festiu

The phrasal construction may not be used with a reduced clause, nor may it contain an expletive negative:

(216) *Estarem més bé a fora del que a dintre
(217) *Dóna més del que no promet

The sequence *del que* is made up of the preposition *de* + *el*, heading an ensuing relative clause. This is exactly parallel to the Spanish *más/menos . . . de lo que* construction; in Catalan also the pronoun is not invariable, displaying number and gender marking when the object of comparison is a noun (see (212)). As the second half of such comparatives is actually a relative, rather than comparative, clause, the tensed verb constraint does not apply, hence the non-occurrence of expletive *no*: the tensed verb may appear with impunity.

The relativized phrasal construction, like the sentential construction, also allows embedding of the second category of comparison, e.g. (218):

(218) Ven menys del que diuen que tothom sap que en Pere afirma que compra[52]
He sells less than they say that everyone knows that Peter claims that he buys

Here the comparison relates to an empty position embedded four clauses down.

Although the two structures, sentential and phrasal, appear to be free alternatives, if the first half of the comparison is negated, the phrasal alternative is normally the only possibility.[53] It has already been shown that expletive *no* may not follow a negative matrix (see (193)). The phrasal version of (193), however, is unproblematic:

(219) No va resultar més fácil del que semblava
It did not prove to be easier than it looked

Similarly, negated versions of, for example, (184) and (211), would of necessity be phrasal in structure:

(220) No aparenta més anys dels que té
He does not look older than he is
(221) No dóna més del que promet
He does not give more than he promises

The phrasal and sentential structures, then, are only truly alternatives in positive expressions of comparison. When the first half of a comparison is negated, expletive *no* becomes intrusive, for reasons already discussed, and the phrasal construction with (some version of) *del que* is the only possibility. This contrasts with the situation in French and Italian where, although it is preferred that expletive *ne/non* should not be preceded by a negative matrix clause, it is possible. The difference may be traced to the fact that in Catalan the expletive negative is identical to the true negative and is not distinguished, as in Italian, by verbal mood, whence the much stronger prohibition. This explains why, despite having an expletive negative element which allows a tensed verb to occur in the comparative subordinate clause, Catalan also retains a phrasal construction, which is common in languages, like Spanish, which have no expletive negative element and therefore require the phrasal construction as the sole means of expressing a comparison containing a tensed verb in the second half. In Catalan, only the phrasal construction may normally express a negated comparison.

In fact, it seems that in all cases the full sentential construction including expletive *no* may be perceived as stylistically more formal than the phrasal alternative. As a result, the *més/menys* . . . *del que* construction appears to be preferred, except in highly formal situations. This may be because of the potential ambiguity of a structure containing an expletive element that is not formally identifiable as such. Alternatively, it may be due to the influence of Castilian, where the phrasal structure is the only one possible. It seems likely that both of these factors are influential.

4.4.2 The comparative of equality

There are two possible construction types for the expression of a comparison of equality:

1 a full sentential construction, e.g. (222):

(222) Tenia tantes[54] banderetes nacionals com països havia visitat
He had as many national flags as he had visited countries

2 a reduced sentential construction, e.g. (223):

(223) No sóc tan ximple com tu[55]
I am not as silly as you

There is no relativized phrasal construction after *tan . . . com* parallel to the *més/menys . . . del que* construction.

The full sentential construction

Sentence (222) exemplifies the full sentential construction, ás do the following:

(224) Tan disciplinadament com (ho fan) els japonesos, ningú no hi treballa a Europa[56]
As disciplinedly as the Japanese work, nobody works in Europe
(225) No costa tant com era de témer
It does not cost as much as was to be feared

(226) Val tant com pesa
It is worth as much as it weighs

Examples (222) and (226) are expressions of partial comparison, the nouns *banderetes* and *països*, and the verbs *val* and *pesa*, being compared, respectively; (224) and (225) are expressions of full comparison, with the adverb and verb, respectively, as the objects of comparison. There is no expletive negative in the clause introduced by *com*. This is as expected, due to the inapplicability of the tensed verb constraint to equative constructions; the tensed verb does not need to be licensed in such clauses. As there is no expletive negative in such constructions, it is unproblematic for the verb of the matrix clause to be negated:

A consideration of other Romance languages 219

(227) No val tant com pesa
It is not worth as much as it weighs

The equivalent sentential construction for the comparatives of inequality is ruled out, as has been illustrated.

As there is no restriction on the appearance of a tensed verb in the equative construction, the compared element may also, as for the comparatives of inequality, be related to a position embedded in an ensuing clause, e.g. (228):

(228) Ven tant com la Maria sap que diuen que compra[57]
He sells as much as Maria knows that they say that he buys

The reduced sentential construction

Sentence (223) exemplifies the reduced sentential construction, the subject *tu* having 'survived' the reduced clause. The following are further examples of this construction:

(229) Sabadell té tanta indústria com Terrassa
Sabadell has as much industry as Terrassa
(230) Tu has enraonat tant com ella
You have talked as much as her
(231) No ho ha fet tan ràpidament com el seu germà
He has not done it as quickly as his brother

Sentences (223) and (229–31) are all expressions of full comparison, involving the adjective, noun, verb and adverb, respectively, as the categories of comparison.

Just as in the case of the full sentential construction, no expletive negative is found in the reduced sentential construction.

4.4.3 The clause introducer

The equative construction and the comparatives of inequality share two structures: the full and reduced sentential constructions. They differ only in that there is an additional construction type available for the expression of a comparative of inequality, the relativized phrasal construction involving *del que*. This is unlike the situation in French or Spanish. Unlike French, Catalan has no universal 'comparative particle' equivalent to *que*. Comparison with Spanish, on the other hand, shows an identical range of comparative clause introducers, three in Spanish (*que, de, como*) and three in Catalan (*que, de, com*). Nonetheless, unlike Spanish, Catalan makes use of an expletive negative following *que* and hence allows a full sentential construction for the expression of a comparison of inequality, where Spanish allows only a phrasal construction. Catalan comparatives of inequality, like their Italian equivalents, appear to be doubly marked for comparison, once via the comparative particle itself, and again by the expletive negative. As in Italian, this is advantageous in extending the structural possibilities for such constructions, in other words, in allowing full clauses, containing a tensed verb, to follow *que* unambiguously.

There are, then, three clause introducers available to act as 'comparative particles' in Catalan. For the comparatives of inequality these are *que* and *de*; a tensed verb may follow *que*, due to the presence of an expletive negative, and also *de*, since it has as its complement *el*, heading an ensuing relative clause. *Com* introduces the subordinate clause of an equative construction, with no restrictions on the presence of a tensed verb.

4.4.4 Summary of the situation in Catalan

Once again, although the preceding discussion of the structural possibilities for the expression of comparison in Catalan has been brief, even a limited consideration of the data has shown that the constraint on the occurrence of a tensed verb in the subordinate clause of a comparative of inequality is equally applicable in Catalan. A tensed verb could not, in theory, follow comparative *que* due to its formal identity with the tensed clause complementizer. However, the availability of an expletive negative *no*, acting as an additional marker of comparison, licenses the appearance of a tensed verb after *més/menys . . . que*, parallel to the situation in French and Italian. Additionally, Catalan allows an alternative phrasal structure, *més/menys . . . del que*, in which the tensed verb may appear unproblematically, since it is in a relative, rather than comparative, clause, to which the tensed verb constraint does not apply. This phrasal structure is formally parallel to the *más/menos . . . de lo que* phrasal construction of Spanish. Functionally, however, it differs greatly. While the phrasal construction of Spanish constitutes the only means of expressing a comparison of inequality including a tensed verb in its second half, in Catalan it acts as an alternative to the full sentential construction. Only when the first half of a comparative of inequality is negated does the phrasal construction become the only one available. I have suggested that this may be due to the formal identity of the expletive negative, which lacks negative force, and the standard negative, a situation which does not arise in French and Italian, whose expletive negatives are, respectively, formally and contextually distinguishable. Although the phrasal construction is required only in negated contexts, it seems it is generally preferred to the sentential construction, which is perceived as highly formal. This may be due to the influence of Castilian.

The expletive negative of Catalan also appears optionally in reduced sentential constructions, where it may be reinforced by *pas*. I have shown that its occurrence is not, in fact, truly optional, but conditioned by the strength of the perceived contrast in the comparison. Where this is weak, *no/no pas* will not occur. While the extension of the expletive negative to such contexts must obviously be linked to its obligatory occurrence in a non-reduced comparative clause, its function is clearly not the same. It does not license the presence of a tensed verb; rather, it serves to signal a strong contrast; hence the possible cooccurrence of *pas*, a non-negative particle which is normally used in Catalan to express or reinforce an adversative nuance. *Pas* may not cooccur with *no* in the full sentential construction, precisely because this is not the function of *no* in such contexts. The use of *no/no pas* in reduced sentential constructions is, in any case, considered highly formal.

As the tensed verb constraint does not apply to equative constructions, a tensed verb may appear following *tan . . . com* and a relativized phrasal option is not required.

Catalan has been shown to share some of the features of both French and Spanish, but to be identical to neither. Formally, it most closely resembles Spanish, in particular with regard to the existence of a phrasal construction. However, the availability of an expletive negative, able to act as an additional marker of comparison and license the appearance of a tensed verb, hence avoiding the effects of the tensed verb constraint in comparatives of inequality, links Catalan more closely to French and Italian. In sharing some of the features of all three languages, Catalan has a greater range of structural possibilities than any of them. Nonetheless, this diversity of construction types has been shown to be amenable to the same analysis as Spanish, French, Italian, Portuguese and Rumanian and thus further supports the thesis that in comparatives of inequality a tensed verb may not occur whenever the comparative particle is formally identical to the tensed clause complementizer.

4.5 COMPARATIVE CONSTRUCTIONS IN GALICIAN, FRIULAN, OCCITAN AND WALLOON

There follows a very brief consideration of the means available for the expression of comparison in Galician, Friulan, Occitan and Walloon, the purpose of which is to demonstrate that the constraint disallowing a tensed verb in the subordinate clause of a comparative of inequality may apply very generally in Romance.

4.5.1 Comparative constructions in Galician

In Galician, a comparative of equality is constructed with *tan . . . coma*, e.g.:

(232) Esta rapaza é tan loira coma ti[58]
   This girl is as blonde as you

The comparatives of inequality are constructed with *máis/menos . . . ca*, e.g.:

(233) Aquel home é máis bo ca min
   That man is better than me
(234) Esta nena é menos grande ca a túa
   This girl is smaller than yours

It is possible for *ca* to be replaced by *do que*, as in (235):

(235) Esta nena é menos grande do que a túa

The meanings of (235) and (234) are identical. However, while *do que* is an optional alternant of *ca* in sentences like (233) and (234), it is obligatory 'cuando figura un verbo en el segundo término de la comparación' (Carballo Calero, 1976: 174–5). Hence only *do que* may introduce the second half of the comparison in a sentence like (236):

(236) E máis doado do que coidabas
   It is easier than you thought

Thus Galician patterns very much like Portuguese, and just as the analysis defended here would predict: *do que* is clearly the sequence preposition + pronoun heading a relative clause, hence a tensed verb may appear after *do que*, since it then occurs in a relative, rather than comparative, clause; a tensed verb may not, however, follow *ca*, since *ca* introduces a comparative subordinate clause and the tensed verb constraint will apply. As Galician lacks an expletive negative element, the relativized phrasal comparative construction is the only means of avoiding the effects of the tensed verb constraint, just as in Spanish. Unlike Spanish, however, and like Portuguese, the synthetic and invariable form of the preposition + pronoun, *do*, has led to *do que* being reanalysed as a simple comparative clause introducer and as a result it may optionally introduce reduced sentential and oblique phrasal comparative clauses, even though they lack a tensed verb. As in all the other languages so far considered, the equative construction is unaffected by the tensed verb constraint.

In Galician, as in Spanish, Portuguese and Rumanian, the lack of an expletive negative to act as an additional marker of comparison in the subordinate clause of comparatives of inequality means that the tensed verb constraint will apply to such constructions; therefore, Galician, like the other three languages, makes use of a relativized phrasal construction to avoid this constraint.

4.5.2 Comparative constructions in Friulan

In Friulan, according to Gregor (1975: 86), comparatives of inequality are constructed with *plui/mancul* 'followed by *di* or *che* (*no*), according to need', a somewhat vague formulation. Iliescu (1972), discussing the Friulan dialects spoken in Rumania, gives *pluy*, *pi*, *puy*, *plu* and *pu* as alternants of *plui* and *pluy pôk* and *mànkul* as an alternant of *mancul*; she states that they are followed by either *di* or *ke no*: 'le second terme de la comparaison est introduit d'habitude par la préposition di . . . . Il peut être introduit aussi par *ke no*' (p. 145). She gives the following example:

(237) Soy mànkul malât di te
    I am less ill than you

Sentence (237) is an example of an oblique phrasal construction.

Neither Gregor nor Iliescu illustrate sentential comparative constructions in Friulan. However, the fact that both agree that alongside the preposition *di*, which appears to serve as the 'comparative particle' in oblique phrasal comparatives, there exists a clause introducer, *che/ke*, followed by an (optional for Gregor) expletive negative element *no*, strongly suggests that Friulan patterns like French and Italian in making use of an expletive negative as a marker of comparison in the subordinate clause of full sentential comparative of inequality constructions to avoid the effects of the tensed verb constraint. Friulan does not appear to have available a relativized phrasal construction, the other possible means of avoiding the effects of the tensed verb constraint.

4.5.3 Comparative constructions in Occitan

In Occitan, a comparative of equality is constructed using *autant . . . que*, e.g.:

(238) Pòrta autant de blad que de cibada[59]
    He carries as much wheat as hay
(239) Es autant valent que son fraire
    He is as brave as his brother

Sentence (238) is an expression of partial comparison, involving the nouns as the categories of comparison; (239) is an expression of full comparison, with the adjective the category of comparison. Both are reduced sentential constructions.

The comparatives of inequality are constructed with *mai/mens . . . que*, e.g.:

(240) Es mai corajos que son fraire
    He is more courageous than his brother

Example (240) is a reduced sentential construction expressing full comparison, with the adjective the category compared.

The following examples are full sentential constructions:

(241) Es mens uros qu'òm non crei
    He is less happy than one thinks
(242) Parla l'occitan melhor que non l'escriu
    He speaks Occitan better than he writes it

Both (241) and (242) are expressions of full comparison, with the adjective and adverb, respectively, the categories being compared. Unlike the reduced construction of (240), however, these contain an instance of an expletive negative in the subordinate clause.[60] Moreover, this expletive *non* is not identical to standard sentential negation in Occitan, which, according to Decomps and Gonfroy (1979: 38), 'n'est formée que d'une seule particule placée après le verbe', e.g.:

(243) Sei pas malaude
    I am not ill

The expletive negative *non*, therefore, is clearly distinguishable from the true negative, *pas*, in Occitan. The function of the expletive *non* in (241) and (242) is, as expected, to act as a marker of comparison and license the appearance of the tensed verbs, *crei* and *escriu*. Without the presence of *non*, both of these examples become ungrammatical.

Occitan appears, then, to pattern like French in avoiding the effects of the tensed verb constraint by making use of a distinct expletive negative element, *non*, to act as a comparison marker and thus allow a tensed verb to surface in the subordinate clause of a comparative of inequality; like French, Occitan has only one comparative particle, *que*, which may not, therefore, itself act as a marker of comparison. As expected, the tensed verb constraint has no effect on the structure of a comparative of equality.

4.5.4 Comparative constructions in Walloon

The following is an example of the comparative of equality construction in Walloon:

(244) Il è ot'tant malin k'l'ôte è bièsse[61]
   He is as sly as the other is stupid

Example (244) is a full sentential expression of partial comparison, with the adjectives *malin* and *bièsse* as the categories of comparison.

Sentence (245) is an example of the comparative of superiority:

(245) I n'a nin pus fin k'l'êwe n'à seû (proverb)
   He is not hungrier than water is thirsty

Sentence (245) is an expression of partial comparison, the nouns *fin* ('hunger') and *seû* ('thirst') being compared. It is a full sentential construction, that is a tensed verb occurs in the comparative subordinate clause. As expected, the tensed verb (*à*) is preceded by an expletive negative element, *ne*. It is the presence of the expletive negative, acting as a marker of comparison, which licenses the appearance of the tensed verb in the comparative subordinate clause, thus avoiding the effects of the tensed verb constraint. Naturally, no such expletive element is required in the equative construction as the tensed verb constraint has been shown not to apply in such contexts.

Walloon, then, is like French, in that it makes use of an expletive negative, rather than a relativized phrasal structure, to avoid the effects of the tensed verb constraint. This tensed verb constraint is, however, clearly applicable

4.5.5 Summary of the situation in Galician, Friulan, Occitan and Walloon

Galician, Friulan, Occitan and Walloon, no less than Italian, Portuguese, Rumanian and Catalan, provide evidence of the existence of a constraint disallowing tensed verbs in the subordinate clause of a sentential comparative of inequality construction whenever the comparative particle and the tensed clause complementizer are isomorphic. Galician behaves like Portuguese and Spanish (and, though less obviously, Rumanian) in favouring a relativized phrasal structure as a means of avoiding the constraint, that is, by completely dispensing with unreduced comparative clauses, replacing them with relative clauses. Friulan, Occitan and Walloon, on the other hand, more closely resemble French, Italian and Catalan in employing an expletive negative element, capable of acting as a marker of comparison, to license the presence of a tensed verb in a comparative subordinate clause. Although consideration of possible construction types has of necessity been very brief, all have been shown to provide evidence to support the general claim that the restriction I have labelled the tensed verb constraint is indeed operative in comparatives of inequality.

4.6 SUMMARY

Comparative constructions in a wide range of Romance languages have now been examined; in each case, the tensed verb constraint has been shown to be equally applicable, its effects being averted either by the use of a relativized phrasal comparative construction or the use of an expletive particle[62] as a marker of comparison. An expletive negative element in the second half of a comparative construction in Romance does, therefore, have an important role to play, not as a marker of negativity, but as a comparison marker, even if the centrality of this function is at times obscured as a result of processes of analogy or 'crossing'. Interestingly, only those languages which have available an expletive particle in other contexts appear to utilize it in comparative constructions. Those which do not make use of such an expletive element elsewhere in their syntax cannot use this means of escape from the tensed verb constraint and thus must use a relativized phrasal construction instead. Some languages, a minority, allow both options: it has been shown that this may be linked to stylistic considerations of perceived formality, as in Italian, where the expletive element triggers the subjunctive mood, a marker of formal style.

A prediction was made in section 1.8 of Chapter 1 with regard to how comparison may be marked in languages with particle comparatives. This was that if, as I have been suggesting, the marker of comparison may be either the comparative particle introducing the comparatives of inequality (when this is different from the particle introducing the equative construction and therefore distinctive) or an expletive negative element (when the same particle introduces both comparatives of inequality and of equality), only those languages in which there is a single comparative particle should utilize an expletive negative as a marker of comparison. While this is certainly the case in French, where *que* is the sole comparative particle and consequently cannot be a marker of comparison, it has been shown that languages like Italian and Catalan, which do possess distinctive comparative particles in comparatives of inequality (*che* and *que*, respectively) capable, therefore, of acting as markers of comparison, also make use of expletive negative elements (*non/no*), even though these do not appear to be required to mark the comparison. In such languages, then, comparatives of inequality seem to be doubly marked. This fact does not, however, vitiate the previous contention, for the following reason. As has been shown, the formal identity of the comparative particle and the tensed clause complementizer results in a restriction prohibiting the appearance of a tensed verb in comparative clauses, due to the possibility of misinterpretation of a comparative clause as a non-comparative clause. In such cases the marker of comparison, the particle, is in effect rendered unable to mark the construction despite being distinctive in relation to the equative particle, just because it is identical to the standard complementizer. Notice that this fact is, as it were, coincidental and unrelated to the system of comparative constructions itself. This formal identity, with its consequence that the particle can only be interpreted unambiguously as a marker of comparison when there is no following tensed verb (a context in which the complementizer could not appear), leads directly to the utilization of an additional marker of comparison, the expletive negative, where this is available. Thus, although such comparatives of inequality appear to be doubly marked for comparison, in fact, when a tensed verb is present the particle can no longer serve this function and the expletive negative becomes, in effect, the sole marker of comparison and a means of distinguishing such comparative clauses from standard tensed clauses; for this reason, I have referred to it as 'licensing' the appearance of a tensed verb.

To return to the original prediction, it seems that it must be modified to some extent, to take account of the 'interference' of the tensed clause complementizer, and might be rephrased in the following terms: languages in which the same comparative particle occurs in comparatives of inequality and equality will strictly require an expletive negative element to act as a marker of comparison in comparative clauses, while languages with two distinctive comparative particles will not be subject to such a requirement; however, if the comparative particle introducing comparatives of inequality is not fully distinct from the tensed clause complementizer and therefore is unable to act unambiguously as a marker of comparison, then languages may mark the comparison doubly by using an expletive negative, where this is available, as an additional marker of comparison.

It was also suggested in Chapter 1, section 1.8, that this fact may mean that the particle comparative languages are a less homogeneous group than Andersen (1983) suggests, with languages making use of an expletive negative as a marker of comparison possibly having a great deal in common with languages exhibiting juxtapositional comparatives. Interestingly, Stassen (1985), though he makes no reference to the use of expletive negatives in this context, does allocate particle comparatives to separate groups according to whether or not they use different comparative particles to introduce comparatives of inequality and equality (see Chapter 1, section 1.5.3). The link I am positing between this fact and the occurrence of expletive negatives suggests that Stassen's groups might be explained by reference to the concept of marker of comparison, which does not appear to play any part in his categorization.

The structural possibilities for the expression of comparison in Romance are extremely diverse. However, the wealth of detail can be predicted and accounted for by the simple generalizations proposed here, that the expression of comparison involves a focus element (the second compared category) and that in comparatives of inequality there must be a marker of comparison. It has been shown that a tensed verb may not occur in comparative clauses unless they are unambiguously marked as such, which leads, in Romance to a restriction I have labelled the tensed verb constraint.

This constraint has been shown to apply quite generally and with entirely predictable results in terms of permissible syntactic structures.

The strands of the argumentation which has led to this conclusion have been various and include consideration of the following: the frequent formal parallelism between the 'comparative particle' and the standard tensed clause subordinator; the availability or non-availability of a single 'comparative particle' for all types of comparison and the consequences of this in relation to how comparison may be marked; the possibility of topicalization of compared categories; the defocussing effect of relative clauses; the existence or non-existence of an expletive negative; the distinctive non-negative use of such a particle; the frequent 'crossing' of the expletive negative into other related structures; its status as a marker of comparison and the wider usage this may entail; the reanalysis of complex sequences as simple 'comparative particles'. Nonetheless, however slight the connection between some of these strands may have seemed, viewed as a whole they interweave to produce a picture, not of complexity, but essentially of simplicity. The constraints on comparison proposed here, that comparative constructions must contain a focus of comparison and that comparatives of inequality must contain a clear marker of comparison, have been shown to have complex consequences, but are themselves simple. Used as an analytical tool, they allow apparently contradictory facts to be reconciled and to follow from quite natural generalizations. Conversely, the data have been shown to support the existence of such constraints.

While only Romance languages, and particularly Spanish and French, have been considered here, the constraint relating to how comparison is marked may well apply much more generally. Its effects, however, are likely to be evidenced in differing ways in different languages, perhaps being conditioned parametrically. Nevertheless, whatever the wider validity of the proposals made here, the notion of a marker of comparison, and the subsequent constraints it imposes on comparative clauses, has, as I hope to have shown, considerable power, both explanatory and predictive.

Finally, there follows a list of the languages considered in this work (excluding Friulan, due to insufficient data), indicating the principal comparative particles available and the predictable consequences for the syntax of their comparative constructions. In each case, the comparative particles referred to are those which may introduce full comparative clauses, i.e. sentential constructions.

Spanish: comparative particle in comparatives of inequality: *que*
comparative particle in the comparative of equality: *como*
Result: marker of comparison is *que*

tensed clause complementizer: *que*
expletive negative available? No

Consequence: (a) a tensed verb may not normally follow comparative *que*
(b) relativized phrasal construction with *de lo que* predominant

French: comparative particle in comparatives of inequality: *que*
comparative particle in the comparative of equality: *que*
Result: marker of comparison is not *que*

tensed clause complementizer: *que*
expletive negative available? Yes (*ne*)
Result: marker of comparison is *ne*
Consequence:

(a) a tensed verb may follow comparative *que*
(b) relativized phrasal construction is rare

Italian: comparative particle in comparatives of inequality: *che*
comparative particle in the comparative of equality: *quanto/come*
Result: marker of comparison is *che*

tensed clause complementizer: *che*
expletive negative available? Yes (*non*)
Result: additional marker of comparison is *non*
Consequence:

(a) a tensed verb may follow comparative *che*
(b) relativized phrasal constructions with *di quanto/di quello che/di come* also frequent (due to formal status of sentential construction)

A consideration of other Romance languages 231

Portuguese: comparative particle in comparatives of inequality: *que*
comparative particle in the comparative of equality: *quanto*
Result: marker of comparison is *que*

tensed clause complementizer: *que*
expletive negative available? No
Consequence:

(a) a tensed verb may not follow comparative *que*
(b) relativized phrasal construction with *do que* predominant

Rumanian: comparative particle in comparatives of inequality: *că*
comparative particle in the comparative of equality: *cum*
Result: marker of comparison is *că*

tensed clause complementizer: *că*[63]
expletive negative available? No
Consequence:

(a) a tensed verb may not follow comparative *că*
(b) relativized phrasal construction with *decît* predominant

Catalan: comparative particle in comparatives of inequality: *que*
comparative particle in the comparative of equality: *com*
Result: marker of comparison is *que*

tensed clause complementizer: *que*
expletive negative available? Yes (*no*)
Result: additional marker of comparison is *no*
Consequence:

(a) a tensed verb may follow comparative *que*
(b) relativized phrasal construction with *del que* also frequent (possibly linked to influence of Castilian)

Galician: comparative particle in comparatives of inequality: *ca*
comparative particle in the comparative of equality: *coma*

Result: marker of comparison is *ca*

tensed clause complementizer: *que*[64]
expletive negative available? No
Consequence:

(a) a tensed verb may not follow comparative *ca*
(b) relativized phrasal construction with *do que* predominant

Occitan: comparative particle in comparatives of inequality: *que*
comparative particle in the comparative of equality: *que*
Result: marker of comparison is not *que*

tensed clause complementizer: *que*
expletive negative available? Yes (*non*)
Result: marker of comparison is *non*
Consequence:

(a) a tensed verb may follow comparative *que*
(b) relativized phrasal construction rare

Walloon: comparative particle in comparatives of inequality: *k'*
comparative particle in the comparative of equality: *k'*
Result: marker of comparison is not *k'*

expletive negative available? Yes (*ne*)
Result: marker of comparison is *ne*
Consequence:

(a) a tensed verb may follow comparative *k'*
(b) relativized phrasal construction rare

This summary of the much more detailed analyses which precede shows clearly that the interrelationship of the comparative particles and expletive elements, on the one hand, and the concept of marker of comparison, on the other, has predictable effects on the syntactic structures available for the expression of comparison in Romance languages.

NOTES

1 *Che* may in this context be replaced by *di*, e.g.:

   Oggi c'è più vento di ieri
   Today is windier than yesterday

2 As in Spanish and French, there exists a small number of morphological comparative adjectives and adverbs:

migliore	più buono
peggiore	più cattivo
maggiore	più grande
minore	più piccolo
meglio	più bene
peggio	più male

   The forms on the left have the semantic content of the analytical forms on the right.

3 Although Battaglia and Pernicone (1965: 167–8) describe *di* followed by a noun phrase as 'il costrutto comparativo più normale e più comune', they also state that 'A volte s'incontra il costrutto con la congiunzione *che* al posto della preposizione *di*', e.g.:

   (a) Io sono molto più stanco che te
       I am much more tired than you
   (b) Tu sei peggio che lui
       You are worse than him

   They describe this construction elsewhere as 'più rara' (p. 501). Notice that these are not examples of reduced sentential constructions, as shown by the form of the pronoun.

4 Examples (3–6) are taken from Lepschy and Lepschy (1988: 113–14)

5 She is, of course, entirely mistaken about Spanish.

6 It should be noted that while the connection between the subjunctive mood and expletive *non* is strong in Italian sentential comparatives, it is not impossible to find literary examples where an indicative verb cooccurs with *non*, for example the following from Boccaccio:

   Io amo molto più lui che egli non ama me
   I love him much more than he loves me

   Moreover, example (2), earlier in the chapter, may allow the indicative in colloquial everyday usage:

   Maria è più intelligente che tu non credi

   I am grateful to Giulio Lepschy for pointing this out. In such cases it must be assumed that *non* is interpreted as a non-negative marker of comparison, despite its formal identity with the standard negative, due to its occurrence in a comparative clause, i.e. a clause following matrix *più/meno*.

7 The full sentential version would, of course, require *non* + the subjunctive:

Quell'espressione si usa più nel nord che non si usi altrove

8 Stassen (1984: 178) states more vaguely that a negative element 'may crop up in comparatives as an independent item, given certain specific circumstances (as in French and Italian . . .)'.
9 Giulio Lepschy (personal communication) points out that he does not consider (41) to be totally unacceptable, but only somewhat awkward; if *quello che* is replaced by *quanto*, then (41) for him is fully acceptable:

Gianni è più grande di quanto non pensassi

10 Seuren (1973: 535) states that *Giovanni è più alto che pensavo* is also possible in Italian, a claim for which I have found no evidence.
11 Giulio Lepschy (personal communication) finds the asterixed examples (61b, 62b, 63a,b) not necessarily unacceptable. He also points out that a differently formulated question is perfectly acceptable, e.g.:

Che sia più intelligente di quanto tu credi/tu non creda?
Could it be that he is more intelligent than you think?

12 In a footnote (p. 89), Napoli and Nespor refer to some French data which they regard as problematic. They note that the following two sentences are acceptable in French:

(a) Jean n'est pas plus beau qu'on ne pense
   Jean is not more handsome than anybody thinks
(b) Jean ne peut pas être plus beau que vous ne pensiez
   Jean cannot be more handsome than you thought

The corresponding Italian examples, however, are not acceptable:

(c) *Gianni non è più bello di quanto non si pensi
(d) *Gianni non può essere più bello di quanto voi non pensiate

They conclude:

> We think the Italian Ss are out for semantic reasons. Thus either the semantics of the French Ss are different from those of the corresponding ones in Italian, or we are wrong and there is indeed some kind of syntactic constraint against two negatives which we do not understand.

They miss the point here. The French examples are sentential constructions, not relativized phrasal constructions like the Italian sentences. Expletive *ne* must appear, therefore, while expletive *non* is optional after *più/meno . . . di quanto*. These sentences are not directly comparable. The true equivalents in Italian are:

(e) Gianni non è più bello che non si pensi
(f) Gianni non può essere più bello che voi non pensiate

These may be slightly less acceptable than the French sentential structures. There are two reasons for this: firstly, French expletive *ne* is not identical to the full negation of the matrix clause, so less ambiguity is produced by its cooccurrence with *ne . . . pas* than is the case with Italian *non*; secondly, the possibility exists in Italian of avoiding the cooccurrence of two *non*s by using a phrasal construction without expletive *non*:

(g) Gianni non è più bello di quanto si pensa
(h) Gianni non può essere più bello di quanto voi pensate

This construction will therefore be preferred. The semantics of the constructions are entirely irrelevant. It is the status of the French and Italian constructions within the range of structural possibilities permitted by the two languages which differs. In the same footnote, Napoli and Nespor note that while the following sentence

(i) Maria non è più intelligente di nessuno
Maria is not more intelligent than anyone

is acceptable, the two sentences below are not:

(j) *Maria non è più intelligente di quanto non è nessuno
(k) *Maria non è più intelligente di quanto non sia nessuno
Maria is not more intelligent than anyone is

They state: 'Why this should be so is not clear to us. We see no semantic reason for excluding the indicative comparative.' However, the reasons for the unacceptability of these two versions are not semantic. The first, (j), is unacceptable because it is semantically equivalent to (i), the inclusion of the tensed verb, è, adding nothing semantically, but adding potential ambiguity syntactically, due to the forced addition of another *non*. The second, (k), is also unacceptable because the subjunctive verb of the subordinate clause will cause the preceding *non* to be interpreted as the expletive element, leaving *nessuno* without its required pre-verbal negative. The second *non* cannot play both roles at once.

13 This construction is parallel to the Spanish equative construction, *tan(to) . . . como*.
14 This means that Italian comparatives, like Spanish, but unlike French, must belong to two separate groups of comparative types under Stassen's (1985) analysis (see Chapter 1).
15 The arguments which have already been adduced in support of this claim with regard to Spanish and French in previous chapters are equally valid for Italian *che*: unlike the tensed clause subordinator, comparative *che* may be followed by a pronoun and by an infinitive:

(a) Io sono molto più stanco che te
I am much more tired than you
(b) Mi piace di più nuotare che fare i tuffi
I like swimming better than diving

As in Spanish, it is therefore possible for a context to occur in which both the comparative *che* and the tensed clause subordinator *che* would be required, potentially allowing a sequence *che che*. Spanish, as has been shown, avoids this in one of two ways: by inserting *no* between the two instances of *que* or by deleting one of them. Battaglia and Pernicone (1965: 569) give an example which appears to show that in Italian the second option is taken:

E meglio ch'egli affronti il viaggio che non se rimane qui
It is better that he should face the journey than that he should stay here

16 In Old French the preposition *de* also served 'as the marker of the standard NP in comparatives' (Stassen, 1985: 249), e.g.:

   plus grant de lui
   more tall than him

17 In fact, since *te* may also appear elsewhere in Italian in contexts where the subject form might be expected, it could also be considered to be an alternative form of the subject pronoun.
18 Recall, however, that the phrasal construction of French is marginal just because it is not required, unlike the phrasal construction of Italian, which is required as an alternative to the more formal sentential construction. This is perceived as formal because of the (usually) accompanying subjunctive verb, which is not required in French as expletive *ne* is formally distinct from the standard disjoint negative *ne . . . pas*. Hence French sentential comparatives are not perceived as formal.
19 Example taken from Willis (1980: 328).
20 According to Hundertmark-Santos Martins (1982: 42), in Old Portuguese *de* replaced both *que* and *do que* in such constructions. This construction would have been parallel to the Modern Italian oblique phrasal construction *più/meno . . . di*.
21 There are a number of synthetic comparatives in Portuguese:

melhor	mais bom
pior	mais mau
maior	mais grande
menor	mais pequeno
melhor	mais bem
pior	mais mal

22 As in Spanish, when *mais/menos* occurs before an indication of quantity or a number, *de* replaces (*do*) *que*:

   Tem menos de quinze anos
   He is less than fifteen years old

23 Example taken from Teyssier (1976: 86).
24 Example taken from Teyssier (1976: 260).
25 Example taken from Willis (1980: 328).
26 Examples (143) and (144) are taken from Teyssier (1976: 260).
27 Example taken from Teyssier (1976: 285).
28 Hills *et al.* (1944: 184) claim that 'if *than* is followed by a clause (containing a verb), the *do que* form is preferable'. This is clearly understating the obligatory nature of the alternation.
29 The form of the equative modifier is *tanto*, invariable with verbs and displaying gender and number marking with nouns, and *tão* with adjectives and adverbs.
30 Example taken from Teyssier (1976: 261).
31 Example taken from Willis (1980: 329).
32 Examples (149) and (150) are taken from Hundertmark-Santos Martins (1982: 43).
33 Example taken from Willis (1980: 329).
34 Example taken from Willis, (1980: 329).

A consideration of other Romance languages

35 This is so even though the comparative particle and the tensed clause complementizer are not fully identical, the former being *ca* and the latter *că*.
36 Adapted from Mallinson (1986).
37 Unless otherwise stated, all the following examples are taken from Mallinson (1986: 165–77).
38 Adapted from Mallinson (1986).
39 Adapted from Mallinson (1986.).
40 According to Baciu (1978: 94) *decît* may sometimes be replaced by *de cum*, e.g.:

Scriu mai correct decît/de cum citeşti tu
I write more correctly than you read

This is similar to the Italian phrasal construction *più/meno . . . di come* and reinforces the parallels mentioned here.
41 As Mallinson (1986: 166) points out, the noun *viaţa* has the definite suffix, despite the normal rule that removes it after most prepositions. This supports my contention that *decît* itself is not a preposition.
42 Example taken from Baciu (1978: 94).
43 Except where otherwise indicated, examples are taken (or adapted) from Badia Margarit (1980).
44 Adapted from Yates (1975).
45 Adapted from Yates (1975.).
46 Example taken from Bonet and Solà (1986).
47 The unacceptability of a tensed verb without the presence of *no* may not be total. Solà (1973: 124) marks the following sentence with ?:

?Pescaran ells més truites que caçareu vosaltres perdius

I am grateful to Max Wheeler for bringing this to my attention. The relative acceptability of this sentence may possibly be due to the strong parallelism of contrasts in the matrix and subordinate clauses.
48 Example taken from Bonet and Solà (1986).
49 Examples (197–9) are taken from Yates (1975: 164).
50 *No* also serves, as in Spanish, to avoid a sequence *que que*, e.g.:

Es millor que te'n vagis que no que et trobi aqui
It is better that you go than that he find you here

Pas may also be inserted after *no*, with no change of meaning.
51 Max Wheeler (personal communication) suggests that it may be the case that *no* (*pas*) is inappropriate when a comparison is being made between a 'given', or 'topic', element and a 'new', or 'comment', one. This would account for the low acceptability of (205) and (206).
52 Example taken from Bonet and Solà (1986).
53 Solà (1973: 124), however, gives the following as fully acceptable:

Tu no has caçat pas més ànecs que jo he pescat truites
You have not shot more ducks than I have caught trout

This is an expression of partial comparison. It may be that such comparisons do not allow a relativized phrasal structure.

54 The equative modifer is *tan* before an adjective or adverb, *tant* when a verbal modifier, and *tant/a(s)*, with gender and number marking, when modifying a noun.
55 Example taken from Yates (1975).
56 Examples (224–6) taken from Bonet and Solà (1986).
57 Example taken from Bonet and Solà (1986.).
58 Examples taken from Carballo Calero (1976).
59 Examples taken from Salvat (1973).
60 It seems that in Limousin, the variety of Occitan spoken around Limoges, an expletive negative with the form of *non pas* may optionally occur in a reduced comparative clause, that is even when a tensed verb is not present. The following examples are taken from Decomps and Gonfroy (1979):

(a) Lo petaron es pus economique que (non pas) l'autò
    The motor cycle is more economical than the car
(b) 'Trapet mai de golhons que (non pas) de truchas
    He caught more gudgeons than trouts
(c) Son darrier libre es melhor que (non pas) lo prumier
    His latest book is better than the first

In each of these examples, although only (b) is actually an expression of partial comparison, a strong contrast is set up between two categories; in (a) *lo petaron* is contrasted with *l'autò*, in (b) *golhons* with *truchas* and in (c) *son darrier libre* with *lo prumier*. It seems the function of *non pas* in such constructions is simply to emphasize this contrast, exactly parallel to *no pas* in Catalan. In both cases this expletive negative sequence is unlike the expletive negative found in full sentential constructions (*non* in Occitan, *no* in Catalan). Its function is not to license the appearance of a tensed verb; in fact, it is disallowed whenever a tensed verb is present. It serves merely to emphasize a perceived contrast, becoming much less acceptable when that contrast is weakened, as has been shown to be the case for Catalan.
61 Examples taken from Remacle (1952, 1960).
62 That the expletive particle is always formally a negative is interesting. It is not obvious from the synchronic perspective why this should be so. The expletive negative found in comparatives is, as I hope to have shown, unconnected with the notion of negativity; indeed, it is almost always formally or contextually differentiated from the true negative. However, the similarity I have noted between particle comparatives which contain expletive negatives and juxtapositional comparatives points to its original function as being that of signalling opposition, for which a formally negative particle is ideally suited.
63 In this case, the comparative particle and the tensed clause complementizer are not fully identical.
64 See note 63.

References

Agard, F. B. and R. J. Di Pietro (1965), *The Grammatical Structures of English and Italian*, Chicago, University of Chicago Press.
Andersen, P. K. (1983), *Word Order Typology and Comparative Constructions*, Amsterdam, Benjamins.
Antinucci, F. and A. Puglielli (1971), 'Struttura della quantificazione', in M. Medici and R. Simone (eds).
Ashby, W. J. (1976), 'The loss of the negative morpheme NE in Parisian French', *Lingua* 39: 119–37.
Ashby, W. J. (1981), 'The loss of the negative particle ne in French: a syntactic change in progress', *Language* 57 (3): 674–87.
Baciu, I. (1978), *Précis de grammaire roumaine*, Lyon, L'Hermès.
Bacri, N. (1976), *Fonctionnement de la négation*, Paris, Mouton.
Badia Margarit, A. M. (1980), *Gramática catalana*, Madrid, Gredos.
Baker, C. L. (1970), 'Double negatives', *Linguistic Inquiry* 1 (2): 169–86.
Battaglia, S. and V. Pernicone (1965), *La grammatica italiana*, Turin, Loescher.
Bergmans, L. (1982), 'Semantic aspects of comparison in Dutch, English and other languages', PhD thesis, University of Louvain.
Bolinger, D. L. (1950), 'The comparison of inequality in Spanish', *Language* 26: 28–62.
Bolinger, D. L. (1953), 'Addenda to the comparison of inequality in Spanish', *Language* 29 (1): 62–6.
Bonet, S. and J. Solà (1986), *Sintaxi generativa catalana*, Barcelona, Enciclopèdia catalana.
Bresnan, J. (1973), 'Syntax of the comparative clause', *Linguistic Inquiry* 4: 275–343.
Bresnan, J. (1975), 'Comparative deletion and constraints on transformations'. *Linguistic Analysis* 1: 25–74.
Bresnan, J. (1977), 'Variables in the theory of transformations', in P. Culicover, T. Wasow and A. Akmajian (eds).
Brettschneider, G. and C. Lehmann (eds) (1980), *Wege zur Universalien Forschung: Sprachwissenschaftliche Beiträge zum 60. Geburtstag von Hansjakob Seiler*, Tübingen, Narr.
Butt, J. and C. Benjamin (1989), *A New Reference Grammar of Modern Spanish*, London, Edward Arnold.
Campbell, R. J., M. G. Goldin and M. Clayton Wang (eds) (1974),

Linguistic Studies in Romance Languages: Proceedings of the Third Symposium on Romance Languages, Washington, Georgetown University Press.

Carballo Calero, R. (1976), *Gramática elemental del gallego común*, Vigo, Galaxia.

Combe, T. G. S. and P. Rickard (eds) (1970), *The French Language*, London, Harrap.

Culicover, P., T. Wasow and A. Akmajian (eds) (1977), *Formal Syntax*, New York. Academic Press.

Damourette, J. (1932), 'Sur la négation en français', *Zeitschrift für französische Sprache und Linguistik* 55: 86–90.

Damourette, J. and E. Pichon (1928), 'Sur la signification psychologique de la négation en français', *Journal de psychologie* 228–54.

De Boer, C. (1954), *Syntaxe du français moderne*, Leiden, Universitaire Pers Leiden.

Decomps, D. and G. Gonfroy (1979), *L'occitan redde e ben: lo lemosín*, Paris, Omnivox.

De Mello, G. (1977), '*Que* and *de* as translations of *than*', *Hispania* 60: 510–11.

Demonte, V. (1977), *La subordinación sustantiva*, Madrid, Ediciones Cátedra.

Doherty, P. C. and A. Schwartz (1967), 'The syntax of the compared adjective in English', *Language* 43 (4): 903–36.

Dubois, J. and F. Dubois-Charlier (1970), *Eléments de linguistique française: syntaxe*, Paris, Larousse.

Enkvist, N. E. (1976), 'Notes on valency, semantic scope, and thematic perspective as parameters of adverbial placement in English', in E. N. Enkvist and V. Kohonen (eds).

Enkvist, N. E. and V. Kohonen (eds) (1976), *Reports on text Linguistics: Approaches to Word Order*, Abo, Abo akademi forskningsinstitut.

Ferrar, H. (1984), *A French Reference Grammar*, Oxford, Oxford University Press.

Flores d'Arcais, G. B. (1970), 'Linguistic structure and focus of comparison in processing comparative sentences', in G. B. Flores d'Arcais and W. J. M. Levelt (eds).

Flores d'Arcais, G. B. and W. J. M. Levelt (eds) (1970), *Advances in Psycholinguistics*, Amsterdam and London, North-Holland.

Friedrich, P. (1975), *Proto-Indo-European Syntax*, monograph no. 1, Butie Mont.

Gaatone, D. (1971), *Etude descriptive du système de la négation en français contemporain*, Geneva, Librairie Droz.

Gougenheim, G. (1939), *Système grammatical de la langue française*, Paris, D'Artrey.

Greenberg, J. H. (1966), *Universals of Language*, Cambridge, Mass., MIT Press.

Gregor, D. B. (1975), *Friulan Language and Literature*, New York, Oleander Press.

Grevisse, M. (1969), *Le Bon Usage*, Gembloux, Duculot.

Hagiwara, M. P. (ed.) (1977), *Studies in Romance Linguistics*, Massachusetts, Newbury House.

Hankamer, J. (1973), 'Why there are two *than*'s in English', *Chicago Linguistics Society* 9: 179–91.
Harris, M. (1978), *The Evolution of French Syntax. A Comparative Approach*, London, Longman.
Hellan, L. (1981), *Towards an Integrated Analysis of Comparatives*, Tübingen, Gunter Narr.
Hendrick, R. (ed.) (1981), *Papers from the Seventeenth Regional Meeting: Chicago Linguistics Society: Proceedings*, Chicago, Chicago Linguistics Society.
Hills, E. C., J. D. M. Ford and J. de S. Coutinho (1944), *Portuguese Grammar*, Boston, D. C. Heath and Company.
Hoeksema, J. (1984), 'To be continued: the story of the comparative', *Journal of Semantics* 3: 93–107.
Huddlestone, R. (1967), 'More on the English comparative', *Journal of Linguistics* 3 (1): 91–102.
Hundertmark-Santos Martins, M. T. (1982), *Portugiesische Grammatik*, Tübingen, Max Niemeyer.
Huttenlocher, J. and E. T. Higgins (1971), 'Adjectives, comparatives, and syllogisms', *Psychological Review* 78 (6): 487–504.
Iliescu, M. (1972), *Le Frioulan à partir des dialectes parlés en Roumanie*, Paris, Mouton.
Jespersen, O. (1917), *Negation in English and Other Languages*, Copenhagen.
Joly, A. (1967), *Negation and the Comparative Particle in English*, Quebec, Université Laval.
Jonas, P. (1971), *Les systèmes comparatifs à deux termes en ancien français*, Brussels, Université de Bruxelles.
Kiefer, F. and N. Ruwet (eds) (1973), *Generative Grammar in Europe*, Dordrecht, Reidel.
Knowles, J. (1984), 'Structural choice in Spanish clausal comparison', *Canadian Journal of Linguistics* 29: 1–19.
Kuno, S. (1981), 'The syntax of comparative clauses', in R. Hendrick (ed.).
Le Bidois, G. and R. Le Bidois (1938), *Syntaxe du français moderne*, New York, Stechert.
Lehmann, W. P. (1974), *Proto-Indo-European Syntax*, Austin, University of Texas Press.
Lepschy, A. L. and G. Lepschy (1988), *The Italian Language Today*, London, Hutchinson.
Leys, O. (1980), 'In defense of the comparative', in Brettschneider, G. and C. Lehmann (eds) (1980).
Mallinson, G. (1986), *Rumanian*, London, Croom Helm.
Mattoso Camara, J. (1972), *The Portuguese Language*, Chicago, University of Chicago Press.
Medici, M. and R. Simone (eds) (1971), *Grammatica trasformazionale italiana*, Rome, Bulzoni.
Migliorini, B. (1984), *The Italian Language*, London, Faber and Faber.
Milner, J.-C. (1978), 'Cyclicité successive, comparatives et cross-over en français (première partie)', *Linguistic Inquiry* 9 (4): 673–95.
Mittwoch, A. (1974), 'Is there an underlying negative element in comparative clauses?', *Linguistics* 122: 39–45.

Moignet, G. (1970), 'La place en système de *que* "comparatif"', in T. G. S. Combe and P. Rickard (eds).
Moignet, G. (1981), *Systématique de la langue française*, Paris, Klincksieck.
Muller, C. (1978), 'La négation explétive dans les constructions complétives', *Langue Française* 39: 76–103.
Muller, C. (1983), 'Les comparatives du français et la négation', *Linguisticae Investigationes* 7 (2): 271–316.
Muller, C. (1984), 'L'association négative', *Langue Française* 62: 59–94.
Napoli, D. J. (1983), 'Comparative ellipsis: a phrase structure analysis', *Linguistic Inquiry* 14 (4): 675–94.
Napoli, D. J. and M. Nespor (1976), 'Negatives in comparatives', *Language* 52 (4): 811–38.
Napoli, D. J. and M. Nespor (1977), 'Superficially illogical "*non*": negatives in comparatives', in M. P. Hagiwara (ed.).
Pinkham, J. E. (1982), *The Formation of Comparative Clauses in French and English*, Indiana, Indiana University Linguistics Club.
Pohl, J. (1970), '*Ne* et les enfants', *Le langage et l'homme*, October: 41–3.
Pohl, J. (1975), 'L'omission de *ne* dans le français parlé contemporain', *Le français dans le monde*, February–March 17–23.
Polizzi, G. (1985), *Della lingua. Grammatica italiana*, Florence, G. D'Anna.
Pottier, B. (1982), 'Comparaison: le même et l'autre', *Modèles linguistiques* 4 (2): 41–8.
Price, G. (1971), *The French Language: Present and Past*, London, Edward Arnold.
Price, S. A. (1982), 'The syntax of Spanish degree clauses', PhD thesis, Salford University.
Regula, M. and J. Jernej (1975), *Grammatica italiana descrittiva*, Bern, Francke.
Remacle, L. (1952), *Syntaxe du parler wallon de La Gleize*, vol. I, Paris, Les Belles Lettres.
Remacle, L. (1960), *Syntaxe du parler wallon de La Gleize*, vol. III, Paris, Les Belles Lettres.
Rivero, M.L. (1970), 'A surface structure constraint on negation in Spanish', *Language* 46: 640–66.
Rivero, M.-L. (1979), 'Wh-movement in comparatives in Spanish', in D. J. Napoli, and W. Cressey (eds).
Saenz, H. (1940), 'The Spanish translations of *than*', *Hispania* 23: 326–30.
Saltarelli, M. (1974), 'Reference and mood in Italian', in R. J. Campbell, M. G. Goldin and M. Clayton (eds).
Salvat, J. (1973), *Grammaire occitane*, Toulouse, Privat.
Sankoff, G. and D. Vincent (1977), 'L'emploi productif du *ne* dans le français parlé à Montréal', *Le français moderne* 45: 243–56.
Seuren, P. A. M. (1973), 'The comparative', in F. Kiefer and N. Ruwet (eds), 528–64.
Seuren, P. A. M. (1984), 'The comparative revisited', *Journal of Semantics* 3 (1/2): 109–41.
Small, G. W. (1924), *The Comparison of Inequality: The Semantics and Syntax of the Comparative Particle in English*, Greifswald, Abel.

Small, G. W. (1929), *The Germanic Case of Comparison, with a Special Study of English*, Philadelphia, Linguistics Society of America.
Solà, J. (1973), *Estudis de sintaxi catalana*, vol. II, Barcelona, Edicions 62.
Solé, Y. R. (1982), 'On *más/menos* ... *que* versus *más/menos* ... *de* comparatives', *Hispania* 65 (4): 614–19.
Stassen, L. (1984), 'The comparative compared', *Journal of Semantics* 3: 143–83.
Stassen, L. (1985), *Comparison and Universal Grammar*, Oxford, Basil Blackwell.
Stechow, A. von (1984a), 'My reaction to Cresswell's, Hellan's and Seuren's comments', *Journal of Semantics* 3: 183–99.
Stechow, A. von (1984b), 'Comparing semantic theories of comparison', *Journal of Semantics* 3: 1–79.
Stockwell, R., P. Schachter and B. Partee (1973), *The Major Syntactic Structures of English*, New York, Holt, Rinehart and Winston.
Studerus, L. (1982), 'Spanish comparison: its dynamic dimension', *Southwest Journal of Linguistics* 5 (1–2): 42–50.
Teyssier, P. (1976), *Manuel de langue portugaise*, Paris, Klincksieck.
Tobler, A. (1905), *Mélanges de grammaire française*, Paris, Picard.
Wagner, R. L. and J. Pinchon (1962), *Grammaire du français classique et moderne*, Paris, Librairie Hachette.
Willis, R. C. (1980), *An Essential Course in Modern Portuguese*, London, Harrap.
Yates, A. (1975), *Catalan*, London, Hodder and Stoughton.
Zaslawsky, D. (1977), 'Une hypothèse sur la structure de certaines propositions comparatives: la bithématisation', *Semantikos* 2 (1): 63–81.

Further reading

Attal, P., C. Muller, J.-P. Boons, A. Borillo and G. Fauconnier (eds) (1984), *Langue française; la négation*, Paris, Larousse.
Bach, E., J. Bresnan and T. Wasow (1974), '"Sloppy Identity": an unnecessary and insufficient criterion for deletion rules', *Linguistic Inquiry* 5: 609–14.
Baldi, P. (ed.) (1984), *Papers from the Twelfth Linguistic Symposium on Romance Languages*, Amsterdam, Benjamins.
Bello, A. (1908), *Gramática de la lengua castellana*, Paris, R. Roger and F. Chernoviz.
Bergmans, L. (1983), 'Some remarks on a proposed "semantic" explanation of "markedness" in the comparative degree', *Leuvense Bijdragen Tijdschrift voor Germaanse Filologie* 72 (4): 415–22.
Besten, H. den (1978), 'On the presence and absence of Wh-elements in Dutch comparatives', *Linguistic Inquiry* 9: 641–71.
Bolinger, D. L. (1972), *Degree Words*, The Hague, Mouton.
Bordelois, I., H. Contreras and K. Zagona (eds) (1986), *Generative Studies in Spanish Syntax*, Dordrecht, Foris.
Bowers, J. S. (1975), 'Adjectives and adverbs in English', *Foundations of Language* 13: 529–62.
Boysson-Bardies, B. de (1976), *Négation et performance linguistique*, Paris, Mouton.
Brame, M. K. (1983), 'Ungrammatical notes 4: *smarter than me*', *Linguistic Analysis* 12 (3): 323–38.
Bresnan, J. and J. Grimshaw (1978), 'The syntax of free relatives in English', *Linguistic Inquiry* 9: 331–91.
Campbell, R. N. and R. J. Wales (1969), 'Comparative structures in English', *Journal of Linguistics*, 215–51.
Campbell, R. J., M. G. Goldin and M. Clayton Wang (eds) (1974), *Linguistic Studies in Romance Languages: Proceedings of the Third Symposium on Romance Languages*, Washington, Georgetown University Press.
Cantrall, W. R. (1977), 'Comparison and Beyond', *Chicago Linguistics Society* 13: 69–81.
Casagrande, J. (1968), 'On negation in French', PhD thesis, Indiana University.

Chevalier, J.-C., C. Blanche-Benveniste, M. Arrive and J. Peytard (1964), *Grammaire Larousse du français contemporain*, Paris, Librairie Larousse.
Chomsky, N. (1971), 'Deep structure, surface structure, and semantic interpretation', in D. Steinberg and L. Jakobovits (eds).
Chomsky, N. (1977), 'On Wh-movement', in P. Culicover, T. Wasow and A. Akmajian (eds).
Clark, H. H. (1970), 'Comprehending comparatives', in G. B. Flores d'Arcais and W. J. M. Levelt (eds), 294–306.
Clark, H. H. (1971), 'More about "Adjectives, comparatives, and syllogisms": a reply to Huttenlocher and Higgins', *Psychological Review* 78 (6): 505–14.
Contreras, H. (1973), 'Spanish non-anaphoric *lo*', *Linguistics* 111: 5–30.
Cresswell, M. J. (1976), 'The semantics of degree', in B. Partee (ed.).
Culicover, P., T. Wasow and A. Akmajian (eds) (1977), *Formal Syntax*, New York, Academic Press.
Flores d'Arcais, G. B. and W. J. M. Levelt (eds.) (1970), *Advances in Psycholinguistics*, Amsterdam and London, North-Holland.
Fodor, J. A. and J. J. Katz (eds) (1964), *The Structure of Language*, New Jersey, Prentice-Hall.
Gaatone, D. (1971), 'Articles et négation', *Revue Romane* 6: 1–16.
Gazdar, G. (1980), 'A phrase structure syntax for comparative clauses', in T. Hoekstra, H. Van der Hulst and M. Mootgat (eds).
Greenberg, J. H. (ed.) (1978), *Universals of Human Language 4: Syntax*, Stanford, Stanford University Press.
Hadlich, R. L. (1971), *A Transformational Grammar of Spanish*, New Jersey, Prentice-Hall.
Hagiwara, M. P. (ed.) (1977), *Studies in Romance Linguistics*, Massachusetts, Newbury House.
Hale, A. (1970), 'Conditions of English comparative clause pairings', in R. A. Jacobs and P. S. Rosenbaum (eds).
Harmer, L. C. and F. J. Norton (1973), *A Manual of Modern Spanish*, London, University Tutorial Press.
Hendrick, R. (1978), 'The phrase structure of adjectives and comparatives', *Linguistic Analysis* 4: 255–99.
Hoeksema, J. (1983), 'Negative polarity and the comparative', *Natural Language and Linguistic Theory* 1: 403–34.
Hoekstra, T., H. Van der Hulst and M. Moortgat, (eds) (1980), *Lexical Grammar*, Dordrecht, Foris.
Horn, L. R. (1978), 'Some aspects of negation', in J. H. Greenberg (ed.).
Jacobs, R. and P. Rosenbaum (eds) (1970), *Readings in English Transformational Grammar*, Waltham, Mass., Ginn.
Jaeggli, O. (1982), *Topics in Romance Syntax*, Dordrecht, Foris.
Kayne, R. S. (1975), *French Syntax: The Transformational Cycle*, Cambridge, Mass., MIT Press.
Kayne, R. S. (1976), 'French relative *que*', in M. Luján and F. Hensey (eds).
Keenan, E. (1987), 'Multiply-headed noun phrases', *Linguistic Inquiry* 18 (3): 481–90.
Klein, E. (1980), 'A semantics for positive and comparative adjectives', *Linguistics and Philosophy* 4: 1–45.

Klein, E. (1982), 'The interpretation of adjectival comparatives', *Journal of Linguistics* 18 (1): 113–36.
Klima, E. S. (1964) 'Negation in English', in J. A. Fodor and J. J. Katz (eds).
Knowles, J. (1978), 'The Spanish correlatives of comparison and sentence recursion', *Lingua* 46: 205–25.
Lakoff, R. (1970), 'Another non-source for comparatives', *Linguistic Inquiry* 1: 128–9.
Lees, R. B. (1961), 'Grammatical analysis of the English comparative construction', *Word* 17: 171–85.
Luján, M. and F. Hensey (eds) (1976), *Current Studies in Romance Linguistics*, Washington, Georgetown University Press.
Manaster-Ramer, A. (1978), 'Comparatives and factives', *Linguistic Inquiry* 9: 308–10.
Marcos Marín, F. (1974), *Aproximación a la gramática española*, Madrid, Cincel.
Möhren, F. (1980), *Le renforcement affectif de la négation par l'expression d'une valeur minimale en ancien français*, Tübingen, Niemeyer.
Napoli, D. J. and W. Cressey (eds) (1979), *Proceedings of the Ninth Linguistic Symposium on Romance Languages*, Washington, Georgetown University Press.
Nathan, G. S. and M. Winters Epro (1984), 'Negative polarity and the Romance subjunctive' in P. Baldi (ed.).
Partee, B. (ed.) (1976), *Montague Grammar*, New York, Academic Press.
Pilch, H. (1965), 'Comparative constructions in English', *Language* 41: 37–58.
Pisarska, A. (1977), 'The element of negation in English and Polish comparative constructions', *Papers and Studies in Contrastive Linguistics* 6: 91–8.
Plann, S. (1982a), 'On F. R. Higgins's analysis of comparative ellipsis', *Linguistic Analysis* 9 (4): 395–403.
Plann, S. (1982b), 'Indirect questions in Spanish', *Linguistic Inquiry* 13: 297–313.
Quintero, C. (1984), 'Resumptive pronoun strategy in Spanish', in P. Baldi (ed.).
Ramsey, M. M. (1963), *A Textbook of Modern Spanish*, New York, Holt, Rinehart and Winston.
Real Academia Española (1962), *Gramática de la lengua española*, Madrid, Espasa-Calpe.
Río, J. Alonso del (1963), *Gramática española*, Madrid, Ediciones Giner.
Rivero, M.-L. (1980a), 'Theoretical implications of the syntax of left-branch modifiers in Spanish', *Linguistic Analysis* 6 (4): 407–63.
Rivero, M.-L. (1980b), 'On left-dislocation and topicalization in Spanish', *Linguistic Inquiry* 11 (2): 363–93.
Rizzi, L. (1979), 'Remarks on variables, negation and wh-movement', mimeographed, Scuola Normale Superiore.
Ross, J. (1980), 'No negatives in *than*-clauses, more often than not', *Studies in Language* 4 (1): 119–23.
Ross, J. and D. Perlmutter (1970), 'A non-source for comparatives', *Linguistic Inquiry* 1: 127–8.

Seuren, P. A. M. (1969), 'Il concetto di regola grammaticale', in *La sintassi: atti de III convegno internazionale di studi*, Rome, Bulzoni.

Steel, B. (1976), *A Manual of Colloquial Spanish*, Madrid, Sociedad general española de librería.

Steinberg, D. and L. Jakobovits (eds) (1971), *Semantics: An Interdisciplinary Reader in Philosophy, Linguistics and Psychology*, Cambridge, Cambridge University Press.

Zierer, E. (1974), *The Qualifying Adjective in Spanish*, The Hague, Mouton.

Index

adpositional comparative 2
Agard, F. B. 148, 151, 160, 177
allative comparative 4
Andersen, P. K. 1–2, 5, 8–9, 21, 22, 23, 48, 228
Antinucci, F. 152
Ashby, W. J. 118

Baciu, I. 207
Badia Margarit, A. M. 211, 213–15
Battaglia, S. 149–50, 151–2, 161, 178–9, 181, 185–6
Benjamin, C. 26, 58, 59
Bergmans, L. 85–6, 107, 110, 115–17, 121, 123, 152, 191
Bolinger, D. L. 26, 58, 173
Butt, J. 26, 58, 59

ca: in Galician 222–3, 231–2; in Rumanian 200–9, 231
Carballo Calero, R. 222
case comparative 2
Catalan comparatives: of equality 218–20; expressing full comparison 210–12, 218–19; of inequality 210–21; expressing partial comparison 210–11, 218; phrasal 216–17, 218–21; sentential 210–15, 218–19
che: in Friulan 223; in Italian 148–50, 154–8, 173, 177, 179, 183–7, 190, 198, 227, 230
com 218–21, 231
coma 222, 231

come 176–80, 190, 209, 230
como: in Portuguese 196–9, 207–8; in Spanish 15–16, 23, 24, 36, 38, 54, 60–1, 128, 136, 144, 184, 190, 207, 220, 230
comparative particle: in Catalan 209–10, 219–21; in French 20, 23, 68, 131–3, 183, 190; in Friulan 223; general 3, 6, 11, 145, 191, 200, 221, 227–31; in Italian 146, 149, 158, 183–4, 190; in Occitan 225; in Portuguese 192, 195–9; in Rumanian 200, 203–9; in Spanish 12, 24, 35, 45, 53, 59–60, 131–3, 184
comparatives: of equality 8–9; of inequality 8–9; oblique 11; phrasal 11–12; relativized phrasal 12; sentential 11–12
comparison: full 9–10, 21; partial 9–10, 21
conjoined comparative 4, 24
Cresswell, M. J. 7
cum 200, 205, 207–8, 231

Damourette, J. 104, 112, 135
de: in Catalan 216–17, 219–20, 231; in French 70–1; in Spanish 27–8, 35, 53, 64, 216, 220, 230
De Boer, C. 68, 127
De Mello, G. 26
decît 200–6, 208–9, 231
Decomps, D. 224
deletion 2

di: in Friulan 223; in Italian 148–9, 157–8, 185–7, 203, 205, 208–9, 230
Di Pietro, R. J. 148, 151, 160, 177
do que: in Galician 222–3, 232; in Portuguese 192–6, 198–9, 203–5, 208–9, 222–3, 231
Doherty, P. C. 10

en 69, 72, 74–5, 91, 103, 115, 123–5, 127, 135
Enkvist, N. E. 48
exceed comparative 4

Ferrar, H. 84, 86, 123
Flores D'Arcais, G. B. 20
focus: of comparison 20–2, 24, 48, 56, 63–4, 74, 76, 91, 113–15, 124–8, 133–5, 143, 145, 229; of contrast 21, 22, 50, 57, 63, 91, 113, 125
French comparatives: of equality 17–19, 83–9, 97–103, 144; expressing full comparison 16–18, 21, 70–89, 133–4, 144; of inequality 16–19, 70–83, 89–97, 142–5; expressing partial comparison 18–19, 21, 89–103, 133–4, 144; phrasal 17–19, 79–83, 88–9, 95–7, 101–2, 133–5, 144–5; sentential 17–19, 71–9, 84–8, 91–5, 98–100, 133–4, 144
Friulan comparatives 223–4

Gaatone, D. 86, 105, 112, 115, 123, 126
Galician comparatives: of equality 222; of inequality 222–3; phrasal 223; sentential 223
Gonfroy, G. 224
Gougenheim, G. 84, 105, 114, 123
Greenberg, J. H. 22
Gregor, D. B. 223
Grevisse, M. 103, 111, 115, 124–7

Harris, M. 103, 110, 119
Hellan, L. 1, 7–8
Higgins, E. T. 8, 112, 121
Hoeksema, J. 1, 11
Hundertmark-Santos Martins, M. T. 197

Huttenlocher, J. 8, 112, 121

Iliescu, M. 223
Italian comparatives: of equality 146, 176–83; expressing full comparison 147–83, 187; of inequality 147–76; expressing partial comparison 150, 177–9, 187; phrasal 147–8, 152–4, 156–74, 177–80; sentential 147–57, 171–80

Jernej, J. 154, 157, 186
Jonas, P. 68, 114, 120
juxtaposition comparative 2, 23, 24

ke 223, 232
Knowles, J. 26
Kuno, S. 21, 44, 50

le 69, 72, 74–5, 91, 114–15, 123–7, 135
Le Bidois, G. 73, 85, 110, 120, 125–6, 131
Le Bidois, R. 73, 84, 110, 120, 125–6, 131
Lepschy, A. L. 148, 153, 156, 159, 176–7
Lepschy, G. 148, 153, 156, 159, 176–7
lo 31–5, 51–4, 57, 63–4, 69, 74, 128, 144–5, 195, 203–5, 208–9, 230
locative comparative 4

Mallinson, G. 201–2, 206–7
marker of comparison 3, 22–4, 60–2, 64, 69, 76–7, 81–2, 91, 95–6, 103, 107, 109, 113–16, 118–20, 123, 129–31, 135–6, 142–5, 147, 151, 154–5, 159, 163–4, 176, 183–4, 185, 188–92, 195, 198–9, 200, 202, 208–11, 215, 220–1, 223, 225–32
Mattoso Camara, J. 193, 195, 197–8
Migliorini, B. 156
Milner, J.-C. 68
Mittwoch, A. 152
Moignet, G. 68, 84, 105, 111, 113, 131
Muller, C. 68–9, 71–2, 77, 81, 86, 96–7, 104–5, 111, 113, 116–19, 121–2, 161

Napoli, D. J. 86, 109, 115, 150, 152–4, 162, 164–6, 180–2, 185–7
ne: in French 20, 23, 60, 61, 68–9, 76–9, 81, 83, 85–9, 91–7, 99–101, 103–30, 133–6, 143–5, 147, 151–2, 154–6, 158, 163–5, 182–4, 189–92, 211, 217, 230; in Walloon 225, 232
negative: expletive 7, 16, 20, 24, 58–60, 61, 69, 103–30, 117, 133–6, 146–7, 151, 159, 183, 191–2, 200, 201–3, 207–11, 213–14, 217–18, 220–1, 223–32
Nespor, M. 86, 115, 150, 152–4, 162, 164–6, 180–2, 185–7
no: in Catalan 211–17, 220–1, 227, 231; in Friulan 223; in Spanish 58–60, 129, 133, 142, 154–5, 184, 190
non: in Italian 146–7, 151–7, 159–76, 180–90, 211, 217, 227, 230; in Occitan 224–5, 232

Occitan comparatives 224–5

particle comparative 2, 5–6, 15–16, 20, 23–4, 60, 106, 131, 136, 227–8
Pernicone, V. 149–50, 151–3, 161, 178–9, 181, 185–6
Pichon, E. 104, 112
Pinchon, J. 111
Pinkham, J. E. 21, 68, 74–5, 123
Pohl, J. 118
Polizzi, G. 151, 160, 178
Portuguese comparatives: of equality 196–8; expressing full comparison 192, 194, 197–8; of inequality 192–6; expressing partial comparison 194, 197–8; phrasal 194–6; sentential 192–4, 196–8
Pottier, B. 112
Price, G. 73
Puglielli, A. 152

que: in Catalan 210, 212–13, 218–20, 227, 231; in French 16, 20, 23–4, 68, 70–1, 73, 95, 124, 128, 131–3, 135–6, 144, 154, 183–5, 190, 198, 207, 219, 227, 230; in Occitan 224–5, 232; in Portuguese 192–6, 198–9, 204–5, 208, 231; in Spanish 15–16, 23, 27–8, 45, 53, 60–1, 64, 129, 131, 133–4, 136, 143–5, 154, 184–5, 190, 196, 198–9, 208, 220, 230

Regula, M. 153, 157, 186
Rivero, M.-L. 26, 58
Rumanian comparatives: of equality 205–8; expressing full comparison 203–4, 205; of inequality 200–5, 207–9; expressing partial comparison 203–4; phrasal 202–7; sentential 201–2, 205–7

Saenz, H. 26
Saltarelli, M. 182
Sankoff, G. 118
Schwartz, A. 10
separative comparative 4
Seuren, P. A. M. 20, 106–10, 155, 161, 185, 189, 191
Small, G. W. 9–10, 110, 185
Solé, Y. R. 26
Spanish comparatives: of equality 13–15, 35–9, 54–8, 62, 143–4; expressing full comparison 12–13, 27–9, 62–3, 143; of inequality 12–14, 27–35, 39–54, 62–4, 143–5, 179; expressing partial comparison 13–15, 39–58, 62–3, 143; phrasal 13–15, 27, 30–4, 39, 50–4, 143, 145, 217, 220; sentential 13–14, 27–31, 36–9, 41–50, 54–7, 143, 145
Stassen, L. 1–2, 4, 6–10, 15, 20, 23–4, 106–8, 131, 155, 160, 185, 189, 198, 228
Stechow, A. von 25, 109–10, 153, 155, 160–1, 165, 189
Studerus, L. 26
subjunctive 105–6, 130, 146, 151–7, 163–5, 171–6, 180–1, 183–4, 189–90, 211, 227

tensed verb constraint 36–9, 45–7, 49, 51, 56, 62–4, 70, 80, 85, 89, 94, 103, 118, 124, 128–30, 134–6, 146–7, 151, 157–8, 163, 173, 183,

185, 188–91, 195, 199–200, 202–4, 207, 209–11, 216, 218, 220–1, 223–9
Teyssier, P. 193, 195, 197
topicalization 14, 47–51, 55–7, 62–4, 93–5, 100–1, 133–4, 143–5, 179, 229

verbal comparative 2

Vincent, D. 118

Wagner, R. L. 111
Walloon comparatives 225–6
Willis, R. C. 193, 195, 197

Yates, A. 213

Zaslawsky, D. 22, 120

For Product Safety Concerns and Information please contact our EU representative GPSR@taylorandfrancis.com
Taylor & Francis Verlag GmbH, Kaufingerstraße 24, 80331 München, Germany

www.ingramcontent.com/pod-product-compliance
Lightning Source LLC
Chambersburg PA
CBHW071821300426
44116CB00009B/1393